# D. H. LAWRENCE

## *The novels*

ALASTAIR NIVEN
*Lecturer in English Studies, University of Stirling*

CAMBRIDGE UNIVERSITY PRESS

CAMBRIDGE

LONDON · NEW YORK · MELBOURNE

Published by the Syndics of the Cambridge University Press
The Pitt Building, Trumpington Street, Cambridge CB2 1RP
Bentley House, 200 Euston Road, London NW1 2DB
32 East 57th Street, New York, NY 10022, USA
296 Beaconsfield Parade, Middle Park, Melbourne 3206, Australia

First published 1978

Printed in Great Britain by
Cox & Wyman Ltd, Fakenham

*Library of Congress Cataloguing in Publication Data*
Niven, Alastair.
D. H. Lawrence: the novels.
(British authors, introductory critical studies)
Bibliography: p.
1. Lawrence, David Herbert, 1885–1930 – Criticism and
interpretation.
PR6023.A93Z756    823'.9'12    77–8475
ISBN 0 521 21744 X hard covers
ISBN 0 521 29272 7 paperback

# General Preface

This study of D. H. Lawrence is the eleventh in a series of short introductory critical studies of the more important British authors. The aim of the series is to go straight to the authors' works; to discuss them directly with a maximum of attention to concrete detail; to say what they are and what they do, and to indicate a valuation. The general critical attitude implied in the series is set out at some length in my *Understanding Literature*. Great literature is taken to be to a large extent self-explanatory to the reader who will attend carefully enough to what it says. 'Background' study, whether biographical or historical, is not the concern of the series.

It is hoped that this approach will suit a number of kinds of reader, in particular the general reader who would like an introduction which talks about the works themselves; and the student who would like a general critical study as a starting point, intending to go on to read more specialized works later. Since 'background' is not erected as an insuperable obstacle, readers in other English-speaking countries, countries where English is a second language, or even those for whom English is a foreign language, should find the books helpful. In Britain and the Commonwealth. students and teachers in universities and in the higher forms of secondary schools will find that the authors chosen for treatment are those most often prescribed for study in public and university examinations.

The series could be described as an attempt to make available to a wide public the results of the literary criticism of the last thirty years, and especially the methods associated with Cambridge. If the result is an increase in the reading, with enjoyment and understanding, of the great works of English literature, the books will have fulfilled their wider purpose.

ROBIN MAYHEAD

FOR HELEN

# Contents

# Acknowledgements

The points of view expressed in this book are my own, but I acknowledge with gratitude the advice I have received from and the discussions I have enjoyed with Michael Black of the Cambridge University Press, Donald Hannah of the University of Aarhus, Denmark, and Robin Mayhead, the General Editor of this series.

For permission to reprint copyright material, I would like to thank the following: William Heinemann Ltd, Laurence Pollinger Ltd, and the Estate of the late Mrs Frieda Lawrence, for extracts from D. H. Lawrence's novels *The White Peacock*, *The Trespasser*, *Sons and Lovers*, *The Rainbow*, *Women in Love*, *The Lost Girl*, *Aaron's Rod*, *Kangaroo*, *The Plumed Serpent* and *Lady Chatterley's Lover**; and Alfred A. Knopf Inc. for extracts of copyright material from *The Plumed Serpent* by D. H. Lawrence. The extract from *Sons and Lovers* by D. H. Lawrence, Copyright 1913 by Thomas B. Seltzer, Inc., all rights reserved, reprinted by permission of The Viking Press; the extract from *Women in Love* by D. H. Lawrence, Copyright 1920, 1922 by D. H. Lawrence, renewed 1948, 1950 by Frieda Lawrence, reprinted by permission of The Viking Press; the extract from *Kangaroo* by D. H. Lawrence, Copyright 1923 by Thomas B. Seltzer, Inc., 1951 by Frieda Lawrence, reprinted by permission of The Viking Press; the extract from 'Study of Thomas Hardy' from *Phoenix: The Posthumous Papers of D. H. Lawrence*, edited by Edward D. McDonald, Copyright 1936 by Frieda Lawrence, © 1964 by the Estate of the late Frieda Lawrence Ravagli, reprinted by permission of The Viking Press; the extract from *England, My England* by D. H. Lawrence, Copyright 1922 by Thomas B. Seltzer, Inc., renewed 1950 by Frieda Lawrence. reprinted by permission of The Viking Press; the extract from *The Rainbow* by D. H. Lawrence, Copyright 1915 by D. H. Lawrence, 1943 by Frieda Lawrence, all rights reserved, reprinted by permission of The Viking Press; the extracts from *The Lost Girl* by D. H. Lawrence, Copyright 1921 by Thomas B. Seltzer, Inc., 1949 by Frieda Lawrence, reprinted by permission of The Viking

* Acknowledgements for this title include New American Library Inc., in addition to those above.

ACKNOWLEDGEMENTS

Press; the lines from 'Ship of Death' and 'Kangaroo' from *The Complete Poems of D. H. Lawrence*, edited by Vivian de Sola Pinto and F. Warren Roberts, Copyright © 1964, 1971 by Angelo Ravagli and C. M. Weekley, Executors of the Estate of Frieda Lawrence Ravagli, reprinted by permission of The Viking Press; the extracts from *Aaron's Rod* by D. H. Lawrence, Copyright 1922 by Thomas B. Seltzer, Inc., 1950 by Frieda Lawrence, all rights reserved, reprinted by permission of The Viking Press; the excerpts from 'Dull London' and 'On Human Destiny' from *Phoenix II: Uncollected, Unpublished and Other Prose Works by D. H. Lawrence*, edited by Warren Roberts, Copyright © 1968 by the Estate of Frieda Lawrence Ravagli, reprinted by permission of The Viking Press; the excerpt from 'Reflections on the Death of a Porcupine' from *Phoenix II* by D. H. Lawrence, Copyright 1925 by Centaur Press, renewed 1953 by Frieda Lawrence, reprinted by permission of The Viking Press; the excerpts from letters from *The Collected Letters of D. H. Lawrence*, edited by Harry T. Moore, Copyright 1932 by the Estate of D. H. Lawrence, and 1934 by Frieda Lawrence; Copyright 1933, 1948, 1953, 1954 and each year 1956–1962 by Angelo Ravagli and C. Montague Weekley, Executors of the Estate of Frieda Lawrence Ravagli, reprinted by permission of The Viking Press.

NOTE

All quotations from the works of D. H. Lawrence are from the Penguin edition.

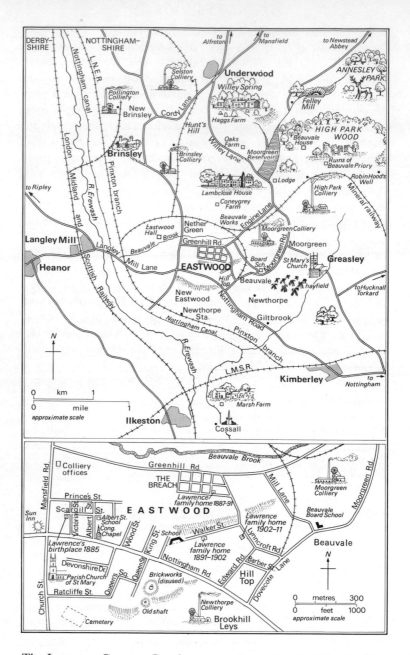

The Lawrence Country. Based on a sketch map by Doris L. Goodhue in *The Intelligent Heart: The Story of D. H. Lawrence* by Harry T. Moore (Penguin Books, 1960).

# 1

# Introductory

D. H. Lawrence was one of the most versatile of all English writers, using almost every literary form in which the English language can express itself. Individual studies of his novels, his stories, his poems, his plays, his travel writings, his criticism, his essays, his translations or his correspondence could occupy a book as long as this one. I have chosen to concentrate upon his ten main novels because, like most readers and critics, I believe these to be the creative core of his achievement. Even so, I leave out any detailed consideration of the two early drafts of *Lady Chatterley's Lover*, now published as novels in their own right, and of *The Boy in the Bush*, a tale of the Australian outback which he wrote in collaboration with M. L. Skinner.

A note of apology for being necessarily selective creeps into almost all books about D. H. Lawrence (some of which I have listed at the end as being especially useful). This is inevitable when his range is so wide and so compelling. The first task of the critic is to sift the most important work from the rest; but even the minor writings of Lawrence point to the volatile energy of his mind and the persistent attempt to stretch his art to its limits. I have concentrated on ten novels, but I have regarded the letters as an essential companion to them, for Lawrence often sums up in a passing remark the mood in which he was writing or the intention he sought to achieve in his fiction. Where it seems to amplify our understanding of a novel I have referred to an appropriate essay or short story.

The stories have not been considered in detail, though the reader new to Lawrence should realize that many of the themes which, in a novel as complex as *Women in Love*, can be single threads in a tapestry of motifs, are often isolated with simple clarity in the shorter fiction. His first collection, *The Prussian Officer and Other Stories* (1914), shows how the subjects which concerned him in his full-length fiction were crucial to him even as a young man, themes of class feeling, of the conflicts between instinct and self-discipline, passion and will, the natural world and the mechanical life which Lawrence believed had usurped it. Fascinating cross-currents can be observed between the shorter fiction and the novels. 'The

Prussian Officer' itself may appear, since it concentrates on the military life, to have scant connection with anything else except 'The Thorn in the Flesh', a tale in the same collection: yet, as a study of the nature of authority and as a drama of possession – the Captain demanding not just the service of his orderly but the man's spirit too – the story anticipates the marital life of Anna and Will in *The Rainbow* and central themes in *Women in Love, Kangaroo* and *The Plumed Serpent*. 'Daughters of the Vicar' and 'Second Best', two more stories in *The Prussian Officer*, anticipate the relationships of Ursula and Gudrun in *Women in Love*, and the former story has close links with *Sons and Lovers*. Yet Lawrence's work is not impoverished by the recurrence of similar themes. No story or novel has the same form. His writing becomes uninteresting only on the rare occasions when he tries to copy another writer's style: M. R. James's perhaps, in his story 'A Fragment of Stained Glass' or the sub-Dickensian descriptions of the Natcha-Kee-Tawaras in *The Lost Girl*. Even when his ideas are self-defeating – some of Birkin's speeches in *Women in Love*, for example – or his sentiments too lyrical, as in his first three novels, his prose is always alive and personal.

Lawrence is sometimes said to bludgeon his readers with an over-insistent tone of voice, but it is as difficult to generalize about his language as about his ideas. He was always looking for new means of expression, just as he wanted to say so many different things that he willingly runs the risk of contradicting himself. Here is a passage, from his short story 'Fanny and Annie' (1922), in which many readers will readily recognize the characteristically Lawrentian tone:

Flame-lurid his face as he turned among the throng of flame-lit and dark faces upon the platform. In the light of the furnace she caught sight of his drifting countenance, like a piece of floating fire. And the nostalgia, the doom of homecoming went through her veins like a drug. His eternal face, flame-lit now! The pulse and darkness of red fire from the furnace towers in the sky. Lightly the desultory, industrial crowd on the wayside station, lit him and went out.

(In *England, My England*, p. 175)

I quote it because it is important to see how Lawrence could shape his own style of English from a common stock of vocabulary. No word here is unusual or strange in itself, yet the rhythms and meaning are wholly Lawrence's. 'Flame-lurid his face': the typical inversion forces our attention on to the descriptive compound adjective. Lawrence's symbolism often expresses itself in natural forces (fire here: elsewhere it might be the sun, the moon, ice, the colours of spring, the ripening of a cornfield) which combine the sense of mysterious illuminating power at the heart of existence with a strong, sometimes almost dangerous physical reality. Here the 'flame-lit' face of Fanny's lover points to an inner sensuality which seems to her almost unattainable. We note the force of the word 'eternal', too, for something of the permanent life of the creation affects all Lawrence's sexual beings. He tried in novel after novel to identify that creative force which he believed to be the deepest realizable mystery of the universe, awaiting understanding by the human species. Yet his best writing does not take off into flights of metaphysical looseness, for a hard social sense accompanies it. 'The pulse and darkness of red fire from the furnace towers in the sky' remind us of the industrial working reality of the town to which Fanny returns and in which her lover has always lived. The flames express the inner glories of the human personality and something of the divine mysteries, but they represent a harsh physical world where social bonds are close-knit and economic deprivation is rampant.

To prevent the prose from becoming too elevated Lawrence moves on to specific social practicalities in the next part of the story:

Compare this with the arrival at Gloucester: the carriage for her mistress, the dog-cart for herself with the luggage; the drive out past the river, the pleasant trees of the carriage-approach; and herself sitting beside Arthur, everybody so polite to her.

(pp. 176–7)

Fanny remembers the gentility of her former employment, even though there was scant distinction made between her and the luggage! The lighter tone here is 'placed' by the deeper note in the earlier passage. This interplay of light and shadow characterizes Lawrence's best writing.

The sense of community can be felt in almost all Lawrence's work. 'Fanny and Annie' expresses it strongly. The first thing Fanny, a stranger among her own folk, is offered on her return is help with her heavy bags and a cup of tea. A keen pride in appearances affects almost everyone: we come across this world of crisp table-cloths and smart dress for Sunday services in many of the novels. Lawrence deeply admired the closeness of industrial people, while believing that the life they were forced to live was degrading. How, in modern industrialized society, could one hang on to the intimacy between people, and between people and the

3

land, which he believed the old agrarian societies had possessed before the economic revolution of the early nineteenth century? Lawrence was too intelligent to believe that the clock could be set back and the lost Eden re-established, and that men would forget about machines. He sought in novel after novel and in many of the stories to find a viable way of coping with modern society and of eventually bringing about a new world where the full potential of men would be realized in conditions of love and harmony. His work has a strongly visionary and idealistic strain in it, combined with a down-to-earth willingness to confront the injustices of society as they actually exist.

My intention in this book is to show, by analysis of language and discussion of themes, that Lawrence contributed in a major way to the nature of the modern novel. Many studies of his work have concentrated on his life, but at no point in his work is Lawrence writing straight autobiography. He used his own experience, but never just remembered or reported it. He worked it into a form in which vestiges of his own past can be easily detected but which exists principally as a work of the imagination. I have noted the traces of autobiographical experience when it has seemed important to do so, but my primary aim has been to demonstrate Lawrence's greatness as an artist. That lies partly in the versatility of his writing and in his determination to face every aspect of modern life, whether this makes his writing social, psychological, political or religious. He knew that he was a great writer, even if he was often sickened by the literary element in his own personality – which, he said in a letter to Helen Corke in 1910, 'like a disagreeable substratum under a fair country, spreads under every inch of life, sticking to the roots of the growing things'. Because he knew he could write better than any of his contemporaries in England, he felt a mission to advance the art of the novel itself. Sometimes, as with his handling of the sexual vocabulary in *Lady Chatterley's Lover*, this compelled him in a specific direction, but at the heights of his art, in *Women in Love* most of all, it leads into experiments with the form of fiction itself.

I hope this book refutes the kind of remark which critics often make about Lawrence, that he 'obeys no rules, there is little conscious artistry about him . . . His novels are wayward and natural rambling landscapes rather than cunningly constructed gardens' (Kenneth Young, *D. H. Lawrence*, p. 4). His work lacks the formal poise of a novel by Henry James, or the kind of shape that lends itself to diagrams, because he did not aspire to write like that.

4

When he strives for conscious literary effect the prose can seem 'painted' and bloodless. We shall see examples of this in the chapter on *The White Peacock*. But artist he undoubtedly was, an artist of the intelligence, often evolving a language where no precedents existed.

Nothing in the circumstances of his birth or childhood made Lawrence's career as a writer inevitable. He was born in Eastwood, an industrial village in Nottinghamshire in the northern midlands of England, on 11 September 1885, the fourth son of parents who had been married almost ten years when he arrived. He was educated at the local Council School and at thirteen went to Nottingham High School. Three years later he took his first job with a firm of surgical goods manufacturers. Many of the details of his childhood and adolescence recur in his third novel, *Sons and Lovers*, though we must not forget, when we read that book, that it is a product of the imagination, not an autobiography; the author's personal history is transmuted by his art into a complex work of fiction. Since his own contemporaries who featured in the novel, and especially his girl-friend Jessie Chambers, failed to see that he was not aiming to be literally true to any single experience, but to use many experiences in order to draw out certain elements which he believed to be true to the whole nature of growing up, it is not surprising that critics and students make the mistake of identifying each incident of the novel with a moment in Lawrence's own life. Most of the events in *Sons and Lovers* derive from occasions in Lawrence's own youth, but in every case they are treated as material to be reshaped and given a new significance.

When Lawrence was eighteen he went to Nottingham University College to take a teaching certificate. At this early age he embarked on his first novel, *The White Peacock*. It was completed just before the death in 1910 of his mother, to whom he was especially close. After gaining his teaching certificate, Lawrence taught for nearly two years at Davidson Road School in Croydon, near London. This period marked his introduction to the south of England and to the literary establishment of the day; it was a time for forming close relationships which affect the shaping of his first novels; and it was the only point in his life when he was employed in an official position. His resignation from the school may be the basis for Ursula Brangwen's similar decision in *Women in Love*; in Lawrence's case the freedom he now had to concentrate on his writing was gained at the expense of a definable social rôle. Ever after, he lived a little in a state of limbo, though his marriage in 1914 to the German noblewoman Frieda von Richthofen-Weekley gave him some sense of permanence and stability. Also, as someone living by his pen, Lawrence was always aware of the need to write a lot and to write well enough to be publishable. In these circumstances it is remarkable that he never played safe in his writing.

The war of 1914–18 affected Lawrence profoundly: more, I think, than has been usually suggested. For much of the time, he was hounded by the authorities in England, suspected of subversion, immorality, espionage and anarchism. Lawrence is in many ways the most English of authors, as his description of the English landscape and language, his wide acquaintanceship with the English social system, and his roots in its industrial life testify; but his bitterness at the way he and his wife were treated during the war, coupled with his horror at what the war represented, meant that he felt betrayed by the country of his birth. When he left England in 1919 it was to live a life of exile for almost the rest of his life.

I have, in this book, discussed the ten major novels. Each rewards discovery in its own right and, despite some moments of repetitiousness within the individual works, none can be said merely to rehash what has been said before. *The White Peacock* and *The Trespasser*, his first novels, have sometimes been seen as appendages to the Lawrence canon, or embryonic studies for his mature work. I have tried to view them as more central than this to his development, as distinguished, concentrated and personal works, though only on the lower slopes of his creative genius. *Sons and Lovers* is a work of consummate narrative integrity, the most personal of his major works and, because of its form, the culmination of that strand of Lawrence's art. He seldom pretends to the omniscient authority which the great Victorian novelists had mastered. Outrage, vigour, preachiness, self-righteousness and scorn can be found throughout his work, but they are tempered by his constant desire to press on beyond the immediate perception or the apparently obvious truism. Doubt and enquiry are far more typical of Lawrence's fiction than dogmatism.

Unhappy as the war years were for the Lawrences, they proved the most creative period of his life. By any reckoning *The Rainbow* and *Women in Love* are the centrepieces of his art. In these two novels, originally conceived as one great work to be entitled *The Sisters*, Lawrence analysed modern society, its mores and its malaise, more profoundly than any of his contemporaries. I have taken the two novels together in order to emphasize their origins in a single creative impulse, but their separateness as works of art, quite different in the forms by which they are expressed, must be asserted too. Much the longest chapter of this book is given to *The Rainbow* and *Women in Love*, for Lawrence's understanding of individuals can in these novels be placed in a larger social and metaphysical scheme which he was still exploring on the final page of the second novel. Almost inevitably the effort these two books cost him led to a period of tiredness and resentment against the whole prospect of imaginative writing, but had he never written another novel his importance in the history of modern literature would have been secured.

*The Lost Girl*, Lawrence's first attempt at fiction after the war was over, shows less sign of the imaginative exhaustion one might expect to find in an author who had completed works on the scale of *The Rainbow* and *Women in Love* and who had suffered acute humiliations at the hands of the authorities. Significantly, however, *The Lost Girl* reworks and completes a script which was begun before the war started. He was reluctant, at this time, to initiate a new novel. This disenchantment with fiction did not last, though it was in the wandering last decade of his life, 1920–30, that he wrote most of his non-fiction: major essays like 'Psychoanalysis and the Unconscious' (1921), 'Studies in Classic American Literature' (1923) and 'A Propos of *Lady Chatterley's Lover*' (1930), the travel books *Sea and Sardinia* (1921), *Mornings in Mexico* (1927) and *Etruscan Places* (published 1934), verse collections such as *Tortoises* (1921), *Birds, Beasts and Flowers* (1923), *Pansies* (1929) and *Nettles* (1930), and the highly personal interpretation of the Book of Revelation, *Apocalypse* (published 1931). The novels which immediately follow *The Lost Girl* – *Aaron's Rod*, *Kangaroo* and *The Plumed Serpent* – have often been taken together. There are good reasons for this, but commenting on them together produces a tendency to overlook their separate qualities. Foreign settings, the felt need to belong to a community produced by a sense of being lost or 'cut off', and theories of potent leadership are common to them all, yet in tone they are quite different. The Lawrence of *Aaron's Rod* has not found any certain answers, seems flippant, even cynical; in *Kangaroo* he becomes more volatile and often angrier, though the novel records an altogether larger response to life; and in *The Plumed Serpent* he discovers in Mexico a blend of ancient ritual and modern rebellion which fires his imagination and stirs his blood.

Of these three novels *Kangaroo* contains the largest measure of autobiography. It records, as no other Lawrence novel does, the author's immediate reaction to people, places and events. Lawrence was attracted by the newness of Australian society in contrast to the antiquity of its landscape. The people there were mainly his own race-kindred. Though he was fascinated by Mexico in *The Plumed Serpent*, the case was different, for not only the terrain but those inhabiting it to whom he was most drawn were fascinatingly but inviolably foreign to him. As for the Italy of *Aaron's Rod*, Lawrence describes only the museum-and-penthouse Italy of the slightly degenerate Anglo-Saxon exile. It could not be a resting place for him. He was tempted to stay in Australia, and he seriously imagined belonging to Mexico, but in the end he was drawn back to Europe where he set his last novel and where he died.

Because I believe *Kangaroo* to be the most undervalued of all Lawrence's novels, and the most personal of his travel writings, I devote a long chapter to it. By contrast to *Kangaroo*, *Aaron's Rod* seems a negative work and *The Plumed Serpent* too inflexibly positive. All three have been criticized for being bitty and broken-backed in structure, but I have attempted to show the necessity for this. If Lawrence was to explore outwards from the core of his own being it inevitably meant a piecing together of fragments in order to create the final wholeness. The process is, in fact, never finally completed: the search for wholeness goes on to the end, necessitating technical experiment.

Lawrence's last novel, *Lady Chatterley's Lover*, marks a return to the England of his first concern. The novel holds out some hope, but it is of a guarded and muted sort. I have suggested that the book has a more than historical value as the novel which 'liberated' English prose from some of its inhibitions. There is a danger, however, that readers will sentimentalize this novel on account of the 'naturalness' of the main relationship, that between Lady Chatterley and her gamekeeper. The novel is as much about the disintegration of modern life and the erosion of the old England. Any way out of the twentieth-century trauma which Connie and Mellors may discover can only be tentative. Even the power of personal relations, Lawrence says in his last novel, may not be enough to resist the anti-life of the present world.

Lawrence died in March 1930. His reputation did not immediately stand very high, but in the last twenty years it has been generally admitted that he enlarged the English novel as no contemporary was able to do. For a time his international reputation was far below James Joyce's, but that, too, is beginning to change, because so many of the issues with which Lawrence dealt intimately concern our own society now. Both as an artist and as a thinker he confronted life in the fullness of his passion and intellect. Our response to his work now should be as alert and vital as if he had written for our own time.

# 2

## *The White Peacock*

In a letter to his friend W. E. Hopkin on 20 February 1911 D. H. Lawrence added this brief postscriptum: 'I was very young when I wrote the *Peacock* – I began it at twenty. Let that be my apology.' *The White Peacock* certainly falls short of the intellectual strengths we find in the later novels, yet it too deals seriously with relationships between the sexes. It has too often been dismissed as worth no more than an historically curious glance. With all its imperfections, its occasional crudities of characterization and its sometimes gratuitously self-indulgent literariness, this first novel reveals a side of Lawrence which he consciously abandoned as he waded into the currents of psychological self-analysis, moral discovery and speculation on the nature of society. From the start he establishes himself as a novelist absorbed in the interior lives of his characters, yet acutely observant of appearances.

The degree of incident in almost all Lawrence's full-length fiction can easily be overlooked, for, with rare exceptions like the attack on Jamiltepec in *The Plumed Serpent*, it resides more in what happens within relationships than in dramatic actions or external adventures. *The White Peacock* exemplifies this. Cyril, who narrates the tale, tells us about his sister, Lettie Beardsall, the man who loves her, George Saxton, and the man she marries, Leslie Tempest. The action of the novel resides in the conversations, in the powerful presence of a gamekeeper called Annable, in the changes of the central relationships from a right to a wrong direction, and in the suggestion that Leslie is representative in compensating for his sexual inadequacy by acquiring a position of power in society. The central theme of Lawrence's first novel concerns the choices facing us as we accept the responsibilities of maturity. All the main characters lead eventually thwarted lives because of the wrong directions they choose to take and most obviously whom they choose to marry. But the most central choice of all is whether to be ourselves, to fulfil what we instinctively believe to be right for ourselves, or whether to follow the requirements of 'society' and to do what it expects of us. For Lawrence, personal honour in the sense of doing what we feel we ought to do by way of self-fulfilment must come before the dictatorship of social duty. Self-fulfilment is not the same as self-gratification, however: to realize one's potential is what matters, not to sacrifice this potential in the pursuit of pleasure.

Not surprisingly for a first novel, *The White Peacock* draws a great deal from personal recollection, and as late as 1926, when he had been living abroad for some time, Lawrence was able to recommend a walk to a friend that would take him 'through the wood to Felley Mill (the *White Peacock* farm)'. Lawrence lived the first twenty-one years of his life in that area of Nottinghamshire which is centred on Eastwood (his birthplace), Greasley, Watnall, Annesley and Underwood, mining villages set in green, often wooded, undramatic countryside. 'That's the country of my heart', he insisted, even when the later years of his life took him to Australia, Mexico and Italy. After a combination of ill-health, violent dissociation from modern England and spiritual enquiry had led him into his voluntary exile, Lawrence naturally looked back on the landscape of his childhood with regretful nostalgia, but while he was writing *The White Peacock* he had no claim to believe that his departure from Nottinghamshire as a home would be irrevocable. He wrote of the only countryside he had experienced first-hand. The result is a novel drenched in an almost adoring devotion to the Nottinghamshire byways. Lawrence seldom failed to evoke a setting richly and dramatically – few descriptions of the Australian outback or the Mexican landscape surpass those of *Kangaroo* and *The Plumed Serpent*, and travel books like *Sea and Sardinia* and *Mornings in Mexico* still bring to life some of the places he visited – but in *The White Peacock* the sense of the seasons passing, of a terrain always changing and evolving, of weather and animal life at first harnessed by and then hostile to man, is a constant element in the novel, and a strong one, despite some immature lushness in the writing.

The relationship of man to nature – where man so often fails to grow naturally from his roots, accepting his nature and fulfilling it in the place he belongs to, with people he is naturally drawn towards – lies at the heart of *The White Peacock* and gives rise to some of the most sustained eloquence in the novel, never more so than in the description of the gamekeeper's funeral.

It was a magnificent morning in early spring when I watched among the trees to see the procession come down the hillside. The upper air was woven with the music of the larks, and my whole world thrilled with the conception of summer. The young pale wind-flowers had arisen by the wood-gale, and under the hazels, when perchance the hot sun pushed his way, new little suns dawned, and blazed with real light. There was a certain thrill and quickening everywhere, as a woman must feel when she has conceived. A sallow tree in a favoured spot looked like a pale gold cloud of summer dawn; nearer it had poised a golden, fairy busby on every twig, and was voiced with a hum of bees, like any sacred golden bush, uttering its gladness in the thrilling murmur of bees, and in warm scent. Birds called and flashed on every hand; they made off exultant with streaming strands of grass, or wisps of fleece, plunging into the dark spaces of the wood, and out again into the blue.

A lad moved across the field from the farm below with a dog trotting behind him – a dog, no, a fussy, black-legged lamb trotting along on its toes, with its tail swinging behind. They were going to the mothers on the common, who moved like little grey clouds among the dark gorse.

I cannot help forgetting, and sharing the spink's triumph, when he flashes past with a fleece from a bramble bush. It will cover the bedded moss, it will weave among the soft red cow-hair beautifully. It is a prize, it is an ecstasy to have captured it at the right moment, and the nest is nearly ready.

Ah, but the thrush is scornful, ringing out his voice from the hedge! He sets his breast against the mud, and models it warm for the turquoise eggs – blue, blue, bluest of eggs, which cluster so close and round against the breast, which round up beneath the breast, nestling content. You should see the bright ecstasy in the eyes of a nesting thrush, because of the rounded caress of the eggs against her breast!

What a hurry the jenny wren makes – hoping I shall not see her dart into the low bush. I have a delight in watching them against their shy little wills. But they have all risen with a rush of wings, and are gone, the birds. The air is brushed with agitation. There is no lark in the sky, not one; the heaven is clear of wings or twinkling dot –.

Till the heralds come – till the heralds wave like shadows in the bright air, crying, lamenting, fretting forever. Rising and falling and circling round and round, the slow-waving peewits cry and complain, and lift their broad wings in sorrow. They stoop suddenly to the ground, the lap-wings, then in another throb of anguish and protest, they swing up again, offering a glistening white breast to the sunlight, to deny it in black shadow, then a glisten of green, and all the time crying and crying in despair.

The pheasants are frightened into cover, they run and dart through the hedge. The cold cock must fly in his haste, spread himself on his streaming plumes, and sail into the wood's security.

There is a cry in answer to the peewits, echoing louder and stronger the lamentation of the lapwings, a wail which hushes the birds. The men come over the brow of the hill, slowly, with the old squire walking tall and straight in front, six bowed men bearing the coffin on their shoulders, treading heavily and cautiously, under the great weight of the glistening white coffin; six men following behind, ill at ease, waiting their turn for the burden. You can see the red handkerchiefs knotted round their throats, and their shirt-fronts blue and white between the open waistcoats. The coffin is of new unpolished wood, gleaming and glistening in the sunlight; the men who carry it remember all their lives after the smell of new, warm elm-wood.

Again a loud cry from the hill-top. The woman has followed thus far, the big, shapeless woman, and she cries with loud cries after the white coffin as it descends the hill, and the children that cling to her skirts weep aloud, and are not to be hushed by the other woman, who bends over them, but does not form one of the group. How the crying frightens the birds, and the rabbits; and the lambs away there run to their mothers. But the pee-wits are not frightened, they add their notes to the sorrow; they circle after the white retreating coffin, they circle round the woman; it is they who forever 'keen' the sorrows of this world. They are like priests in their robes, more black than white, more grief than hope, driving endlessly round and round, turning, lifting, falling and crying always in mournful desolation, repeating their last syllables like the broken accents of despair.

Their bearers have at last sunk between the high banks, and turned out of sight. The big woman cannot see them, and yet she stands to look. She must go home, there is nothing left.

(pp. 182–4)

The cortège moves down the hillside, disturbing the birds and animals, like an ancient procession of Druid priests engaged in a pagan rite. We have here the first stirrings of that tone in which Lawrence evokes the climactic sacrifice in his story 'The Woman Who Rode Away' seventeen years later, for the scene of death seems both to distress the surrounding nature and to complement it. Death is part of the whole life which this passage celebrates. Elsewhere in the novel, Lawrence becomes over-literary in his evocations, but is less so here. The excitement of a personal response to nature, the hint almost of a sexual 'rapport', supports the lushness of the phrasing. 'Thrilled', 'thrill', 'thrilling' – Lawrence's characteristic repetition has an exuberance that pulls against the effect of occasional archaisms and prettinesses like 'perchance', 'a favoured spot', 'a golden, fairy busby'. Even the rhetoric of 'Ah, but the thrush is scornful, ringing out his voice from the hedge!' is justified by the acute scrutiny revealed a moment later: 'You should see the bright ecstasy in the eyes of a nesting thrush, because of the rounded caress of the eggs against her breast!'

The coffin itself, hacked from the surrounding woods, seems, despite its rawness, to be still part of the setting: 'the men who carry it remember all their lives after the smell of new, warm elm-wood'. The tragic family follows on, just as the lambs rush to their mothers. We can see here why Lawrence admired Hardy, whose influence is stronger in *The White Peacock* than in the other novels. What Lawrence has to say of Egdon Heath in *The Return of the Native* may be taken as his view of natural energy generally.

Here is the sombre, latent power that will go on producing, no matter what happens to the product. Here is the deep, black source from whence all these little contents of lives are drawn. And the contents of the small lives are spilled and wasted. There is savage satisfaction in it; for so much more remains to come, such a black, powerful fecundity is working there that what does it matter?

Three people die and are taken back into the Heath; they mingle their strong earth again with its powerful soil, having been broken off at their stem. It is very good. Not Egdon is futile, sending forth life on the powerful heave of passion. It cannot be futile, for it is eternal. What is futile is the purpose of man.

('Study of Thomas Hardy', written 1914)

George's crushed manhood at the end of *The White Peacock*, Cyril's apparent wanderlust, Leslie's spiritual impoverishment and Lettie's self-imprisonment should be read against this kind of feeling. As Emile Delavenay says in *D. H. Lawrence: The Man and His Work*, Hardy was chief among the contemporary authors whose prose and poetry constituted 'the constant background' to Lawrence's life at the time he was writing his first novel. Hardyesque touches abound throughout *The White Peacock*, in small moments like Lettie's observing the old household custom of swinging an unbroken strip of apple-peel as much as in the portrait of Annable's abrupt death and timeless funeral. In later novels Lawrence moved away from Hardy's influence, believing that human character was more subtle than Hardy perceived, but at the start of his career his admiration of the older writer affected his work significantly.

The interaction of man and his setting becomes almost the governing feature of Lawrence's first book. When, at the beginning of the novel, George imprisons and then destroys a small bee with callous levity – ' "Oh, dear – pity!" said he and crushed the little thing between his fingers' (p. 14) – we recognize that the incident demonstrates a masterful side to George's character. As the novel unfolds, this becomes part of a whole pattern. Several episodes of animal suffering point symbolically to an innate cruelty which Lawrence perceived in many people: episodes which anticipate the crucial chapters 'Mino' and 'Rabbit' in *Women in Love*. Drowning a cat, the rabbit hunt, throwing stones at the rats in a pool, 'a chicken been and walked into the fire' (p. 238), are all part of this destructiveness. Annable, consciously the champion of the natural world, protects the rabbits that the Saxons and the Beardsalls hunt to the death. His care for them resembles Mellors's concern for his chickens and his dog in *Lady Chatterley's Lover*. But as gamekeepers both men have to kill when necessary.

Lawrence did not ignore the predatoriness instinctive in both animals and men. We need to avoid sentimentalizing his view of nature. In 1925 he was provoked by an incident in New Mexico to write an essay, 'Reflections on the Death of a Porcupine', which made clear what had been implicit in much of his fiction before then:

In nature, one creature devours another, and this is an essential part of all existence and of all being. It is not something to lament over, nor something to try to reform ... We did not make creation, *we* are not the authors of the universe. And if we see that the whole of creation is established upon the fact that one life devours another life, one cycle of existence can only come into existence through the subjugating of another cycle of existence, then what is the good of trying to pretend that it is not so? The only thing to do is to realize what is higher, and what is lower, in the cycles of existence.

Among the people in *The White Peacock*, Annable presents the 'higher cycle' spiritually. He does not kill (as George does) for self-gratification. He discriminates; in a sense, he judges. Nevertheless, he provides the critic with his greatest problem. His place in the action is small, yet his influence colours the development of the whole work, for the narrator establishes him in our minds as a standard for personal fulfilment. Annable, after many years of social revulsion, has achieved a measure of that uninhibited completeness and naturalness to which Cyril aspires, which Lettie and George deny in themselves and which Leslie is incapable of understanding.

I thought him rather a fine fellow,' said I.
'Splendidly built fellow, but callous – no soul,' remarked Leslie dismissing the question.
'No,' assented Emily. 'No soul – and among the snowdrops.'
Lettie was thoughtful, and I smiled.

(p. 157)

Annable, this 'man of one idea: – that all civilization was the painted fungus of rottenness' (p. 172), displays the power of physical and sexual mastery, humbling even the assertive George, who is the only other character in the novel approaching him in masculine authority. Though Lawrence shows Cyril as enthralled by Annable's animal potency – 'a good animal before everything' (p. 178) – he also shows the poverty and grim insecurity of the widow and children who survive him. He does not want us to see the gamekeeper's life as a final success, but as a wasted potential. 'I'm like a good house, built and finished, and left to tumble down again with nobody to live in it' (p. 175). Lawrence admires Annable's vitality, but does not present him as the complete manifestation of the ideal life. Lawrence never entirely reconciled his veneration of physical excellence with his own striving for intellectual distinction, and certainly in Annable we recognize only half a man.

Nor, in his first novel, has Lawrence overcome the problem of giving us the keeper's history without making it appear slotted into the main narrative like a romantic fantasy. *The White Peacock* is full of other obvious pieces of narrative machinery (such as the frequent summaries of action through the quoting of letters). Annable's account of his marriage to Lady Crystabel seems one of the most obvious. Lawrence illustrates through the story a number of issues which concerned him again – the emasculation of the male by the patrician lady, the effeteness of life lived through art alone, the sexual fertility of natural man – but he has not learned yet, as he did by the time he wrote *Lady Chatterley's Lover*, that such themes are best shown directly through the things people do and say, rather than through an artificial recollected narrative for which he has ill prepared the ground.

Lawrence constantly spoke out against the kind of woman whose will to dominate a man transforms him into a merely social being or into an intellectual without a body. Annable tells his tale accompanied by the shriek of a peacock, an overt symbol that helps him and Cyril to identify the beauty and vanity of womanhood, the devilish cause of his downfall. Lawrence's title is emblematic in the same way as Webster's play *The White Devil*. Innocence and vanity, integrity and a yearning for admiration are linked in several characters, but most of all in Lettie.

'I know how a man will compliment me by the way he looks at me' – she kneeled before the fire. 'Some look at my hair, some watch the rise and fall of my breathing, some look at my neck, and a few – not you among them – look me in the eyes for my thoughts. To you, I'm a fine specimen, strong! Pretty strong! You primitive man!'

(p. 40)

In Lettie Beardsall Lawrence embarks on one of his characteristic studies of female psychology. His success does not lie so much in her physical description as in the manner of her conversation and behaviour, and the way he chronicles her self-stunting existence. Though Lawrence excelled at noticing the externals of female appearance – the clothes that Ursula and Gudrun Brangwen wear in *Women in Love*, for example, state their personalities – he never conveys quite the same physicality in women as he does in men. The first portrait of Lettie itemizes her attractions in slightly too flat a manner.

She was tall, nearly six feet in height, but slenderly formed. Her hair was yellow, tending towards a dun brown. She had beautiful eyes and brows, but not a nice nose. Her hands were very beautiful.

(p. 21)

The description is external, observed rather than felt. Nothing can be described in phrases like 'a nice nose' and 'very beautiful' hands. When, a moment later, George enters the room from milking and feeding cows, he is described in a dynamic movement rather than in a static set of descriptive phrases, with the emphasis less on general features, more on private marks and personal gestures. Lawrence seems almost to linger over the details, the moisture on George's body, his legs apart, the rubbing of his towel beneath his shirt, the swelling of his arms as he moves them, the rise and fall of his breasts, 'wonderfully solid and white', 'the sudden meeting of the sun-hot skin with the white flesh in his throat' (p. 27). Yet although George's presence in the novel is physically more vigorous than Lettie's, she never falls far from the centre of interest. Indeed, Lawrence suggests that George's magnetism increases the closer he is to Lettie. Their relationship grows to the accompaniment of music and walks in the country, at first tentative and later almost obsessive, as they more earnestly endeavour to shield it and deny it.

They gazed at each other for a moment before they hid their faces again. It was torture to each of them to look thus nakedly at each other, a dazzled, shrinking pain that they forced themselves to undergo for a moment, that they might the moment after tremble with a fierce sensation that filled their veins with fluid, fiery electricity.

(pp. 43–4)

Here, at the beginning of his writing career, Lawrence confronts the problem of expressing sexual intensity through undercurrents and suggestions. Though *The White Peacock* is often too allusive, too knowingly literary in its reference, it wholly succeeds with this central relationship, which expands and intensifies yet also denies and ultimately obliterates itself.

'The sun loved Lettie, and was loath to leave her' (p. 59). Lawrence shows Lettie moving away from the natural world for which she was created into a social universe where her brightness still shines, but more harshly and with greater shallowness. When still young they take part in the harvesting. As George gathers the ripe upstanding corn a kind of sexual energy charges the atmosphere between him and Lettie (as it does between Will and Anna in the harvesting scene in *The Rainbow*):

'Do you know,' she said suddenly, 'your arms tempt me to touch them. They are such a fine brown colour, and they look so hard.'

He held out one arm to her. She hesitated, then she swiftly put her finger-tips on the smooth brown muscle, and drew them along. Quickly she hid her hand into the folds of her skirt, blushing.

He laughed a low, quiet laugh, at once pleasant and startling to hear.

'I wish I could work here,' she said, looking away at the standing corn, and the dim blue woods. He followed her look, and laughed quietly with indulgent resignation.

'I do!' she said emphatically.

'You feel so fine,' he said, pushing his hand through his open shirt front, and gently rubbing the muscles of his side. 'It's a pleasure to work or to stand still. It's a pleasure to yourself – your own physique.'

She looked at him, full at his physical beauty, as if he were some great firm bud of life.

Leslie came up, wiping his brow.

'Jove,' said he, 'I do perspire.'

George picked up his coat and helped him into it, saying: 'You may take a chill.'

'It's a jolly nice form of exercise,' said he.

George, who had been feeling one finger-tip, now took out his pen-knife and proceeded to dig a thorn from his hand.

'What a hide you must have,' said Leslie.

Lettie said nothing but she recoiled slightly.

Lawrence's prose here is crisp, alert and detailed; it never wanders into abstraction and distils the essence of the contact and feeling between the three characters. With remarkable simplicity he shows George's simple contentment with himself, without making it weakness or vanity. The physical details say it all – a fondness for his own body ('gently rubbing the muscles of his side') and yet a confident mastery of it ('now took out his pen-knife and proceeded to dig a thorn from his hand'). Lawrence suggests the inappropriateness of Leslie's interruption without spelling it out. The apparent mildness of the writing understates its asperity, for in the limp middle-class jocularity of Leslie's few words ('Jove', 'perspire', 'jolly nice', 'what a hide') and in Lettie's silent recoil Lawrence locates a whole tragedy of wrong partnerships. Leslie's language also recalls E. M. Forster's 'social' people in his novels of the same period, for example Tibby in *Howards End*.

*The White Peacock* is demonstrably nostalgic, 'full', as Richard Aldington says, 'of tender and wistful regret for youth's passing'. The sorrow of the novel contributes to its compassion. Lawrence's handling of the relationship between Lettie and George is honest, yet full of pity. The girl who likes things 'to wink and look wild' (p. 72) and who has 'read all things that dealt with modern woman' (p. 92) frustrates the spirit she knows to be within her, yet becomes reconciled, perhaps because, in the Hardy manner, she senses fatalistically that 'We can't help ourselves, we're all chessmen' (p. 143) in a submissive life in which 'she lived gleefully in a little tent of present pleasures and fancies' (p. 71). Lawrence does not chart Lettie's descent into marital domesticity as though it were a violent capitulation after months of debilitating siege. The moments of tension between Lettie and Leslie are rare – an irritation with her engagement ring, a revulsion at the sight of her own hands – but we sense a denial of possibilities whenever the two are together. Lettie closely resembles Cathy, in Emily Brontë's *Wuthering Heights*, whose marriage to Linton similarly offends against her natural being. Leslie is 'not one of your souly sort' (p. 104); he is suited to a life of cars, business, dilettante class politics and the attendant paternalism. Yet, as with Gerald Crich in *Women in Love*, Lawrence does not load the moral dice too heavily against him. Leslie flounders through life, bolstered up by a series of social gains, but totally inadequate to grasp the real fruits of existence. He is bewildered by Lettie's moments of doubt about their future together. In the last part of the novel Lawrence pities rather than reproaches this advocate of machinery whose car is forever burning up the country lanes, who sleeps apart from his wife, entertains lavishly and has never glimpsed any reality that is not confined by social proprieties.

Lawrence implies that the nature of Leslie's inadequacy is partly sexual. Two factors prevent the author from making this explicit. First, a novelist in 1911 writing his first book could not easily free himself from the inhibitions about language and subject matter which still lingered from Victorian morality. (Three years later

Forster wrote *Maurice*, his study of a homosexual relationship, but it remained unpublished until after his death in 1970.) Though sexual situations could be delicately conveyed in serious fiction – non-consummation of marriage in George Eliot's *Middlemarch*, for example – it was hardly possible for Lawrence at twenty-five to challenge the norms and still expect to be published. As his writing matured it became unavoidable that his fiction should express his view of sex without reserve: but the legal prosecutions of *The Rainbow* and *Lady Chatterley's Lover* were the penalty for doing so. The second reason for Lawrence's reticence in *The White Peacock* was of his own making. The device of a first-person narrator who observes everything that is described in the novel makes it impossible for wholly private scenes to be analysed. The depiction of Leslie, therefore, seems more diffident than it could have been had Lawrence used some other narrative device.

A scene from the chapter entitled 'The Irony of Inspired Moments' illustrates the weakness of Lawrence's character analysis in his first novel. It begins in one tone, then after a pause in the narration it moves to a more sombre mood. The characters here are Leslie and Lettie.

He came down to supper, bathed, brushed, and radiant. He ate heartily and seemed to emanate a warmth of physical comfort and pleasure. The colour was flushed again into his face, and he carried his body with the old independent, assertive air. I have never known the time when he looked handsomer, when he was more attractive . . . He talked and laughed more gaily than ever, and was ostentatious in his movements, throwing back his head, taking little attitudes which displayed the broad firmness of his breast, the grace of his well-trained physique. I left them at the piano; he was sitting pretending to play, and looking up all the time at her, who stood with her hand on his shoulder.

(pp. 202–3)

Lawrence (or Cyril) here concentrates on Leslie's physical qualities; but the exceptional grace and vitality of his appearance indicates his heightened sensuality. He is 'radiant', 'assertive', 'attractive', 'ostentatious', like a peacock flaunting himself, sexually alert. But, hampered by having the story told by an uninvolved third person, Lawrence can only end the act like a curtain falling in the theatre and move to the next:

In the morning he was up early, by six o'clock downstairs and attending to the car. When I got down I found him very busy, and very quiet.

(pp. 203)

The tone has changed from expectation to defeat: 'He was remarkably dull and wordless' (p. 203). Lawrence signifies that
something has happened, but cannot make clear what it is. When
Lettie appears in the breakfast room, the tension is conveyed by the
prose well enough, but we can only guess at the reason.

> He stood in the doorway a moment, looking at her with beseeching eyes.
> She kept her face half averted, and would not look at him, but stood pale
> and cold, biting her underlip.
>
> (p. 204)

A crucial change of direction has taken place for Lettie and Leslie,
but we are seriously in the dark about its nature. Has Leslie
molested Lettie? ('I knew you were angry', he goes on to say.) Has
he been an unsuccessful lover? ('I don't see why – why it should
make trouble between us', he adds, perhaps relegating sex to a
minor place in a relationship, as Clifford Chatterley more explicitly
does in Lawrence's last novel.) Have they made love, and Lettie
now repents it? ('You make my hands – my very hands disclaim
me', she says (p. 205), as though she is ashamed of something.) Has
she rebuffed his advances? (The aftermath shows Lettie withholding herself physically from Leslie, averting her face and hardly
moving.) Lawrence shows that something major has occurred, for
there can be no other explanation of the change of tone in the
chapter; but his art is not yet able to deal with it head on.

Lettie, unlike the Brangwen sisters, or Alvina Houghton in *The
Lost Girl*, or Constance Chatterley, lacks what Lawrence later came
to recognize as the most vital part of human nature, the courage to
dare, to be herself, and the whole of herself. Perhaps because he
saddles himself with an inadequately conceived narrator-figure in
Cyril, Lawrence tends only to show Lettie in the early stages of her
history. Once she has married Leslie, the mechanics of the narration
are such that we can only see her intermittently, at dinner parties,
during visits home or through letters. Cyril loses the immediacy of
contact with his sister that has allowed him (by stretching probability to its limits) to witness every major stage of her friendships
with George and Leslie. If the novel becomes rushed in its final
stages it is partly because the author does not know how to maintain
interest in Lettie when she has moved outside Cyril's world. We
never doubt, however, that she has made the wrong choice in
marrying Leslie, has become a mere social success and is denied an
essential part of her being. Lawrence illustrates through Lettie's
mistake a general principle that concerns him throughout his life:

our first duty is not to win social approbation, to find economic security or even to perpetuate the species in our own likeness, but to fulfil to the last jot the potentialities of our own selfhood.

Lettie's wrong choice mirrors thousands like it; in particular it looks forward to Mrs Morel in *Sons and Lovers,* a character fashioned upon Lawrence's own mother:

This peculiar abnegation of self is the resource of a woman for the escaping of the responsibilities of her own development. Like a nun, she puts over her living face a veil, as a sign that the woman no longer exists for herself; she is the servant of God, of some man, of her children, or maybe of some cause.

(p. 323)

It is as though Lettie and George block their own arteries, withering and crumpling in the desiccated second-best of their marriages to Leslie and Meg. Lawrence may in later years have felt that *The White Peacock* stopped too soon, not merely because of his own inexpertise in handling the narrative but because he had not shown in Lettie and George any capacity to develop *after* their fatefully wrong choices have been made: they just seem to wither or stagnate. We see Lettie in the later chapters preening herself like a captive peacock on show to an admiring public, and George drained and ruined by the brutal marriage into which he has forced himself. Their lives are wretchedly hollow. The capacity for growth, which Lawrence later came to believe could never be utterly destroyed in a truly living person, has in this novel been stunted. His central characters prove themselves to be fatally ordinary. If Lawrence afterwards took people like Annable rather than Lettie or George as his model for human action, it may be that a consequent loss of probability occurred in his work. The likelihood of what happens to Lettie and George, given the type of society in which they live, seems so disturbingly right that one more readily accepts Lawrence's life-affirming beliefs in *The White Peacock* than one always does in the more intellectually demanding later novels. He knew that if our first duty is to realize our natural selves, our prime danger is that we acquiesce too easily in being social beings – we want to be well off, to marry 'suitably', to be 'acceptable', or 'successful'.

Lawrence cannot confidently parallel what happens to Lettie and George with the narrator's own struggles to find a meaning in his life. He portrayed too much of his own adolescent uncertainties in Cyril's character. That he had some sort of personal identification with him is clear if we recall that Beardsall was the maiden name of Lawrence's mother. The strongly loving matriarch, the weak father (who, in the novel, has been wholly severed from the family and rather pathetically dies after an attempted reunion), the passionate ties with what is familiar in the local landscape, coupled with an untapped longing to find other sides to life, all combine to give us an embryonic Paul Morel, the main character in *Sons and Lovers*. It must be said, however, that Lawrence largely fails to make his narrator as interesting as the people he talks about, despite his own obvious closeness to him. At the beginning of the story he gives a sense of frightened desolation to Cyril Beardsall:

I felt the great wild pity, and a sense of terror, and a sense of horror, and a sense of awful littleness and loneliness among a great empty space. I felt beyond myself as if I were a mere fleck drifting unconsciously through the dark.

(p. 52)

This is like Emily Brontë's language, insistent, lofty and brooding; but it seems both here and on later occasions oddly empty, for Cyril never projects himself long enough into his own narration for us to care about him much. Lawrence makes Cyril's rôle in the novel so neutrally and discriminatingly observing of the main triangle that he ceases to have a sustained vitality of his own.

Lawrence probably diagnosed this failure, for he did not repeat the first-person narrative technique in any subsequent novel. The only relationship Cyril forms, since Emily is so shadowy a figure, is with George, to whom he acts as an intellectual mentor. Though Lawrence may irritate some readers with Cyril's name-dropping, it is evident that the author has an intelligent young man's interest in the life of the mind:

Day after day I told him what the professors had told me; of life, of sex and its origins; of Schopenhauer and William James.

(p. 75)

The truth of the relationship lies less in matters of the mind than of the body. A physical intimacy develops between the two men, just as it does between Crich and Birkin in *Women in Love,* and we perceive it entirely through Cyril's admiring gaze. To Cyril, George's eyes 'were beautifully eloquent – as eloquent as a kiss' (p. 106); he advises him to leave his neck showing if he wants to please Lettie; and when George is very tired he tenderly ministers to him.

In my heart of hearts, I longed for someone to nestle against, someone who would come between me and the coldness and wetness of the surroundings.

(p. 254)

For a while George serves just such a purpose, but though something like a homosexual undercurrent in their friendship must be acknowledged and becomes overt when the two men bathe together, Lawrence has not sufficiently absorbed us in Cyril's affairs for us to be greatly interested in the relationship. Drying himself, Cyril watches George, 'For he knew not I admired the noble, white fruitfulness of his form' (p. 257); and he momentarily recalls the story of Annable, casting himself, no doubt, in the rôle of Lady Crystabel, who had also had that rather voyeurist interest in Annable, and had nearly destroyed her lover by thinking of him as a Greek statue. Lawrence feared or hated the 'aesthetic' streak in people which made life something to watch, and art something to possess mentally; and we see the beginning of this in *The White Peacock*.

Lawrence vigorously evokes one aspect of Cyril's personality, his intense attachment to his home and surroundings. Since the novel was written whilst Lawrence was taking the first steps away from the country of his growing up, it inevitably reflects the pain of seeing familiar views with the freshness of a last look.

I thought of the time when my friend should not follow the harrow on our own snug valley side, and when Lettie's room next mine should be closed to hide its emptiness, not its joy. My heart always clung passionately to the hollow which held us all; how could I bear that I should be desolate!

(p. 83)

Even in this honest writing there is a hint of mannered extravagance and self-consciousness: 'how could I bear that I should be so desolate!' *The White Peacock* does not sink under the weight of its self-indulgence – it is too intelligent and 'felt' for that – but it sometimes strays into the morass of prose poetry. At its worst, the mannered phrases derive more from Lawrence's reading of Ruskin, William Morris and Walter Pater than from his first-hand observation.

The tender-budded trees shuddered and moaned; when the wind was dry, the young leaves flapped limp. The grass and corn grew lush, but the light of the dandelions was quite extinguished, and it seemed that only a little time back had we made merry before the broad glare of these flowers. The bluebells lingered and lingered; they fringed the fields for weeks like purple fringe of mourning. The pink campions came out only to hang heavy with rain; hawthorn buds remained tight and hard as pearls, shrinking into the brilliant green foliage; the forget-me-nots, the poor pleiades of the wood, were ragged weeds. Often at the end of the day, the sky opened, and stately clouds hung over the horizon infinitely far away, glowing, through the yellow distance, with an amber lustre.

(p. 252)

Though Lawrence's vision and feeling are not in doubt, he is rather too obviously straining after the tone in which to express it, and the effect is to distance the reader instead of involving him. Moments of true detail – the dry wind causing the young leaves to flap limply, the pink campions heavy with rain – are obscured by the wilful elegancies: 'purple fringe of mourning', 'pearls', 'the poor pleiades of the wood', 'stately clouds', 'an amber lustre'. An awful literariness creeps into some of the conversations, too, occasionally to ludicrous effect. When Cyril tells Emily that 'You think the flesh of the apple is nothing, nothing. You only care for the eternal pips' (p. 86), we can only laugh. The novel constantly displays its taste and sensibility, but seems too often to use names like jewels on a rich fabric, more for the dazzle they will give than as an integral part of the material. Clausen, Ibsen, Wordsworth, Burne-Jones, Hardy, Aubrey Beardsley, Gorki, Maeterlinck: important artists, some philosophical, some social-minded, some merely decorative, but all mentioned by Lawrence in his first novel too much like evidence of culture.

When he came to write *The Rainbow* and *Women in Love*, Lawrence was able to develop many themes at once and to locate them in a penetratingly observed social setting. *The White Peacock* lacks the density of these later novels. The countryside is at times described with lyrical exactness, but the attempts to convey a distinctive community only half succeed. When, for example, Lawrence talks of the miners' strike at the opening of Part Two he seems to nod with a dutiful conscience towards their plight but to be more interested in demonstrating Leslie's supercilious reaction. Sometimes he achieves a genuine variety of social life – when George entertains his cronies at the Mill after threshing day, for example – but *The White Peacock* lacks the maintained vitality of community existence which Lawrence caught three years later in *Sons and Lovers*.

What, then, is the achievement of *The White Peacock*? Few who read the novel are likely to be unmoved by George's drift into alcoholic failure or by Lettie's weak decision to marry the man whose name insipidly resembles her own. Both George and Leslie prepare

25

the way for Gerald Crich. The novel has important links with later works, yet a sturdy independence in its own right. Had Lawrence died, as so many of his generation did, in his early youth, this novel would still be read as a minor work of real distinction. It has, to a degree remarkable in a first novel, a sense of how life could be and of how it more normally is.

# 3

## The Trespasser

In his second novel Lawrence seems to have experimented with forms and methods quite different from those of *The White Peacock*. The first novel attempts to evoke a complex pattern of relationships between a number of people; the second concentrates with furious intensity on the affair between Siegmund MacNair and Helena Verden. *The White Peacock* takes place over a period of years; *The Trespasser*, though framed by a prologue and epilogue set some months after Siegmund's suicide, happens essentially within one week. The rooted familiarity of the first novel, full of landscapes and impressions which Lawrence himself had known throughout his life, is exchanged for the Isle of Wight, which Lawrence knew personally only from a holiday enjoyed there in the summer of 1909. Where *The White Peacock* laments the inevitable farewells that have to be made to the country of one's youth, *The Trespasser* looks forward with the despair of melancholy adolescence to the crisis and desolation of middle age. The main relationships are dealt with more intensely than in *The White Peacock*. The result fluctuates wildly and is normally written off by critics as a very minor work indeed. Containing some of Lawrence's most extravagantly unleashed prose, it tempers the rhapsodies with a new symbolic suggestiveness and manages to blend moments of intimate pain into what the author realistically thought, immediately after writing it, was 'a decorated idyll running to seed in realism'.

Lawrence wrote *The Trespasser* at a particularly unhappy and disoriented stage of his life. Death and illness in the close-knit family circle, uncertainty about his career, scant fulfilment in personal relationships – against that background he met Helen Corke, a colleague at the school in Croydon where he taught from October 1908 to March 1912. She was later to write her own version of the love affair she had briefly enjoyed with a music master, Herbert Baldwin Macartney, in the summer of 1909. (Their stay on the Isle of Wight took place at the very moment Lawrence was there.) Helen Corke's novel, *Neutral Ground* (1933), is at heart an autobiographical account of the relationship between

Ellis, the heroine, and her violin teacher, whom she calls 'Domine', and it covers much the same territory as *The Trespasser*. In 1975 her autobiography, *In Our Infancy*, appeared complete with the brief journal about the week on the Isle of Wight which she had written shortly after the Macartney affair sixty-six years earlier. This journal, and Helen Corke's direct account, became the basis of *The Trespasser*. Though Lawrence was, therefore, writing at second hand, basing his novel on events in which he had no share (even down to small details like the discovery of a light-bulb on the beach), he knew Helen Corke extremely well: was in love with her and concerned to help her through her grief and horror, even her guilt. He saw her as the kind of woman who must exert her will on men, but he pitied her for this. She, meanwhile, had a personal view of him as a kindred spirit occupying the 'neutral ground' between the opposed poles of heterosexuality and homosexuality.

The truth of the novel lies as much in its general tone of un-happiness and discontent as in the particular analysis of its central relationship. Lawrence records in *The Trespasser* much of his sense of wonder at discovering his own sexuality, but the typical bewil-derment of early youth is there too. Doubts about religion, the purpose of life and the possibility of finding either spiritual equality or emotional ease in the arms of a woman run through the novel. Stylistically, as he noted himself in a letter to Edward Garnett (29 January 1912), it is 'too florid, too *chargé*', but both in theme and presentation *The Trespasser* marks a crucial stage in Lawrence's development.

In *The White Peacock* Lawrence had made a character's reaction to music one touchstone of his or her sensitivity. In his second novel he draws specifically on motifs in Wagner's *Ring*. Siegmund and Helena, the protagonists in *The Trespasser*, resemble Siegmund and Sieglinde, and Tristan and Isolde, though in Lawrence's story it is the man who is married. Siegmund in the *Ring* is des-troyed by the gods because he has a forbidden love. Lawrence used Wagner not as a rigid model for his own work, but as a standard for comparing his own values. He entirely rejects Wagner's trans-cendental view that to die of love is a triumph. For Lawrence it is bitter and sordid, but he shares something of Wagner's contempt for ordinariness and low materialism, the mere restrictiveness of conventional social marriage, and the sense that a passion is some-thing to give oneself to, whatever the result.

In *The Trespasser* music is a central motif, thrilling the atmo-sphere on the Isle of Wight as though it were Prospero's enchanted isle. Siegmund plays, but not as a grand maestro or a famous soloist. Lawrence exactly catches the everyday nature of his working life by making him, like Aaron Sisson in the London chapters of *Aaron's Rod*, a member of a theatre orchestra, doomed mostly to scratch away at sentimental melodies from musical comedies or popular operas. His music lies a long way off from art. For the first time Lawrence uses the word 'mechanical' with insistence: Siegmund is a victim of the city and of the suburban responsibilities forced upon the city-dweller. His music affords little compensation for the mean existence he lives with his embittered wife and hostile family. Lawrence carries much more conviction in placing Siegmund and Helena at the start of *The Trespasser* than he does in the hectic central part of the book, for he was living in an outer London suburb himself at the time he wrote the novel and was surrounded by colleagues whose domestic lives were little different from Siegmund's. A detail like 'The table was spread with a dirty cloth that had great brown stains betokening children' (p. 15) seems more acute and considerably starker than the kind we find a few pages later when Siegmund and Helena are on their way to the Isle of Wight: 'White with the softness of a bosom, the water rose up frothing and swaying gently' (p. 21). Lawrence returns to this soul-crippling world in the final chapters, once more finding a truth of observation which often eluded him in the core of the novel.

Lawrence often reaches the apex of his powers when analysing his characters' growth *towards* emotional maturity. In *The Trespasser*, however, he is concerned only with the climax and destruction of a relationship. He establishes Siegmund's adulterous passion for Helena as a fact but makes little attempt to demonstrate what it is founded upon. The mechanical nature of Siegmund's working day, the martyred attitude of his wife, 'the grave, cold looks of condemnation from his children' (p. 18) obviously show his need to escape, but they do not in themselves explain why Helena Verden so enchants him. Critics must beware of being too literal, but Lawrence asks too much of us if he intends the sheer ecstasy of the language to carry all before it. For Siegmund, he says, 'Helena was a presence. She was ambushed, fused in an aura of his love' (p. 23). Throughout *The Trespasser* Lawrence is on the verge of expressing in the central relationship a kind of semi-mystic communion of souls. It eludes him partly because of inadequate language and partly because he does not here provide the perspective through which, in later novels, the main characters are defined. The thinly drawn friendship of Helena and Louisa, with its mild hint of lesbianism, or the largely feminine household in which Siegmund's authority has been dimmed almost to extinction, do not provide enough history for the main adultery to seem inevitable.

Helena may be seen as another version of Lettie Beardsall. Less tempted by society than Lettie, considerably less witty and ultimately less self-aware, she nonetheless has the same tendency to transform what really is into what she feels it ought to be. 'With her the dream was always more than the actuality. Her dream of Siegmund was more to her than Siegmund himself' (p. 30). Helena, Lettie, and Miriam in *Sons and Lovers* respond to life in much the same way, refusing what it specifically offers and preferring a fantasy world. In this lies both their fascination and their danger. Lawrence invokes Helena's rarity of imagination but makes it clear that a soul such as hers turns its back on the creative side of life by substituting its own mock creativity. The end-product of this process would be someone like Hermione in *Women in Love*, who wants to mould her man into an imagined shape rather than to accept the real personality he presents. Lawrence makes it explicit that Helena's fancies lead eventually to Hermione's life-rejection:

'That yellow flower hadn't time to be brushed and combed by the fairies before dawn came. It is tousled . . .' so she thought to herself. The pink convolvuli were fairy horns or telephones from the day fairies to the night fairies. The rippling sunlight on the sea was the Rhine maidens spreading their bright hair to the sun. That was her favourite form of thinking. The value of all things was in the fancy they evoked. She did not care for people; they were vulgar, ugly and stupid, as a rule.

(p. 43)

Has Helena really seen the flowers or the sunlight? Has she not, by her conjurer's art, turned life into fiction, experience into dream? An imagination like hers may be exquisite, but it is life-denying too. Lawrence turns his own inclination for lavish prose to clever effect. The fairies and the Rhine maidens suggest the merely fanciful, even the absurdity, in Helena's response to life.

Like Miriam in *Sons and Lovers*, Helena offers herself in sexual sacrifice. Lawrence was later to suggest a positive virtue and even thrill in the notion of orgasmic sacrifice, as 'The Woman Who Rode Away' and *The Plumed Serpent* make explicit, but in the early novels (later, too, in *Lady Chatterley's Lover*) he sees it as an abuse of the total partnership of body, will and spirit which sex ought to entail.

Helena, who is often described in the novel as though she were a religious image ('He saw the silver of tears among the moonlit ivory of her face' – p. 37), gives herself to Siegmund with a fundamental chastity. 'She belonged to that class of "dreaming woman" with whom passion exhausts itself at the mouth' (p. 30). The failure of their relationship is Helena's responsibility, just as Lettie makes the crucially wrong decision in *The White Peacock*. Moments of fulfilment come in which Helena and Siegmund seem as though moulded to each other in perfect union, but Lawrence laments the impermanence of the ecstasy and the constant dominance of time. In the early novels he seems to come reluctantly to a sense that women, as lovers, must betray. He sums up Helena's tyranny in a single sentence:

She wanted to sacrifice to him, make herself a burning altar to him, and she wanted to possess him.

(p. 56)

On many occasions in *Sons and Lovers* we are asked to see Miriam in the same way:

She would obey him in his trifling commands. But once he was obeyed, then she had him in her power, she knew, to lead him where she would.

(*Sons and Lovers*, p. 364)

Just as Miriam yearns for the clean innocence of nunhood, so Helena sees her relationship with Siegmund as a combination of self-immolation, worship and a sort of possession which is not so much demonic as in the spirit of Donne's famous sonnet:

> Take mee to you, imprison mee, for I
> Except you'enthrall mee, never shall be free,
> Nor ever chast, except you ravish mee.

The use of the colour white repeatedly applied to Helena sustains the notion of a Christian innocent, and so she sees herself. The implications of her quasi-religious approach to sexual union appal Lawrence, for the object of such devotion necessarily loses his humanity and becomes an idol or a god. Helena sees life as though it were directed by a master artist, with a rhythm and flow orchestrated like a symphony. She observes the pattern of existence, and the details that make up the pattern, but she misses entirely the mood and tone that the pattern evokes.

31

'I want to absorb it all,' he said.

When at last they turned away:

'Yes,' said Helena slowly; 'one can recall the details, but never the atmosphere.'

He pondered a moment.

'How strange!' he said. 'I can recall the atmosphere, but not the detail. It is a moment to me, not a piece of scenery. I should say the picture was in me, not out there.'

Without troubling to understand – she was inclined to think it verbiage she made a small sound of assent.

'That is why you want to go again to a place, and I don't care so much, because I have it with me,' he concluded.

(p. 66)

In snatches of dialogue like this Lawrence crystallizes the exact nature of what he wants to say in *The Trespasser*. He forgets about decorating his language and offers instead an explicit summary of the two characters, Helena all detachment and precision, Siegmund sucking experience into his innermost being.

Lawrence often seems, in *The Trespasser*, to be groping towards ideas which he will properly realize in later novels. Helena looks towards Miriam; perhaps also towards Gudrun in *Women in Love*, with her view of human destiny and her response to Wagner and the Teutons. Lawrence's initial intention of calling the novel *The Saga of Siegmund* was not without irony. Siegmund may have a Nordic name, but he feels part not of one culture or even of one section of time, but of the eternal essence of things. 'Why should I be parcelled up into mornings and evenings and nights?' he asks (p. 68). 'He was sea and sunlight mixed, heaving, warm, deliciously strong' (p. 52). Lawrence constantly associates Siegmund with the central original forces of the universe, likening his heart-beats to the 'great expulsions of life' which cause existence. He attempts more in Siegmund than he is able to achieve, for he intends him to be a life-force, the first Adam on earth, and also a human being crushed between the brutalities of modern society and Helena's refining dreams. His narcissism recalls both George and Annable in *The White Peacock*: 'his body was full of delight and his hands glad with the touch of himself' (p. 58). In Siegmund's meeting with Hampson, we catch a glimmer of the male admiration which draws Cyril and George together. Lawrence gives too fragmented and jerky a portrait of Siegmund, however. Little light is thrown on his character by recalling his childhood illness: if it is to suggest his need for mother-love, which occasional references to Helena as a Madonna-figure would endorse, then the theme is certainly not sustained. Similarly, Lawrence gives inadequate grounds for Siegmund's retreat into himself during his last hours on the island.

Siegmund would like to transcend time, relishing what the present moment gives in a totally physical, sensual, immediate and whole-hearted, therefore integral, response to what life offers now. Helena wants to turn it into something else, so as not to surrender to it. Lawrence never allows his reader to forget the irony of this, for the action of *The Trespasser* is dominated by an ever-ticking clock. The idyll on the Isle of Wight must end within a week. Lawrence, like Thomas Mann, whose *Death in Venice* (1913) he anticipates in the slow fatal journey to the island (a precursor, too, of Kate's boat-trip across the lake in *The Plumed Serpent*), is aware from the outset that the authority of time over man inevitably renders puny and ephemeral even the grandest devotion.

Amidst the journeying of oceans and clouds and the circling flight of the heavy spheres, lost to sight in the sky, Siegmund and Helena, two grains of life in the vast movement, were travelling a moment side by side.

(p. 46)

This could easily be the opening sentence of a novel by Thomas Hardy: the same sense of the crushing vastness of the universe, the same pathetic insignificance of human existence. To some extent Lawrence follows a Hardy-like course throughout the novel; he stresses how life goes on after Siegmund's death so that, within a short time, it is as if he had never lived. The strings of his violin shrink and snap, his wife finds a new life and Helena is courted by another man. Lawrence never attains quite the purity of fatalism which informs Hardy. Siegmund finds utter fulfilment and commitment in single moments, Wordsworthian spots of time. He commits suicide not because they were only short-lived but because they will never happen again. He has glimpsed the uttermost potential of human existence, the interfusion of two beings in their passion; for the Lawrence of this novel, that makes life meaningful. Later, notably in some of Birkin's utterances in *Women in Love*, Lawrence was to recoil from this notion of interfusion in love, wanting people to remain separate and themselves even in the intensity of their passion; but a conviction that lovers can and ought to merge their beings in each other forms part of the romanticism of *The Trespasser*, inherited perhaps from Wagner's *Tristan*.

In time Siegmund may be forgotten, but Lawrence refuses to see time as the final arbiter. He is struggling towards the mystery which he defines more closely – so far as he can ever define it – in the last pages of *Women in Love*. He gives Siegmund the best words he can to express this sense – which becomes fundamental in Lawrence's later work – that there is a source in the universe from which we can never be consciously or wholly separated.

'Ah, well!' thought Siegmund – he was tired – 'if one bee dies in a swarm, what is it, so long as the hive is all right? Apart from the gold light, and the hum and the colour of day, what was I? Nothing! Apart from these rushings out of the hive, along with swarm, into the dark meadows of night, gathering God knows what, I was a pebble. Well, the day will swarm in golden again, with colour on the wings of every bee, and humming in each activity. The gold and the colour and sweet smell and the sound of life, they exist, even if there is no bee; it only happens we see the iridescence on the wings of a bee. It exists whether or not, bee or no bee. Since the iridescence and the humming of life *are* always, and since it was they who made me, then I am not lost. At least, I do not care. If the spark goes out the essence of the fire is there in the darkness. What does it matter? Besides, I *have* burned bright; I have laid up a fine cell of honey somewhere – I wonder where? We can never point to it; but it *is* so – what does it matter, then!'

(pp. 143–4)

This is intuitive or metaphorical writing, but it strives to find a language for the metaphysical instinct that Lawrence felt gave a final value to life.

If Lawrence believes in 'the essence of the fire' which never goes out – whatever happens to the mere individual – then Siegmund's suicide becomes irrelevant and scarcely a defeat at all: merely an acknowledgement that his best moment has passed. Yet surely Lawrence does expect us to see it almost as a sin, certainly a defeat? I think he finds himself at the end of *The Trespasser* caught in a dilemma from which he has no obvious escape. On the one hand he talks semi-mystically of an eternal existence which renders human individuality insignificant and death meaningless, but on the other hand he presents Siegmund (as he has earlier shown George Saxton and Lettie) as unable to grow any further. He has reached, quite literally, the end. His development is blocked because he cannot find within himself the capacity to go on. That, in Lawrentian terms, is denial of the spirit. Lawrence, I suspect, saw for himself the paradox he had created and makes attempts to bridge it by quoting (inaccurately, as it happens) from Shakespeare. As Siegmund prepares to die:

34

' "But for that fear of something after-death" ', he quoted to himself.

'It is not fear,' he said. 'The act itself will be humble and fearsome, but the after-death – it's no more than struggling awake when you're sick with a fright of dreams. "We are such stuff as dreams are made of".'

(p. 186)

The artifice here diminishes the austere quality of the closing chapters, but Lawrence attempted in his gesture towards Hamlet and Prospero more than the kind of literary allusiveness with which *The White Peacock* is studded. He tries to prove that the 'wonderful kindness in death' which Siegmund anticipates has some justification, but he fails to convince us that suicide can really be the next natural stage in Siegmund's spiritual development, as valid in its way as Aaron's wandering off to 'flower' elsewhere at the end of *Aaron's Rod*. Lawrence has insisted too much on the sense of nothingness which Siegmund feels after leaving Helena for the last time.

Much of the best writing in *The Trespasser* occurs in the final chapters. It is a relief to exchange the rhapsodic prose of earlier passages for the bitterness and severity of the close. The clusters of prose beautiful have sometimes been intentional – Helena's Rhine maidens, for example, or Siegmund's swim to the white rocks of the headlands which he sees for a moment with her eye for fantasy – but too often they are lush for the sake of it, evoking thoughts of overripe fruit rather than magical islands.

They faced the lighted chamber of the west, whence, behind the torn, dull-gold curtains of fog, the sun was departing with pomp.

(p. 27)

Lawrence abandons such orchestration in the last sixty pages. His observation and feeling perfectly correspond in the scenes following Siegmund's return home. A chill, silent hostility affects the whole family, even Gwen, the child of his heart. Beatrice, the wife, is a prime example of Lawrence's skill in drawing character with a few swift strokes. We may recognize her again in aspects of Mrs Morel or in the bitter wife of *Aaron's Rod*, all rueful for lost passion; but she has a life of her own, full of pent-up resentment, dreary motherhood and loneliness.

In the morning Beatrice was disturbed by the sharp sneck of the hall door. Immediately awake, she heard his quick, firm step hastening down the gravel path. In her impotence, discarded like a worn out object, she lay for the moment stiff with bitterness.

'I am nothing, I am nothing,' she said to herself. She lay quite rigid for a time.

(p. 19)

Beatrice listens, watches, abuses her husband or comforts her children, but she never shares her life with anyone. Adjectives like 'stiff' and 'rigid' typify her; a favourite verb associated with her is 'fixed'. When Lawrence wants to indicate Mrs Morel's first change of heart towards her young husband, in the opening chapter of *Sons and Lovers*, he again uses the adjective 'rigid'. Lawrence may detest her subservience to the family, but he pities her, too. Her unwillingness to think about Siegmund after his death springs not just from heartlessness but from pain.

'I don't care for *The Trespasser* so much as the first book', Lawrence wrote in a letter shortly after it was published in 1912. Knowing both how uncertainly he had put into words the sexual and philosophical beliefs he was searching for at this stage of his life and how much of the novel was based on Helen Corke's reminiscences rather than his own, his reaction does not seem surprising. Of course, *The Trespasser* is more deeply unhappy than *The White Peacock*. Its unsettling character is another reason why few readers bother to return to it. Too full of experiences Lawrence had not lived through himself, yet written amid bouts of desperation, the novel lacks consistency. Despite its patchiness, however, it forms a watershed in Lawrence's development, for within it he wrestles with the new discoveries of beginning maturity. If we look at what his contemporaries were writing at the same time – Ford Madox Ford's *The 'Half Moon'* (1909), E. M. Forster's *Howards End* (1910), Katherine Mansfield's *In a German Pension* (1911), Compton Mackenzie's *Carnival* (1912) – we see how personal Lawrence's art had already become and how he had the capacity now to advance the English novel in directions it had not previously approached.

# 4

## *Sons and Lovers*

The new direction in which Lawrence moves in *Sons and Lovers* may not be immediately clear. That the novel is longer than the first two, more obviously autobiographical, does not make it an innovatory work. Indeed, the element of self-exploration makes it in one respect a very traditional kind of novel – the *Bildungsroman* attempted by many romantic artists. Its confidence, intensity and strange mixture of self-mistrust and self-knowledge does, however, mark a new stage in Lawrence's writing. He dramatized much of his early life in this novel – his family background, his education, his first sexual relationships – but he always kept before himself the need to create a work of the imagination. *Sons and Lovers* is a great work of self-analysis by a young writer looking back on the recent years of growing up: but it is always first and foremost a novel, not an autobiography.

Lawrence establishes an honesty of method right at the start. '"The Bottoms" succeeded to "Hell Row"' (p. 7). Visitors to Eastwood can still see the streets to which the opening paragraph of *Sons and Lovers* refers, and drive round the pock-marked countryside where the coalpits, 'some of which had been worked in the time of Charles II' (p. 8), bear witness to the struggle for survival of generations of miners' families. The colliers and their donkeys burrowed down 'like ants into the earth, making queer mounds and little black places among the corn-fields and the meadows' (p. 8) – a continuous history, in other words, of desecrated country-side and anonymous service to a vast capitalistic enterprise. Lawrence shows from the start (as in the 'queer mounds and little black places') that the village of Bestwood and the coal and iron fields of Nottinghamshire and Derbyshire monstrously deform the landscape in which they are set. Companies such as Carston, Waite and Co. have moved in like barons palatine from a former age, to command the lives of everyone here. Managers, workers and their families are all degraded by the urbanized life which industrialization brings about. A companionship of work-sharing dies out. Lawrence wrote his novel while the process was still taking place.

Throughout *Sons and Lovers* Mrs Morel, the protagonist's mother, is a matriarch to her family. When Lawrence first introduces her to us she seems to gather to herself all the repression and despair of the thousands of married women who are condemned to rear their children in narrow terraced houses beside squalid alleys and congested ashpits. She is pregnant for the third time with a child she can hardly bear to bring into her miserable world, the short days of ecstatic married life having long since faded into a permanent evening of household drudgery and stifled hopes.

> But for herself, nothing but this dreary endurance – till the children grew up! . . . This coming child was too much for her. If it were not for William and Annie, she was sick of it, the struggle with poverty and ugliness and meanness.
>
> (p. 12)

Lawrence portrays in Mrs Morel a person with a soaring capacity for life – though she can stunt the life in others. She recognizes the instinctive dignity of the miner, which she calls 'noble', but instead of taking it at its simple value she almost fantasizes about it. 'He risked his life daily, and with gaiety' (p. 19), she thinks, seeming to revel more in the idea than the fact of Morel's danger. As with Lettie and Helena, reality eventually breaks through fantasy; the disillusionment which follows embitters her irrevocably. Yet her determination not to be ground down never deserts her even in her final almost gladiatorial battle with cancer. That Lawrence first presents her to us at the nadir of her moral strength is important for several reasons. First, he concentrates in her the dreariness of all the women who inhabit the 'Bottoms' and 'Hell Row'. Secondly, by placing her in this deepest trough of despair at the start of the novel, Lawrence emphasizes the enormity of Mrs Morel's achievement in coming to terms with her life. Throughout the novel she seems always to be climbing uphill to the high plain of her final encounter with death. If *Sons and Lovers* has an epic scale, then this is illustrated as much by Mrs Morel as by her younger son. Thirdly, Lawrence weaves together the fates of mother and son so closely in this novel that he makes the birth and early life of Paul the cause of Mrs Morel's revival. Like the matriarch in Shakespeare's *Coriolanus*, 'The thought of being the mother of men was warming to her heart' (p. 44). The novel belongs as much to this Volumnia as to her son, for there is no part of Paul Morel's sexual development or social advance in which his mother is not implicated.

*Sons and Lovers* traces the careers of the three Morel boys – William, Paul and Arthur – their sister Annie, and their parents,

Gertrude Coppard and Walter Morel. William leaves home to find his fortune in London, he squanders his sexual life on a shallow girl called Lily, and eventually he dies; Arthur enlists in the army, and Annie marries; but the focus of the novel remains firmly fixed upon Paul Morel and his mother. Paul's relationship with his parents, whose love for each other had withered long before he was born, with Miriam Leivers, the companion of his adolescence, and Clara Dawes, the married woman who initiates him into adulthood, these are the subject matter of the book, coupled with his complex attitude to the village and society in which he has been reared and his growing awareness of his own creative instincts when life seems to hold only years of work in a surgical-stocking factory. Perhaps the central intensity of the novel springs from Lawrence's investigation of new experiences – Paul's first job, first love, first confrontation with death. Each encounter recreates Paul's sensibility. The stimulus of innovation, old attitudes constantly challenged, leads to deepened perceptions. In strictly autobiographical terms the novel is obviously open-ended, for Paul at its conclusion stands only on the threshold of adult life, but a powerfully emotional solution seems nevertheless to have been reached.

In one of the most lyrical passages of *Sons and Lovers* Lawrence evokes the mood of Paul's conception. The father of the unborn child seems hardly to be there. After one of their fiercest rows Mrs Morel is thrown from her house by her drunken husband and wanders across the garden almost delirious with anger and shock, the cold white light of the full moon falling upon her.

With an effort she roused herself to see what it was that penetrated her consciousness. The tall white lilies were reeling in the moonlight, and the air was charged with their perfume, as with a presence. Mrs Morel gasped slightly in fear. She touched the big, pallid flowers on their petals, then shivered. They seemed to be stretching in the moonlight. She put her hand into one white bin: the gold scarcely showed on her fingers by moonlight. She bent down to look at the binful of yellow pollen; but it only appeared dusky. Then she drank a deep draught of the scent. It almost made her dizzy.

(p. 35)

He represents in this episode in the garden the sexual consummation of Mrs Morel: the moon, the stiff white flowers, the perfume, the pollen. The formalism of the scene as Mrs Morel bends down to the cup of the lily particularly recalls the Annunciation to the Virgin Mary as it appears in a number of Renaissance paintings, in which Gabriel carries a lily as he brings the news to Mary of the child within her. Lawrence uses the iconography of Botticelli or Raphael to bestow on Mrs Morel a Madonna-like grace; and Paul's most positive source of revulsion against Miriam later in the novel will be his sense that she consciously emulates Christ's mother and seems to want to make him both her son and her lord. The beatific imagery works on the one hand to dignify Mrs Morel and on the other to belittle Miriam, both of them in similar rôles – a slight inconsistency of which, perhaps, Lawrence remained unaware. More importantly, however, the passage shows Lawrence imagining beyond his own experience. *Sons and Lovers* is sometimes spoken of as though it were entirely autobiographical, but a passage like this (taking place before Paul is born) reminds us that we are considering a novel and a work of art.

The household into which Paul is born struggles not only against the surrounding social conditions but against its own divisiveness. D. H. Lawrence believed that industrial life in England stained each member of society with a mark as indelible as a brand, shrinking humanity and narrowing vision: to live in the mechanical servitude demanded by the gods of industrialization, productivity and consumption, was to live a wasted existence. Lawrence found all the ambitions of a modern secular state – a high material standard of living, an efficient bureaucracy, a booming consumer economy – essentially life-denying. He did not intend Paul's determination to better himself by winning middle-class approval to seem snobbish, but the reader may note it as an early stage in Lawrence's own rejection of everything which is affected by the industrial process. Though there may have been in Lawrence himself an equivocal response to high society, it was unjust of Bertrand Russell to claim of him that 'he had a snobbish pride' and that 'he had such a hatred of mankind' (Russell's *Autobiography*, vol. II, *1914–44*, p. 23 and p. 20). Lawrence's gradual move away from the restrictions of the Nottinghamshire coalfields, as projected through Paul Morel, was first and foremost a cry of rage against being born into the prison of the working class. In later work, however, he was to recognize the loss – particularly in comradeship – that moving away entailed.

Mr and Mrs Morel illustrate this class motif, he from mining stock, she from a burgher family separated by only two generations from a solid Protestant prosperity. Their union was founded on a sexual fascination, which is frankly recognized and well rendered, but is also evanescent; when it goes, the barrier of class between them is as potent as the curse upon Oedipus. Initially Gertrude

Coppard enjoys the frank manners of the working man and is intrigued by the difference of custom – 'She had never been "thee'd and thou'd" before' (p. 19) – but inevitably a gulf opens up between them. The class instinct has been deeply absorbed on both sides, though there is more to it than that:

There began a battle between the husband and wife – a fearful, bloody battle that ended only with the death of one. She fought to make him undertake his own responsibilities, to make him fulfil his obligations. But he was too different from her. His nature was purely sensuous, and she strove to make him moral, religious. She tried to force him to face things. He could not endure it – it drove him out of his mind.

(p. 23)

The battle which Lawrence talks of here is basically between two conflicting temperaments. Mrs Morel has an emotional power far beyond her husband's, as the verbs Lawrence uses here make clear: 'she fought . . . she strove . . . she tried to force'. But the clash springs from their class roots too, for Mrs Morel tries to give her husband the qualities of the burgher family from which she has come. Serious, productive, Nonconformist, venerating hard work and moral rigour, she stands for an ethic which Walter Morel, in his essentially physical existence, neither wants to observe nor understands. Even small details of rearing a family become crises in the perpetual fight. When, for example, Mrs Morel discovers that her husband has cut off Paul's curls – 'Yer non want ter make a wench on 'im' (p. 24) – it is as though an intruder has desecrated the relationship of mother and child. Constantly in these early chapters Lawrence emphasizes how Mrs Morel almost unconsciously excludes her husband from the bond which unites her to her children, and to Paul especially. 'She felt as if the navel string that had connected its frail little body with hers had not been broken' (p. 50). Only with her death is this umbilical union really severed. Because she believes Walter Morel to be weak and passive she drives him further into weakness and passivity. In doing so, though, she has some sense of her own guilt and is aware that she scars herself no less than her husband. Lawrence asserts that Mrs Morel 'lost none of her worth' (p. 25). He chooses the word 'worth' for the moral weight it carries, but perhaps we should be alive no less to its faint hint of chilling Calvinism. Lawrence in later life believed that he should have been more generous to his father in *Sons and Lovers* and, by implication, more severe with his mother's streak of self-righteousness. To have been so explicit, however, might well have unbalanced the novel. Mr Morel does not emerge merely as an idle sot and Mrs Morel is the most flawed of Madonna-figures. A careful tension is sustained between them in which the criticism of the woman and the pity for the man may be detected by any sensitive reader.

In talking of Gertrude Morel's inherent Protestant ethic and her husband's basically physical disposition, one hints at a fundamental historical struggle which the two of them play out. Lawrence managed to make them both convincingly realized characters, with a special poignancy since they were so clearly derived from memories of his own parents, and prototypes of the social drama, the conflict between industrial and pre-industrial values, which in some way informs almost everything he wrote. Lawrence had a highly developed sense of human evolution: the Morels are among his major characters who testify to this. Walter embodies, in the early part of the novel, what Lawrence regarded as the vigour, dignity and comradely virility of western man before the coming of industrialization. His disintegration partly represents the erosion of that 'natural' state by the forces of an industrial society. Gertrude, if we apply the analogy to her, represents those 'virtues' which have helped to make the industrial society possible: piety, prudence, temperance, hard work, saving and veneration of respectability. Inevitably the victories of the novel are hers, for her side has, so far, won the historic battle which Lawrence personifies in her and her husband. Morel's weaknesses are all those of pre-industrial man; her strengths are those of industrial society. Lawrence felt ambivalent at this stage towards both sides, and only in *The Rainbow* and *Women in Love* properly sorted out his views 'for' the pre-industrial society. That is probably why he felt in later years that he had been ungenerous to his father, or to Walter Morel. He meant he had not clarified his sympathy for what Morel's weaknesses actually represented.

Early in the novel Lawrence describes an incident which underlines the poignant isolation of Walter Morel. The husband has just flung a drawer at his wife and struck her on the forehead.

As he looked at her, who was cold and impassive as stone, with mouth shut tight, he sickened with feebleness and hopelessness of spirit. He was turning drearily away, when he saw a drop of blood fall from the averted wound into the boy's fragile, glistening hair. Fascinated he watched the heavy dark drop hang in the glistening cloud, and pull down the gossamer. Another drop fell. It would soak through the baby's scalp. He watched, fascinated, feeling it soak in; then, finally, his manhood broke.

(p. 54)

Was Lawrence being unsympathetic to his father here? It is difficult to think so. Certainly Morel's weakness of spirit follows his violence of temper, but what Lawrence evokes here is like an initiation rite in which the blood-sacrifice unites mother and child, priestess and acolyte, before the dull eyes of the pagan onlooker. Shortly before this moment, in an episode similar in intensity and other-worldliness to her contemplation of the lilies, Mrs Morel has ritually cast out the feeling of not wanting her new baby by holding him up to the setting sun and commanding him to look at the dark centre of creation. She names him 'Paul' in this second, a baptism by fire in which the absent father has no part. Lawrence invokes from the simplest domestic detail a scale of relationship which obliges us to see in the Morel family not only their particular struggle or the recreated image of his own family but an archetype for his view of family life. The mother destroys her husband in the act of creating the new generation, exposing his incipient weakness by driving a wedge into it until eventually he breaks away like a fallen rock. Morel is helpless before her strength and power, reduced to an impotence which Lawrence stresses in talking of him as 'a husk' (p. 62) who 'did not seem to ripen with the years' (p. 142), 'an outsider' (p. 82) who goes 'thudding over the deadening snow' (p. 482) on the morning of his wife's death, elderly, drained and afraid. At the start of the novel Morel is flamboyantly attractive, his physical grace blending with an awkward charm. The phrases Lawrence uses to describe him at this stage all emphasize his natural vigour, what, in later novels, would be seen as a quality of the blood: 'a certain subtle exultation like glamour in his movement' (p. 17), 'this man's sensuous flame of life, that flowed off his flesh like the flame from a candle' (p. 18). This union of bodily grace with something more mysteriously incandescent makes Morel one prototype of the magnetically animal figure whom Lawrence so often creates: less literarily conceived than Annable, simpler and more impassioned than Gerald Crich, without the intellectual and moral conviction of Mellors, but a figure initially to be admired.

Mrs Morel, Delilah-like, cripples her husband's self-esteem and bleaches his manliness. The sexual desire between them is the last part of the relationship to wither, occasionally flaring up for a moment before the desolation descends again. By the end of the novel Morel has been repeatedly described as a 'ruin', and quite early on Lawrence stresses that the family life flourishes most naturally when the father is out.

Nothing had really taken place in them until it was told to their mother. But as soon as the father came in, everything stopped. He was like the scotch in the smooth, happy machinery of the home. And he was always aware of the fall of silence on his entry, the shutting off of life, the unwelcome. But now it was gone too far to alter.

(p. 81)

Only his simple hobbies bring him back into the family fold, relished by the children because they can take part in the mysteries of cobbling or fuse-making. A primitive bond seems momentarily reconstituted at such moments. A similar bond exists between Morel and his fellow colliers. He is more at home in the pit than in the household over which his wife presides. Some of his happiest moments are provided by the routines of getting up and preparing for work. He is a man of natural passions in whom the principles of a strict social morality can only be artificially implanted. Lawrence's sympathy for Walter Morel in this novel may be greater than he himself fully realized.

Mrs Morel's revulsion for her husband's coarseness and her anger at the squandering of his wages in drink drifts into a weary indifference, almost as though an unconscious truce had been declared between the warring parties. She dedicates herself to her children and finds moments of consolation in the countryside and the seasons. Lawrence suggests that Paul's commitment to the arts is inherited from his mother. Her delight in sunsets, harvests, her sunflowers, in a little item bought at the market with a furtive sense of luxury, lasts until the end of her life. These are the 'still moments when the small frets vanish, and the beauty of things stands out, and she had the peace and strength to see herself' (p. 49). At times like this we recognize, through Paul's eyes, that Mrs Morel's married life was grounded in the absence of fulfilment. Lawrence has conceived in Mrs Morel a properly tragic figure, for she is obliged, like Lettie in *The White Peacock*, to live her life at only a fraction of its potential. The Lawrentian vision of tragedy is defined in this novel by waste, repression and denial. Yet we must avoid being so generous to Mrs Morel that we sentimentalize her into a martyred victim of social injustice and an inadequate husband. Lawrence moves us gravely in his account of Mrs Morel's protracted death, but he knows too that her ambition for her children – 'perhaps her son would be a Joseph' (p. 49) – could be a destructive force.

Consider the lives of the four Morel children. Annie has only a shadowy existence, the Electra to Paul's Orestes when they prepare their mother's last sleeping draught. Arthur is the member of the family who gravitates most naturally to the father, for his interests are in no way intellectual. Lawrence deals sympathetically with Arthur, so unlike Paul that he settles for early marriage, a place in the army, and a steady existence within limited horizons. William, the eldest of the family, occupies a more central place in the novel and justifies the plural in the title. By giving prominence to William in the early sections, Lawrence intensifies Paul's isolation in his first years. Paul grows up under William's shadow; after his brother's death the mother eventually transfers her intense maternity to him, underpinning it with a sense of her own guilt at having watched over the dead rather than the living in the intervening months. William has represented for both parents the possibilities in life which they themselves have never experienced. Neither Mr Morel's ability to shuffle away from tragedy nor his wife's stoic transference to Paul of her matriarchal love can completely eliminate the shock of his death. Lawrence makes William a unifying force in the family. Though his mother may frown austerely upon his girl-friends, the atmosphere when William returns for Christmas overflows with pride in the son who has gone to London, and warmth that the household is complete again. Paul never replaces William in this way, though the care he displays to avoid becoming a victim to any girl has partly been instilled in him by witnessing his elder brother's slavish devotion to Lily and his mother's admonitions against such a relationship. It is all too easy, after reading *Sons and Lovers*, to believe that Lawrence's obsessive wanderings through the world once he had broken with Eastwood were in surrogate search for the family bonds that had been severed with his mother's death. Passionately though he had loved his mother, as Paul loved Mrs Morel, one part of Lawrence remained conscious and alone. His own elder brother, William Ernest Lawrence, drifted carelessly away from his roots once he settled in London, but while he lived he always occupied the main place in his family's heart. Between D. H. Lawrence and his family, even between Bert (as they called him) and his mother, a detachment existed of which everyone was instinctively aware. The situation is accurately recaptured in *Sons and Lovers*.

It is time, therefore, to talk of Paul Morel himself. Lawrence's characteristic method for the exposition of character is through small incidents which, though they do not contribute directly to the development of the plot, collectively give the salient details of a personality. Paul's burning of the doll Arabella will serve as an example of this.

He made an altar of bricks, pulled some of the shavings out of Arabella's body, put the waxen fragments into the hollow face, poured on a little paraffin, and set the whole thing alight. He watched with wicked satisfaction the drop of wax melt off the broken forehead of Arabella, and drop like sweat into the flame. So long as the stupid big doll burned he rejoiced in silence. At the end he poked among the embers with a stick, fished out the arms and legs, all blackened, and smashed them under stones.

'That's the sacrifice of Missis Arabella,' he said. 'An' I'm glad there's nothing left of her.'

Which disturbed Annie inwardly, although she could say nothing. He seemed to hate the doll so intensely, because he had broken it.

(p. 76)

The start of the passage reads like a perverted parody of the incident when a drop of Mrs Morel's blood fell from her brow on to the baby Paul, but this time violence ripples through the prose with ominous foreboding. The words of the earlier passage were passive and even gentle – 'gossamer', 'glistening' (used twice), 'fascinated' (also twice) – but now Lawrence evokes not a religious initiation but an act of heathen ju-ju. The language is stark, plain nouns and blunt aggressive verbs expressing Paul's furious inner state. Paul's rage is inarticulate as yet, but Lawrence makes it clear through the senseless obliviousness of his behaviour that the young boy feels both trapped and desperate. His frustration breaks out in extravagant attacks on the mining community, as when, for example, he is sent to collect his father's wages.

They're hateful, and common, and hateful, they are, and I'm not going any more. Mr Braithwaite drops his 'h's', an' Mr Winterbottom says 'You was.'

(p. 93)

Once again we must avoid the easy temptation to read a bitter snobbery into Lawrence's words. Paul is not shouting down the ill manners of the colliers but crying out at the unfairness of being apparently doomed to a strait-jacketing existence without culture or self-respect. To his child's mind Mr Braithwaite's dropped aspirates testify to a life of ugly constraint. The words he utters are childlike, and partly influenced by his mother's notions of 'refinement'. Lawrence does not mean us to think that these are his mature sentiments about mining life. Morel and his comrades at work are evidence that he had a much more appreciative understanding of the mines. Nevertheless, Paul mouths a kind of anger which simmers in his personality throughout *Sons and Lovers*, helping to explain his treatment both of Miriam and Clara.

Even in the dreariness of Bestwood Paul Morel finds evidence that life is not composed only of squalid industrialism. A butterfly on the rhubarb leaves, sunflowers peeping over a red brick wall, the moon rising, these become symbols of the world outside to which one day he must escape. Periodically he can find this world on his own doorstep, by retreating to Haggs Farm. There life is lived as in the traditional England before the coming of industrialization: the England which Lawrence later eulogized in the opening paragraphs of *The Rainbow*. Opportunities to escape, however, come infrequently. At the point in the chapter 'Paul Launches into Life' when he is about to take up his first job, Lawrence describes Paul looking out of the window, 'a prisoner of industrialism' (p. 113), on to a valley ripe for harvesting. The incident is carefully placed, an ironic commentary on the young man's aspirations towards a freedom that his clerical duties in a factory are scarcely likely to bring him. Lawrence also crystallizes at this point Paul's realization that freedom is not just a theoretical state that can be attained in the imagined world far beyond Bestwood or the stocking factory, but that it must be defined comparatively. The corn-filled valley and, beyond it, the mysterious Annesley woods, have been his playground as he grew up; now they must be left behind. As he gazes out of the window a brewers' waggon comes rolling along the road.

The brewers' waggons came rolling from Keston with enormous barrels, four a side like beans in a burst bean-pod. The waggoner, throned aloft, rolling massively in his seat, was not much below Paul's eye. The man's hair, on his small bullet head, was bleached almost white by the sun, and on his thick red arms, rocking idly on his sack apron, the white hairs glistened. His red face shone and was almost asleep with sunshine. The horses, handsome and brown, went on by themselves, looking by far the master of the show.

Paul wished he were stupid. 'I wish,' he thought to himself, 'I was fat like him, and like a dog in the sun. I wish I was a pig and a brewer's waggoner.'

(p. 114)

Lawrence's eye for vividly particular detail enhances the symbolic intention of such a passage. Through descriptive incidents like this, Lawrence creates in *Sons and Lovers* a feeling for the agricultural society of England which can be equated with Hardy's.

Indeed, the passage reflects Lawrence's respect for Hardy. But the primary purpose of what Lawrence writes here is not to evoke the social fabric of English life. The waggoner and his waggon seem to merge into a single organic unit, existing in Paul's eye as evidence that some compatibility between man and nature is possible. The waggoner, like Joe Boswell when we first meet him in Lawrence's novella *The Virgin and the Gipsy*, possesses physical nobility. He is 'throned aloft', led by his horses as though he were a king. He does not compete with the horses, or protect himself from the elements or intellectualize his situation, but just contentedly exists. 'His red face shone and was almost asleep with sunshine' – the alliteration lends the man grace and simplicity. The attainment of such harmony and passivity seems almost godlike to Paul, faced as he is by either years of imprisonment in the factory or struggle to escape. In all his novels Lawrence deplores the constraints of existence, hating the fact that man pitches himself against life rather than allowing himself to be absorbed in an indolent natural rhythm. At moments like this he feels cursed by the weight of his own intellect.

Paul Morel's induction into the firm of Thomas Jordan, Manufacturer of Surgical Appliances, is not without wit. 'It seemed monstrous that a business could be run on wooden legs' (p. 116). A wry joke is slipped in when Mr Jordan asks the young boy to translate a letter from the French and Paul fumbles on the word 'doigts', translating it in the end as 'fingers' instead of 'toes', to the horror of the hosiery manufacturer. Lawrence's comic sense had fuller rein in the short stories and the plays, but should not be underestimated in the major novels too. He evokes the busy life of the factory with an affectionate rather than a satirical eye. Of course, the routine is dreary and the people exploited, but, taking his cue from Dickens, he criticizes by letting the monotony contrast unfavourably with the courageous resilience of the workers. Fanny, the hunchback, Polly and Connie and Mr Pappleworth could all have come from the pages of *Our Mutual Friend*. At Jordan's factory Paul is thrown into contact with young girls for the first time. Shyness on his side, giggles on theirs, soon give way to a mutual liking. Lawrence does not appear to have found the life at Jordan's factory (Haywood's, as it was in real life) wholly awful, but as he only spent a few months there, he probably left before its dreariness took hold.

A crucial element of *Sons and Lovers* is the sexual development of Paul. The adolescent awkwardness he feels at Jordan's makes him conscious of physical qualities and emotional defences that he had never rationalized in himself before, but Lawrence alerts the reader to this from the start. We find the powerful hold of Mrs Morel over her son at the root of all Paul's attempts in the novel to find a right relationship. When Paul is a baby, Lawrence constantly mentions the physical contact of mother and child – against her bosom, by her side, even asleep with her.

Sleep is still most perfect, in spite of hygienists, when it is shared with a beloved. The warmth, the security and peace of soul, the utter comfort from the touch of the other, knits the sleep, so that it takes the body and soul completely in its healing. Paul lay against her and slept, and got better; whilst she, always a bad sleeper, fell later on into a profound sleep that seemed to give her faith.

(p. 87)

In his last novel, *Lady Chatterley's Lover*, we find Lawrence still convinced of the importance of touch in human relationships. Here is Mrs Bolton in that novel, speaking of her dead husband:

. . . the touch of him! I've never got over it to this day, and never shall. And if there's a heaven above, he'll be there, and will lie up against me so I can sleep.

(*Lady Chatterley's Lover*, p. 170)

The language in both passages expresses the consolation and submission which, coupled with a renewal of belief in the partner, are at the heart of sexual feeling. In Paul's case, he is not just a son to his mother and a lover to Miriam and Clara; the rôles can be reversed as he becomes at times almost his mother's beau and seeks from both the other women a kind of substitute maternalism. We should be wary of pouncing on this Oedipal theme so readily that we assume that Lawrence is deeply influenced by Freud. As Frank Kermode has observed, 'The degree to which the personal relationships in the novel comply with Freud's account of mother-fixation is surely a tribute to the accuracy of Freud's generalization rather than a proof of Lawrence's indebtedness' (*Lawrence*, p. 20). Nevertheless, the exclusiveness and intensity of the relationship between Mrs Morel and Paul as he grows older are compatible with the thesis that Freud expounded contemporaneously with Lawrence. On one page alone we find phrases such as these: 'his heart contracted with pain of love of her', 'a rare, intimate smile, beautiful with brightness and love', 'the excitement of lovers having an adventure together', 'they stopped to hang over the parapet' (p. 117). The clichés of youthful ardour take on a special colour when applied to Paul and his mother. Destructive and obsessive it may sometimes be, but their love for each other can also be rhapsodic.

Lawrence's own personal relationships up to the time he started writing *Sons and Lovers* are too well documented to need extensive repetition here. The last weeks of 1910 were, however, of central importance to his literary development. In October he began *Sons and Lovers*, which he initially called *Paul Morel*; in November he broke finally with Jessie Chambers, the friend on whom he based the character of Miriam Leivers; and on 10 December Mrs Lawrence died after months of illness. Lawrence wrote his first major novel by refashioning situations he had just experienced. This helps to account for the severity with which he treats Miriam. She is introduced into the novel almost a third of the way through. Lawrence allows no slackness in either the planning or the language of this moment. Paul, significantly accompanied by his mother, walks to the Leivers' farm through an Eden of peewits, herons, bluebells, new-mown hay, apple blossom and red gillivers. The girl he meets is fourteen years old, 'very fine and free . . . shy, questioning, a little resentful of the strangers' (p. 156). As they play together afterwards Paul encourages the timid Miriam to let a hen peck from her hand. Once again a small detail establishes a major theme, for Paul is the teacher and Miriam learns to dare by his example. Miriam is often seen as a bitter rival to Paul's mother, the two predators fighting for the soul of their victim. But if likenesses are to be drawn, are not Miriam and Paul himself almost mirror-images? For both of them their mother is their closest companion, and a strange separation exists between them and their siblings. The romantic streak which makes Paul tell over the day's happenings to his mother as though they were tales from the Arabian nights is reflected in Miriam, who feels herself one moment to be the Lady of the Lake and the next a swine-girl forever doomed to hide the princess within her. Most of what Lawrence says about her at the start of 'Lad-and-Girl Love' could be as easily applied to Paul:

> she . . . quivered in anguish from the vulgarity of the other choir-girls and from the common-sounding voice of the curate; she fought with her brothers, whom she considered brutal louts; and she held not her father in too high esteem because he did not carry any mystical ideals cherished in his heart but only wanted to have as easy a time as he could, and his meals when he was ready for them.
>
> She hated her position as swine-girl. She wanted to be considered. She wanted to learn . . . For she was different from other folk, and must not be

scooped up among the common fry. Learning was the only distinction to
which she thought to aspire.

(p. 178)

Paul feels the attraction of a like mind but perhaps sees too much
of himself in Miriam. His ultimate rejection of her is at least partly
an angry attack upon himself. Miriam, nevertheless, has a personality of her own, even more dreamy than Paul's and uplifted by a
spiritual conviction which goes far beyond Mrs Morel's chapel
morality. Miriam has inherited this from a mother who 'exalted
everything – even a bit of housework – to the plane of religious
trust' (p. 182), but she brings a private purity of vision to her
understanding of life. Miriam's error, Lawrence implies, is to
believe only in the theories of life, not the practice. She can acknowledge no acceptable fallibility or permissible weakness in human
behaviour, but only extremes of good and imperfection.

Lawrence chooses the right setting to intimate early on in Paul's
and Miriam's relationship the sexual tension between them. As
they play on a swing Paul acts with masculine authority, Miriam
with fear and reluctant submission to his will.

She felt the accuracy with which he caught her, exactly at the right
moment, and the exactly proportionate strength of his thrust, and she was
afraid. Down to his bowels went the hot wave of fear. She was in his
hands. Again, firm and inevitable came the thrust at the right moment.
She gripped the rope, almost swooning.

(pp. 187–8)

This may not be the language of passion or sentiment but it is undoubtedly akin to the male confidence of sexual intercourse.
Lawrence establishes that all Paul's actions are physically controlled: 'accuracy', 'exactly at the right moment', 'in his hands',
'inevitable', 'the right moment'. Miriam appears by instinct to
resist. Struggle is therefore implicit in their relationship from the
start. As they grow emotionally and move towards the crisis of
their sexual personalities these early moments can be seen in retro-
spect as establishing the prototype for everything that develops
from them. Lawrence's character-analysis in this novel is wonderfully consistent. The girl who, shortly after we meet her, appears
to stifle her youngest brother with a surcharge of love almost inevitably becomes the adult woman whose natural response to Paul's
temperament is to cradle his head to her bosom and to spoil him
like a baby. Paul accedes to this even as another part of him fights
inwardly to avoid it. The confusion in Miriam is that she gives her

love with massive sacrificial generosity but withholds herself. Paul gives his physical being but cannot commit his spirit to what he terms 'a soul union' (p. 339). This schism between one's selfhood, the part of one which cannot easily be shared (though all of Lawrence's novels seek to find a state where it may be shared), and one's values, which remain in the gift of each individual, is a premise upon which Lawrence builds the structure of relationships in *Sons and Lovers*. Perhaps the main subject matter of the novel is the gulf between theory and inner experience, the attempts to reconcile what we withhold from others with what we willingly surrender to them. 'If he could have kissed her in abstract purity he would have done so' (p. 232), says Lawrence about Paul midway through the novel, but he knows too well the absolute divorce which exists between will and intention.

Bitter though his perception of her sometimes is, Lawrence portrays Miriam with great consistency. She carries with her a barely conscious aura of sanctity which infuriates Paul. When he throws a pencil in her face out of sheer rage, 'There was a silence. She turned her face slightly aside' (p. 195). This Christ-like humility is not a studied pose but Miriam's acceptance that she is to be martyred on the cross of male passion to which she must give herself, first soul, then body, for the glory of God and the salvation of men. Paul, with his instinct for shared experience, feels almost violated by this purity and yet understands that through Miriam he gains insight into his own personality. The irony of their situation is that Miriam, too, believes in the principle of shared experience, but seems to crush her partner in her desire that he should have the same intensity of perception as herself. There is no midway meeting point for Miriam. It is as though she summons Paul to the high altar of her own creed and implies that, until he has communed with her before the Host of experience, there has been no sharing.

She wanted to show him a certain wild-rose bush she had discovered. She knew it was wonderful. And yet, till he had seen it, she felt it had not come into her soul. Only he could make it her own, immortal. She was dissatisfied.

Dew was already on the paths. In the old-oak wood a mist was rising, and he hesitated, wondering whether one whiteness were a strand of fog or only campion-flowers pallid in a cloud.

By the time they came to the pine-trees Miriam was getting very eager and very intense. Her bush might be gone. She might not be able to find it; and she wanted it so much. Almost passionately she wanted to be with him when he stood before the flowers. They were going to have a communion together – something that thrilled her, something holy. He was walking beside her in silence. They were very near to each other. She trembled, and he listened, vaguely anxious.

Coming to the edge of the wood, they saw the sky in front, like mother-of-pearl, and the earth growing dark. Somewhere on the outermost branches of the pine-wood the honeysuckle was streaming scent.

'Where?' he asked.

'Down the middle path,' she murmured, quivering.

When they turned the corner of the path she stood still. In the wide walk between the pines, gazing rather frightened, she could distinguish nothing for some moments; the greying light robbed things of their colour. Then she saw her bush.

'Ah!' she cried, hastening forward.

It was very still. The tree was tall and straggling. It had thrown its briers over a hawthorn-bush, and its long streamers trailed thick right down to the grass, splashing the darkness everywhere with great split stars, pure white. In bosses of ivory and in large splashed stars the roses gleamed on the darkness of foliage and stems and grass. Paul and Miriam stood close together, silent, and watched. Point after point the steady roses shone out of them, seeming to kindle something in their souls. The dusk came like smoke around, and still did not put out the roses.

Paul looked into Miriam's eyes. She was pale and expectant with wonder, her lips were parted, and her dark eyes lay open to him. His look seemed to travel down into her. It was the communion she wanted. He turned aside, as if pained. He turned to the bush.

'They seems as if they walk like butterflies, and shake themselves,' he said.

She looked at her roses. They were white, some incurved and holy, others expanded in an ecstasy. The tree was dark as a shadow. She lifted her hand impulsively to the flowers; she went forward and touched them in worship.

'Let us go,' he said.

There was a cool scent of ivory roses – a white, virgin scent. Something made him feel anxious and imprisoned. The two walked in silence.

(pp. 197–8)

In this crucial passage Lawrence eschews any kind of spurious religiosity. Though his setting is romantic and the occasion a conjoining of spirits, each phrase comments tellingly on the relationship between Miriam and Paul. Lawrence insinuates from a potential cliché situation and from images of traditional ardour a rigorously critical attitude to the two lovers. Not that Paul is Miriam's only lover here, for she is intimate both with nature and with her hidden Christ. This is a further paradox in their relationship.

for Miriam's desire to enjoy a total sharing with Paul seems to him vitiated by the whole-heartedness of her mystical attachments. He becomes the agency by which her transcendentalism is fulfilled: 'Only he could make it her own, immortal.' Lawrence transforms a country stroll into a quest for a grail or a religious rite enacted in an enchanted forest. We respond for a moment to the urgency of Miriam's search; the dew and the mist lend an element of holy unreality to the setting. The symbolism is carefully balanced, however. The masculine oaks, the phallic pines, and the clinging honeysuckle with its special scent all serve a specific sexual function in the passage, leading the reader to Miriam's bush. A wild rose, it presides with solitary dignity over its neighbours even as it strangles them. 'It had thrown its briers over a hawthorn-bush, and its long streamers trailed thick right down to the grass, splashing the darkness everywhere with great split stars, pure white.' The rose-tree images Miriam herself, and the alliterative melody helps sustain a near-erotic suggestiveness: 'great split stars', 'large splashed stars'. Lawrence, through Paul, himself recoils from what is only an act of witness, not of physical consummation. 'He turned aside, as if pained.' Miriam remains entranced before the white bridal roses but Paul feels 'anxious and imprisoned'. A moment of religious dedication on her part and of sexual revelation on his merge into a final sense of disharmony. 'The two walked in silence.' A conjoining of spirits has taken place, certainly, but eventual separation is implicit in the writing, too.

This girl with Veronese's 'St Catherine' on her wall tries to make of Paul her own private Christ-figure. 'Make me love him splendidly, because he is Thy son', she cries (p. 212); Paul strives to escape this suffocating religiosity. ' "I'm so damned spiritual with *you* always!" he cried, ". . . And I don't want to be spiritual" ' (p. 232). Miriam waits patiently for her lover's awakening – with some justification, for Paul is not without religious emotions. He experiences intense awe before the orange moon, and, though Lawrence describes him midway in the novel as 'setting now full sail towards agnosticism', we sense always 'a reaching to something' (p. 279) which can only be described in the vocabulary of religious experience. This 'something' cannot, Paul believes, be intellectualized or even rendered through conscious awareness. Like the flight of a crow across the sky, it is because it is. A truly religious moment for Lawrence – as he makes clear in *The Rainbow* – must be separated from time or space; it is perfect, unaware, total as an occurrence that needs neither preparation to achieve nor faith to translate. Mrs Morel recognizes this for a moment in Lincoln Cathedral. 'What was, *was*' (p. 294). Miriam never understands such mysticism. For her, religions involve acts of commitment, demonstrations of faith, valiant strivings to be worthy and effusive prayers for enlightenment. The letter which Paul sends her at the end of chapter 9 – 'See, you are a nun' (p. 307) – serves both as homage to her piety and as a necessary sign of her incapacity to understand him. Paul and Miriam are both religious beings, but each struggles for knowledge in a separate world.

Lawrence introduces Clara Dawes as the third in the trio of women who initiate Paul Morel into the mysteries and practicalities of life but who in the process nearly stifle him. Whereas Miriam was based on Jessie Chambers, Clara seems to be a composite portrait of several people in Lawrence's life, including his wife, Frieda (the incident on the river bank in Nottingham reflects his first meeting with her); Helen Corke; his first fiancée, Louie Burrows; and a Mrs Dax. Alice Dax was the wife of an Eastwood chemist, and Lawrence began to consort with her as early as 1908. Handsome, socialist, sexually liberal, she was both more sophisticated and less demanding than Jessie Chambers, who appears to have remained in ignorance of the sexual nature of Lawrence's relationship with Mrs Dax even while she was reading the early draft of *Sons and Lovers*. The contrast between the two women as they are portrayed in the novel is absolute. Where Miriam is a Madonna and a saint, Clara 'reminded him of Juno dethroned' (p. 320). This slightly pagan suggestiveness stays with Clara throughout her part of the novel. She is called 'the Queen of Sheba' by the factory girls (Miriam likes to think her own regal counterpart is Mary, Queen of Scots) and she brings with her a literal earthiness which the lily-scented Miriam forgoes.

It is worth looking at the different way in which Lawrence talks of Paul's first sexual consummation with Miriam and then with Clara. The move towards Miriam is gradual and cumulative, that towards Clara swift and certain. In Miriam's case it is harvest time, the harvest significantly of cherries, the symbol of the Passion with which the Virgin Mary is often associated.

Cherries touched his ears and his neck as he stretched forward, their chill finger-tips sending a flash down his blood. All shades of red, from a golden vermilion to a rich crimson, glowed and met his eyes under a darkness of leaves.

(p. 348)

In this passage Lawrence does not just evoke a mood of sexual alertness but paints word-pictures of intimate sexual detail. Indeed, he saves such passages from basking in their own poetry by the specificity of the symbolism. An almost callous note further holds in check the dangers of prose beautiful.

> Beside her, on the rhubarb leaves, were four dead birds, thieves that had been shot. Paul saw some cherry-stones hanging quite bleached, like skeletons, picked clear of flesh.
>
> (p. 348)

This macabre touch casts a moment of sterility and despair over the scene which is picked up in Paul's post-coital thoughts of pain and death. As the vivid sunset gives way to the grey evening shadows, Miriam and Paul wander towards the fir-trees and the pines. The scene perceptibly darkens and what the lovers now act out has the remote austere impersonality of a Stone Age rite. Afterwards, as the cleansing rain falls, Paul lies surrounded by dead pine-needles, the apartness of their sexual intimacy stressed by Lawrence's vocabulary, 'thick', 'oblivious', 'dreary', 'smeared', 'strange'. Shadows of death and impermanence fall upon the scene. The consummation with Clara is presented with as much symbolic statement, but it is of an opposite kind. The greyness of the first episode gives way to the brilliant scarlet of the second, 'red clay', 'red earth', 'red decline' (pp. 376–7). The emotional colouring is as vivid as the physical. Paul and Clara peer in on the private solitude of two fishermen and then come to the steep bank of red clay on the slope of which the roots of two beech-trees form a natural cradle. Here they make love. Afterwards, as they rise from the perfect afternoon stillness, they are surrounded not by dead pine-needles but by 'many scarlet carnation petals, like splashed drops of blood' (p. 379). The scene looks forward to the woodland lovemaking of Connie and Mellors in *Lady Chatterley's Lover*. For Paul at least the occasion is one of joy and victory.

Lawrence slightly rushes his treatment of Paul and Clara. He hints at their eventual separation as specifically as he did earlier with Paul and Miriam. From the start Clara looms monumentally in Paul's life, eventually threatening to swamp him.

> There was no himself. The grey and black eyes of Clara, her bosom coming down on his, her arm that he held gripped between his hands, were all that existed. Then he felt himself small and helpless, her towering in her force above him.
>
> (p. 403)

For fear of being strangled he loosens the bonds. Clara's return to her husband is one of the puzzles of the novel. That the affair with Paul has been as much a baptism of life for her as it has been for him may be true, but Clara's urge to humble herself before Baxter, to be self-sacrificial, can only be explained if we accept that she believes herself to be finally mated to her husband. Lawrence often writes about marriage as though the link it forged was a more potent factor than any unhappiness it might produce in either partner. Alvina in *The Lost Girl*, Aaron in *Aaron's Rod* and Kate in *The Plumed Serpent* all refuse to break the link, even if they do not always know how to deal with it. Only Connie Chatterley and Oliver Mellors, of Lawrence's principal characters, seriously envisage divorce, but even they, at the end of *Lady Chatterley's Lover*, will not find it easy to dissolve their marriages.

As *Sons and Lovers* moves towards the end Paul Morel has a growing sense that his life is like a circle, a process more of repetition and return than of a thrusting forward. Perhaps a foreboding of possible failure affected Lawrence even as he wrote the novel, an obscure awareness of his own dark talents and the possibility that they would never grope towards the light. Certainly that is the burden of the closing chapters, 'The Release' and 'Derelict'. Having resisted Miriam's enfolding love, and unsubmerged by Clara, Paul is nearly dragged to self-annihilation by his mother.

Sometimes they looked in each other's eyes. Then they almost seemed to make an agreement. It was almost as if he were agreeing to die also.

(p. 477)

The novel comes full circle in this return to Mrs Morel's centrality.

She who has given life to Paul now seems to draw him out of it. Only by a supreme effort of will does he turn away from death, 'the tear in the veil, through which his life seemed to drift away' (p. 495). That he manages to make this effort of will – the clear implication of the novel's closing words – must partly be attributed to the liberating influence which Clara has had for him. She may at times have overpowered him, but we must not make light of Lawrence's words at their moment of separation. 'Together they had received the baptism of life, each through the other' (p. 439). Clara provides Paul with a measure of self-esteem and a certainty of his own sexual abilities.

Significantly, too, he returns to the town to take up a profession and so to integrate himself in a full social life. In this he resembles Ursula Brangwen in *The Rainbow*, who commits herself to teaching. But in *Women in Love* Ursula gives up her job and moves out

57

of the social world. In his last novels Lawrence gives many instances of people who have withdrawn from social occupations: in each case the gain in individual freedom must be weighed against the loss of a community rôle and a consequent weakening of their value to the reader as moral exemplars. Paul's decision to re-enter a responsible social life gives a pleasing positive tone to the end of *Sons and Lovers*.

In his third novel Lawrence scrutinized himself more intimately than in any other book. He wrote later that 'I shall not write quite so violently as *Sons and Lovers* any more' (to A. D. McLeod, 10 January 1914), 'in that hard, violent style full of sensation and presentation' (to Edward Garnett, 30 December 1913). I do not believe the book to be violent or sensational; it is, rather, anxious and self-doubting, an unrivalled exposition of self in the twentieth-century novel. In a sense that neither Miriam Leivers nor Mrs Morel would understand, it is a deeply religious work, for it talks of the sanctity of the personality and the ecstasy it may obtain. In a foreword to the novel which Lawrence sent Garnett in January 1913 from Gargnano in Italy, he speaks of the Father, the Son and the Word made Flesh.

The Father was Flesh – and the Son, who in Himself was finite and had form, became Word. For form is the uttered Word, and the Son is the Flesh as it utters the Word, but the unutterable Flesh is the Father.

Lawrence speaks here less of Christian mysteries than of his own novel. Its sacred value lies for him in its attempt to render seen and actual the half-grasped wonders of experience. Lawrence never abandoned his search for 'the unutterable Flesh', the complete revelation towards which Mrs Morel, Miriam and Clara have led Paul a little way.

# 5

## The Rainbow and Women in Love*

In the same letter to Edward Garnett in which he announced his abandonment of the style of *Sons and Lovers*, Lawrence referred to the new novel on which he was working. He had been engaged on it at least since the beginning of 1913 and had not finally decided upon a title. In his letters he returns many times to *The Sisters* as a possible name, which suggests that his intention then was to focus the novel on the two girls equally; but he also refers to the new work as *The Wedding Ring*. The central subject of the book was to be wholeness, wholeness of being and wholeness of society; and the second contemplated title shows how concerned he was to find a central image of completeness. The ring is a circle and a perfect shape; like the rainbow it has its mystery. For the new novel was, he told Garnett, to be '*very* different from *Sons and Lovers*: written in another language almost'. This other language he is generally thought to have mastered; for the two novels *The Rainbow* and *Women in Love*, which he originally conceived as one, are the core of his achievement and the work by which he is always likely finally to be judged.

Lawrence married Frieda Weekley on 13 July 1914 and war against Germany broke out less than a month later. Frieda, who left her English professor husband and her three children to live with Lawrence, was a German baroness of the von Richthofen family. No marriage could more dramatically have sustained the view that the brilliant young author was perverse, obnoxious, revolutionary and probably treasonable. Lawrence did not care much how others viewed his relationship with Frieda, yet within himself he knew (despite a wry little note on the day of his marriage that 'I don't feel a changed man, but I suppose I am one') that the commitment to her tested his capacity for permanence in feeling. For months he had struggled with the new book, unable to 'get my soul into it. That was because of the struggle and the resistance between Frieda and me'. Living with Frieda demanded emotional,

* In the quotations, R = *The Rainbow*, W = *Women in Love*.

social and sexual adjustment. The headlong plunge into war disturbed him greatly, too, though when he refers to it a few days after it was declared in a trivial dismissing phrase – 'What colossal idiocy, this war' (letter to J. B. Pinker, 5 September 1914) – we see that he had no more apprehension than anyone else in his generation of the real catastrophe that was upon mankind. Nevertheless, out of these two events, marriage and war, was forged much of the tone of *The Rainbow* and *Women in Love*, two novels over which he laboured as at the birth of a new being. In a foreword written much later to an American edition of *Women in Love* he made this point explicitly:

It is a novel which took its final shape in the midst of the period of war, though it does not concern the war itself. I should wish the time to remain unfixed, so that the bitterness of the war may be taken for granted in the characters.

The creation of what we know now as two separate novels spans a continuous arc of experience from March 1913 to November 1916. Whatever form the final novels were to take, it is clear that Lawrence envisaged from the start a major work on the establishment of new relations between men and women; that to render this theme he must create a new kind of novel; that central to the conception would be a young girl, initially called Ella, later Ursula; and that her evolution would match Lawrence's own. The new work would convey something of his fears for his country and his loathing of the social system which, among its other evils, had brought about the war. Between 1913 and 1916 Europe changed. 'And I am changing, one way or the other', Lawrence wrote to Garnett on 29 January 1914. 'I am going through a transition stage myself.'

No summary can do justice to these deeply interior novels, for if they are about the dissolution of old values they do not simplistically assert new ones. In no other English fiction are social and personal themes interconnected in so metaphysical a context. 'You must read it – it is really something new in the art of the novel', Lawrence told A. D. McLeod on the eve of *The Rainbow*'s publication, for at all times of his life he was passionate about the present state of the novel. Both in his 'Study of Thomas Hardy', written at the same time as he was struggling with *The Sisters*, and in later polemics like 'The Novel' (*Phoenix II*), he argues for a break with 'these wearisome sickening little personal novels!' which he saw his contemporaries producing. No one character should be at the centre of fiction, 'but some unnamed and nameless flame behind them all'. Paul Morel had known that that flame existed; but *Sons and Lovers* was perhaps the apotheosis of the kind of novel from which Lawrence now sought to break free, probing densities of character in a specific social milieu. In *The Rainbow* and *Women in Love* he creates characters whom he carefully describes so far as physical detail is concerned – colours and textures of clothes were never so important to him as here – but they are placed in a community less geographically exact than *Sons and Lovers*, and they are not characters in an accepted dramatic or novelistic sense: sharply distinguished separate entities. Their essences of being attract Lawrence now: the stirring life within the seed, the kernel within the nut. 'In the great novel, the felt but unknown flame stands behind all the characters, and in their words and gestures there is a flicker of the presence. If you are *too personal, too human*, the flicker fades out, leaving you with something awfully lifelike, and as lifeless as most people are.' These remarks from his essay 'The Novel' were written in the 1920s, but they say something of the lambent intention which Lawrence had before him as, in the period of his richest creativity, he shaped out of a single conception these two novels.

The lifeblood of western European culture has always been the family. In some of his novels, notably in *The Trespasser, Aaron's Rod* and *Lady Chatterley's Lover*, Lawrence placed the central relationships in opposition to the paralysis of marriage and, indeed, after *The Sisters* he never again wrote a novel in which children have a crucial rôle. His interest in other civilizations (in, for example, *The Plumed Serpent*) derived partly from his desire to find alternatives to the western nuclear family unit. For the moment, however, the deep absorption in family values to which *Sons and Lovers* bears witness affected him strongly. Written contemporaneously with a number of other family sagas – John Galsworthy's *The Forsyte Saga* (begun 1906, completed 1921) and Arnold Bennett's *Clayhanger* trilogy (1910–16) are the best-known examples – Lawrence's *The Rainbow* and *Women in Love* approach family life from many more angles than its mere social function. In their diversity and historical sense they resemble master studies of family life in the nineteenth century like George Eliot's *Middlemarch* (1871–2) and Leo Tolstoi's *Anna Karenina* (1875–6) more than any novel of Lawrence's own time.

The two books can be contrasted as well as co-ordinated in the way they look at a particular family. This is partly a question of symbolic patterning. Lawrence used a number of basic images in *The Rainbow* (the sun and the moon, for example, as well as the rainbow itself, and the related arch and doorway). These help to give an archetypal aspect to the novel but can seem rather heavy-handed, and he abandoned some of them before the end. *Women in Love* retains the more versatile images (the rind image, or the use of animal behaviour to indicate natural truths) but scraps the tendency to self-conscious symbolic detailing in the first book. We shall see evidence of the heaviness and of the scrupulosity later. As a family saga, the story of the Brangwens, Lawrence relates *The Rainbow* by the comparatively traditional diachronic method in which the actions of several generations are narrated in the sequence in which they happen. *Women in Love* chronicles the dissolution of that same family, the questioning attitude of one Brangwen generation to its elders as it sloughs the bonds of family responsibility and is initiated into different commitments. The narrative technique is synchronic, a more sophisticated method by which actions can be analysed separately though they take place at the same moment, and which allows for less descriptive but more probing insights into interior character: the author sees human experience less as a long chain of cause and effect over time, more as a series of concentric circles which coexist. (This more complex narrative method can be linked philosophically with the beliefs of the religion of Quetzalcoatl which fascinated Lawrence in *The Plumed Serpent*; and some account of it is given in chapter 9.)

Lawrence focusses on the Brangwens with increasing closeness, rapidly sketching their past history in the opening pages of *The Rainbow*, then slowing down from generation to generation, so that the second novel relegates the saga aspect to a secondary rôle and concentrates only on Ursula and Gudrun Brangwen, now in their middle twenties. A family tree is helpful, taking 1840 as a starting point. Victorian and Edwardian England produced many families like the Brangwens, always moving up or down but never stagnating. In *The Rainbow* Lawrence concentrates only on some of the Brangwens: Tom and Lydia, Will and Anna, and Ursula. In *Women in Love* Ursula and Gudrun share equal prominence with two outsiders – Rupert Birkin, whom Ursula marries, and Gerald Crich, whom Gudrun rejects. Both men are part of the subtle opening out of the author's perspective which is part of the development of his concept: increasing concern with individuals set in a broadened world of public issues and social diversification.

The first paragraphs of *The Rainbow* are crucial, a genuine

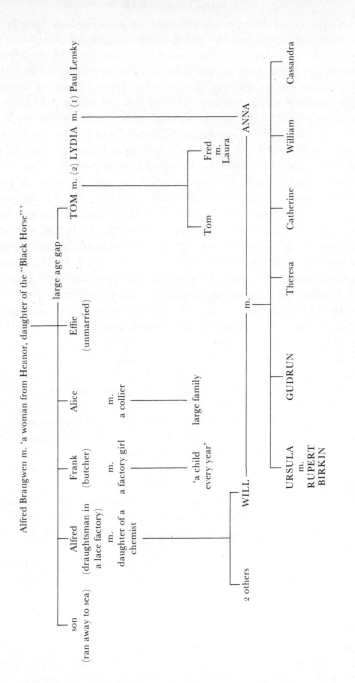

Alfred Brangwen m. 'a woman from Heanor, daughter of the "Black Horse"'

son
(ran away to sea)

Alfred
(draughtsman in
a lace factory)
m.
daughter of a
chemist

Frank
(butcher)
m.
a factory girl

Alice
m.
a collier

Effie
(unmarried)

←——— large age gap ———→

TOM m. (2) LYDIA m. (1) Paul Lensky

'a child
every year'

large family

WILL

2 others

m.

URSULA
m.
RUPERT
BIRKIN

GUDRUN

Theresa

Catherine

William

Cassandra

ANNA

Tom

Fred
m.
Laura

prologue much richer in content than the prologue Lawrence later wrote for *Women in Love* but which artistic judgement caused him to suppress. 'The Brangwens had lived for generations on the Marsh Farm', we learn at the start of the book, 'in the meadows where the Erewash twisted sluggishly through alder trees, separating Derbyshire from Nottinghamshire.' An English landscape *par excellence* and, in a novel much less concerned with precise details of place than its predecessors, a portion of England which Lawrence obviously knew well. Once again he is writing of his own country, but not this time of his own stock: 'always, at the Marsh, there was ample', and 'ample' was hardly what the young Lawrence had known in the Eastwood collieries. Like all sagas, *The Rainbow* concerns several ages in the chronicling of its central history, but Lawrence's intention was far from Galsworthy's. He intended the Brangwens to be representative of their types, as well as individuals whose special passions would be worth examining, but he hoped, too, to show them as part of the evolutionary process by which man in England had arrived at his contemporary condition.

In the soft natural origins of man's existence have been built villages and farms. A society has crystallized. The people in that society are Janus-like, one face towards the future with 'that air of readiness, for what would come to them, a kind of surety, an expectancy, the look of an inheritor' (R, p. 7), one face towards the land. Lawrence emphasizes in these first pages the close harmony between the early Brangwens and their land. 'But heaven and earth was teeming around them, and how should this cease? . . . they knew the intercourse between heaven and earth' (R, pp. 7–8). The dying away of this marriage with the land is a gradual process once the Brangwen people, especially their women, have glimpsed an alternative life of the mind and of refined manners. The land, however, has not died, and twice in the novels it exerts a powerful vengeance on its betrayers, rising in muddy flood over Tom Brangwen and drowning a member of the Crich family, its overlord and ravager.

All the main themes are laid in this opening chapter: relations between men and women, ideal friendship between man and man, the intrusion of industry and class (the colliery blackening the hillside, the canal cutting the land in twain), the growth towards a new order for the spirit and welfare of man. But Lawrence so intermerged these different strands that one cannot easily pluck them from the text as separate entities. As in the intricacy of animal anatomy each artery within the novels exists only because the others do. When Lady Cynthia Asquith asked Lawrence what *The Rainbow* was about he replied:

I don't know myself what it is: except that the older world is done for, toppling on top of us: and that it's no use the men looking to the women for salvation, nor the women looking to sensuous satisfaction for their fulfilment. There must be a new world.

(Letter, 7 February 1916)

The emphasis on the newness of the world which Lawrence urged upon his readers is significant. *The Rainbow* and *Women in Love* do not advocate a back-to-nature idyll; Birkin does not seek to imitate Adam in the Book of Genesis; Eden contained not just the serpent but the seed which, nourished by man, flowered into the disaster of human history. Lawrence desired a world which will transcend the past. In *The White Peacock* he had perhaps idealized the lost Eden, but this was not his intention now. Though the novels refer back to Eden many times, the language Lawrence uses draws as much from Revelation as it does from Genesis. Constantly the two books look beyond a mythic idealization of man's origins to a new dawn. It might be that in this new dawn the moments of ecstasy, which we know from perfect sexual union or transfiguring religious experience can be realized by human beings, will become not just single spots of time but also the certain truth of existence. By pairing *The Rainbow* and *Women in Love* and by reviving the convenient umbrella title, *The Sisters*, which Lawrence had in mind during much of their composition, we can follow a course in his view of man which is not nostalgic – for that would bring us back to the place from which we started – but forward-moving, tentative and exploratory. The pastoral harmony with which the work begins is replaced at the end by a vision of a possible unity which Birkin utters only cautiously because he perceives it as through a glass darkly. Indeed, Lawrence becomes more tentative and more cautious as we read on. The opening of *The Rainbow* presents a world which, though idealized to some extent, the author believes once existed but sees as irrecoverably forfeited. *The Rainbow* as a whole is written with an often desolate but certain view of modern life. In *Women in Love* Lawrence writes in a more exploratory, enquiring manner, often raising issues which *may* lead somewhere but which, equally well, may be *culs-de-sac*. Two quotations, one from the start of *The Rainbow* and one from the close of *Women in Love*, may help to explain this. The first speaks of a lost race, our ancestors, vigorous in their affirmation of life. The second proposes the possibility that man may be replaced by a higher, better species. As rhetoric it is splendid – until we ask what use it is to us, living now, to picture the life of some imaginary mutation.

So much warmth and generating and pain and death did they know in their blood, earth and sky and beast and green plants, so much exchange and interchange they had with these, that they lived full and surcharged, their senses full fed, their faces always turned to the heat of the blood, staring into the sun, dazed with looking towards the source of generation, unable to turn round.

(R, p. 9)

. . . the timeless creative mystery would bring forth some other being, finer, more wonderful, some new, more lovely race, to carry on the embodiment of creation.

(W, p. 538)

In the seventh paragraph of *The Rainbow* Lawrence distinguishes the Brangwen women from their menfolk. They 'looked out from the heated, blind intercourse of farm-life, to the spoken world beyond. They were aware of the lips and the mind of the world speaking and giving utterance' (R, p. 8). In other words, the women question the claim of the natural world to be the sum total of experience. With Eve as their prototype they recognize that the fruit on the tree may taste good, and thus they instil in their partners an unease which begins to break up the timeless intimacy of men and land. Lawrence's suspicion of the uttered word is important here – as though the temptation to which the women first, and sometimes their men, fall victim, resides within language itself. Though constantly struggling to find a means of articulating his own sense of the inner life in men and the creative presence inherent in all existence under the sun, Lawrence remained deeply sceptical of the claims of language to render such subjects properly; language forced men into a verbal mental existence, the culmination of which he depicts in *Women in Love* in the prattle of the Café Pompadour or the dry barrenness of the theoretical Loerke. The women among the ancient Brangwens hear, like Wordsworth's solitary reaper, the sounds of another world. There is knowledge to be discovered and they yearn 'to be of the fighting host' (R, p. 9). That element remains, for good or bad, in every important woman in the two novels, in Lydia, Anna, Ursula, Gudrun and Hermione, the need *to know*. The men recognize this aspiration in their women and so enshrine in them all moral principle and spiritual wisdom.

The men placed in her hands their own conscience, they said to her 'Be my conscience keeper, be the angel at the doorway guarding my outgoing and my incoming.' And the woman fulfilled her trust, the men rested implicitly in her, receiving her praise or her blame with pleasure or with anger, rebelling and storming, but never for a moment really escaping in their own souls from her prerogative.

(R, p. 19)

By their ambition the women take possession of the inner lives of their men. Anna will take possession of Will in just such a way. Perfect harmony is destroyed and equilibrium upset. What Ursula and Birkin struggle to re-establish is this perfection of balance.

'Why should we consider ourselves, men and women, as broken fragments of one whole?' Lawrence asks in *Women in Love*. 'It is not true' (W, p. 125). He posits an eternal fluid in which life had its origin; as individual life separated out from that creative effluence so distinctions of sex emerged. Polarization became a condition of existence. Lawrence has been accused of a mysticism aspiring to a state of metaphysical and bodily fusion between the sexes which even Hinduism does not believe possible in an earthly existence. The charge is unjust. In Lawrence's messianism there is a strongly moral premise: that men and women, if the will to achieve it is there, can balance as sun and moon balance.

There is now to come the new day, when we are beings each of us, ful- filled in difference. The man is pure man, the woman pure woman, they are perfectly polarized. But there is no longer any of the horrible merging, mingling self-abnegation of love. There is only the pure duality of polariza- tion, each one free from any contamination of the other. In each, the individual is primal, sex is subordinate, but perfectly polarized. Each has a single, separate being, with its own laws. The man has his pure freedom, the woman hers. Each acknowledges the perfection of the polarized sex- circuit. Each admits the different nature in the other.

(W, p. 225)

This is the core of Lawrence's beliefs about sexual relationships. The passage does not convey a nostalgia for the lost unity, the source of undifferentiated life from which all individuals derive and in which, before the birth of individual consciousness, we once germinated. Lawrence insists, instead, on the *total difference* of man and woman; and he denounces love, in the 'mental' and possessive form by which most people understand it, as a mistaken attempt to blur the distinctions. He denies the impulse (inherent in much romantic fiction and still trusted by many people) to blend two personalities into one, losing their identity. (Compare the old

67

myth of Platonic love: that the two lovers recognize in each other a lost half, and their union brings back a complete single being.) Lawrence challenges some of the premises on which a great deal of western literature exists. He appeals instead for total separateness between people, true individuality: not equality, but what he calls 'disquality'. This applies not just in social rights but in spiritual attitudes, too. That is why Ursula and Birkin, who come nearest to this ideal, remain separate beings, still arguing, but arguing creatively, at the end of *Women in Love*. They recognize that the equilibrium and the complementary nature of their partnership depends upon their *separateness* as human beings, not on an impossible mystic blending of their souls. Lawrence writes of conscious people. He would, for example, have had little sympathy with the drug-induced etherealism of later generations. In everything he wrote lies the crucial truth that we are separate, different beings one from another; he considered escapist and absurd any attempt to merge beings, to become identical with the sexual partner, or to find a plane of existence in which people's distinctive qualities are suspended.

The problem which Lawrence tries to resolve in *The Rainbow* and *Women in Love* is this: if all people are irrevocably separate from each other, is there any achievable harmony in the universe? He cannot accept the tragedy of a final human isolation, where each man is his own island and there is nothing more to be said. Lawrence is not an existentialist writer, though the premise that all people are inalienably distinct might mistakenly lead one to suppose that he is. He argues that the polarization of the sexes at the start of human evolution was a condition of human development, but, as he says before the start of the last passage quoted, 'the separation was imperfect even then'. Part of its imperfection lay in the woman's taking possession of the man's soul. There is much talk in both novels of possession – the man's desire to possess the woman's body, the woman's to possess the man's spirit, parents to possess their children, managers to possess workers, society to possess its material goods. Possession disrupts equilibrium. In a significant chapter of *Women in Love*, 'A Chair', Ursula rejects ownership as a valve worth pursuing, and at the end of the novel she and Birkin possess nothing they treasure. Certainly in their case we must avoid the cliché that 'they possess each other', for that is precisely what they are fighting to resist. Ursula retains vestiges of a healthy possessiveness in her affection for Birkin, but it is hardly ever aggrandizing or tyrannous.

Early in *The Rainbow* the enthralment of the two sexes, man's soul to woman, woman's body to man, marks the destruction of the primeval admixture from which they irrevocably came. There can be no reconstitution of that creative beginning: if the fluid survives, it is only in the life of the soul or in the moment of mutual orgasm. Yet some Brangwens sense that balance and wholeness need not be extinct just because humanity has evolved as sexually divided. Their agonies are much bound up with their inner certainty that balance and wholeness are waiting to be achieved. To see how they attempt to achieve it brings us to a specific scrutiny of *The Rainbow*.

## 'THE RAINBOW'

Tom Brangwen's and Lydia Lensky's is the first relationship which Lawrence examines, and perhaps in no other novel did he establish the perspective of a central relationship so firmly. The opening paragraphs of the novel talk of the history of the rural society into which Tom is born. They suggest that its organic dissolution has been hastened by the coming of industrialization to the community, though the Brangwens themselves remain farming people with an increasing level of material well-being.

The building of a canal across their land made them strangers in their own place, this raw bank of earth shutting them off disconcerted them. As they worked in the fields, from beyond the now familiar embankment came the rhythmic run of the winding engines, startling at first, but afterwards a narcotic to the brain. Then the shrill whistle of the trains re-echoed through the heart, with fearsome pleasure, announcing the far-off come near and imminent.

(R, pp. 12–13)

The world Tom inherits straddles old and new values, for industry has not just disrupted it but virtually drugged it. He, much the youngest of the family, is especially close to the women, which helps to account for his special sensitivity. He is greatly moved by Shelley's poetry, for example, wherein the sky-bound spirit finds expression. Like all the Brangwens he feels an innate separateness from the people brought up around him, hating the other boys for 'their mechanical stupidity' (R, p. 16). That word 'mechanical' becomes one of the signposts of Lawrence's attitudes throughout the two novels, denoting all that is spiritless and uncreative. Tom Brangwen, the young aristocrat of the instincts, goes through the torments of sexual awakening. To him, as to Paul Morel, women have meant mother and sister for so long that he feels it a violation of their sex to want another kind of woman. Lawrence never loses touch with the psychological realities of adolescence. 'A hot, accumulated consciousness was always awake in his chest, his wrists felt swelled and quivering, his mind became full of lustful images, his eyes seemed blood-flushed' (R, p. 28). Yet Tom's attempts to satisfy these yearnings with stray girls who come his way have no enchantment. That comes with Lydia Lensky.

Lydia enters the novel like one of Thomas Hardy's heroines, alone on a country road with 'her curious, absorbed, flitting motion, as if she were passing unseen by everybody' (R, p. 29). That shadowy ghost-like quality is the first indication we have that she is different from any other woman in Brangwen's ken. Her black bonnet and coat are typical specifics in Lawrence's method of pointing a character, attributing to her qualities of darkness and mystery which will never be completely dispelled. For Lydia's foreignness is essential. She introduces to the novel another world – to Tom it is 'the world that was beyond reality' (R, p. 29) – and whatever strength of spirit she may bring with her, she, too, is one of the alien influences which produce the break-up of the unconscious pastoral harmony. For a long time in the novel Lawrence does not name Lydia, thus enhancing her strangeness. When we learn more of her we find she is a Polish widow who came to England in the company of her late husband, a failed radical. Importantly, in a novel which has much to do with the contemporary state of England, Lydia feels the English people 'as a potent, cold, slightly hostile host among whom she walked isolated' (R, p. 51). No one, of course, can feel foreign to oneself: for Lydia, England is foreign, she the norm. Lawrence needed that duality of viewpoint to explore his own society. His marriage to Frieda helped him to understand the foreign view. That Lawrence chooses Poland for Lydia's background does not matter much, though he needed to use a country about which his readers would have few cultural stereotypes in mind. Italy or France would not have done so well. For Lydia, Poland is 'a great blot looming blank in its darkness' (R, p. 52); so too for many readers. Yet this darkness within her being never totally deserts her. It is that part of her which remains 'other', and Tom never gains access to it. Thus there exists between them a natural distance which Lawrence believes desirable. The other couples in *The Rainbow* and *Women in Love* have to work to maintain this separateness against their impulses to possess or overwhelm each other.

This sense of connection between the generations can be seen not just in matters of inheritance but in the imagery of the novels. With Lydia and Tom, Lawrence initiates several patterns of language which will be taken up in Will, Anna, Gudrun and especially Ursula. Lydia walking among the trees with 'the bluebells around her glowing like a presence' (R, p. 53); Tom proposing to her with a bunch of yellow flowers in his hand: we think ahead to Will crossing a field of dandelions on his way to work – a 'bath of yellow glowing' (R, p. 206) – or to Ursula, whom Lawrence frequently associates with flowers and the creative radiance of the sun's colour. Both sisters will respond, too, to the moon, whose action can be either tranquil and presiding or violent and fleeting, as it is on the night of Tom's proposal when 'the moonlight blew about . . . the terror of a moon running liquid-brilliant into the open for a moment, hurting the eyes before she plunged under cover of cloud again' (R, p. 49). The marriage of sky and earth is nearly rent apart in moments like these, as though the creative wholeness of the universe were as vulnerable as man. Lawrence never indulges in the natural imagery for its own sake, though it can be too heavy for the mood it needs to set. After Tom and Lydia marry, for example, she retreats so often into her private silence that 'his heart seemed under the millstone of it, she became herself like the upper millstone lying on him, crushing him, as sometimes a heavy sky lies on the earth' (R, p. 64). These grim images of a sky suffocating the earth, of a stone preventing the life of the seed which grows beneath it from pushing up into life, recur in similar forms many times in the novels. Certainly they express Lawrence's sense of the dual threat to man's aspirations – the incompatibility of man and the natural world, and the corresponding incapacity of one partner's will to settle with the other's – but some readers will find them too monumental and lacking in delicacy.

'As if crushed between the past and the future, like a flower that comes above ground to find a great stone lying above it, she was helpless' (R, pp. 54–5). Lydia's and Tom's relationship is not as unfertile as this central image might suggest. In *The Trespasser* and *Aaron's Rod* Lawrence gives examples of genuinely and finally blocked marriages. Among all the Brangwens there are moments when they discover a wholeness of intimacy which, in its total sexual and spiritual harmony, excludes all else. Crucially, such moments render further aspirations of any kind purposeless, for 'there was nothing beyond, they were together in an elemental embrace beyond their superficial foreignness' (R, p. 59). In all his writings, I believe Lawrence strains for the realization of this moment, transcending the accepted 'foreignness' and with no 'beyond'. Perhaps in seeking its permanent realization he attempts to step outside time, for the 'beyond' must always exist in a conscious world. In later novels and tales, especially *Kangaroo* and *The Plumed Serpent, St Mawr* and 'The Woman Who Rode Away', he may partly be seeking a world where, if static time is impossible, he may at least discover the sense of suspended time. In *Women in Love* Gudrun feels terrorized by the tick of the clock, 'one of the things that made her heart precipitate with a real approach of madness' (W, p. 522), and both Ursula and Birkin attempt time's destruction through the power of their sustained intimacy. 'Those who die, and dying still can love, still believe, do not die' (W, p. 540), says Lawrence at the end of *Women in Love,* and while it would be absurd to think of him trying to find a way to evade the biological fact of death he does seek for a means whereby we shall not think of death as a tyranny which dissolves everything that matters and makes it meaningless. In this perception he gets clearer what Siegmund, in a consoling thought before his suicide, calls 'the after-death ... so wonderfully comforting, full of rest, and re-assurance, and renewal' (*The Trespasser*, p. 186). In some of the poems which he wrote just before he died, Lawrence dwelt further upon this theme: in 'The Ship of Death', for example, he talks of renewal after the waters of death have closed over the life's bark.

> The flood subsides, and the body, like a worn sea-shell
> emerges strange and lovely.
> And the little ship wings home, faltering and lapsing
> on the pink flood,
> and the frail soul steps out, into the house again
> filling the heart with peace.

'Those who die, and dying still can love, still believe, do not die.' The love generated flows to those who have witnessed and understood it. But for this to happen the love and belief of the partners must be selfless and undominating. Tom's and Lydia's shines brightly in this way. Their relationship (emulated by Anna and Will in the next generation only in the early stages of their marriage) constantly flows and recoils like the breathing movement of life itself. The process of 'connexion' and 'severance' (Lawrence's terms, R, pp. 62, 63) lasts until their passions steady into the constancy of a love which does not entail any attempt by either partner to possess the other. All this Tom intuitively recognizes in his reverie at Anna's wedding later in the novel when he speaks of marriage as though it were the only truly creative state in which mankind can exist: 'If I am to become an Angel', he says, 'it'll be my married soul, and not my single soul. It'll not be the soul of me when I was a lad: for I hadn't a soul as would *make* an Angel then' (R, p. 139).

We ought to pause for a moment to see how this concept of life's ebb and flow (as evident in 'The Ship of Death' over twenty years later as it is here in *The Rainbow*) affects Lawrence's prose style. A major writer needs to find the form for what he wants to say. From the start of *The Rainbow* Lawrence finds a prose rhythm which, when appropriate, illustrates the flow and recoil which he believed to be a vital component of life.

They felt the rush of the sap in spring, they knew the wave which cannot halt, but every year throws forward the seed to begetting, and, falling back, leaves the young-born on the earth.

(R, pp. 7–8)

Critics commonly invoke the Bible when this kind of Lawrentian prose is quoted, and certainly words like 'begetting' have an Old Testament resonance. Lawrence did more than draw upon one of the great fountains of his language, however. He gave to that language his own contribution. A sentence like this just quoted comes unmistakably from his pen. Why? There are certain recognizable Lawrence touches – 'they felt . . . they knew' rather than one verb to cover both, for example – but essentially the movement of the prose expresses the sense, a thrust forward and dropping back to speak for the flow and ebb of existence. One cannot always defend Lawrence against charges of self-indulgence or jerkiness in his language, but those who level them should be careful that they do not confuse a necessary fragmentation of style for sheer wayward-ness. Lawrence hated the connection–severance manner in which most of us live, but as an artist he had to find an appropriate prose form for it. Where the Brangwen marriages are concerned, he largely succeeded.

The coming of children brings a new dimension to each partner. Some bitterness comes into the relationship, with recriminations. 'Paul', says Lydia Lensky of her first husband, 'used to come to me and take me like a man does. You only leave me alone or take me like your cattle, quickly, to forget me again' (R, pp. 93–4). War; truce; peace. A marriage involves struggle and even conflict, Lawrence insists, if it is to have any reality. Tom and Lydia make something strong and life-enhancing out of their struggle:

Their coming together now, after two years of married life, was much more wonderful to them than it had been before. It was the entry into another circle of existence, it was the baptism to another life, it was the complete confirmation. Their feet trod strange ground of knowledge, their footsteps were lit up with discovery. Wherever they walked, it was well, the world re-echoed round them in discovery. They went gladly and forgetful. Everything was lost, and everything was found. The new world was discovered, it remained only to be explored.

(R, p. 95)

The emphasis on discovery in so many of the phrases cannot be overlooked. Yet though Lawrence does not deny that hurtful separations can intensify the fondness of being together again, he avoids leaving the matter sentimentally at that. Two years are lost in a short life. The bitterness of this loss can never be ignored, but neither can the fact that what they find in its place is a transformation of what they have lost. Lawrence's ambivalence is not the result of confused thinking but of the genuine paradox in human experience that victories are hard won. Tom and Lydia use their struggles positively, as Ursula and Birkin are doing at the end of *Women in Love*, to create something rich, durable and even triumphant. Will and Anna, on the other hand, show how the struggles of marriage can be debilitating and eventually self-consuming.

Anna Lensky is entirely Polish by birth. The foreign part of her nature accounts for her reserve and exclusiveness, but instead of forging closer ties between daughter and mother it seems to distance them from each other. Lawrence describes the connection that does exist between them as 'anxious' (R, p. 71), never placid. After an unpromising beginning to their relationship Anna becomes, instead, Tom's 'great and chiefest solace' (R, p. 66): 'they were like lovers, father and child' (R, p. 64). An element of loving partnership happens in only a few of Lawrence's parent–child studies. We have seen, for example, how Paul Morel is both son and lover to his mother. The intimacy between Tom and Anna stems partly from Lydia's remoteness and privacy, but it is founded in natural affection, too. For a man who never had a family of his own and whose experience of children was virtually negligible after he left Eastwood, D. H. Lawrence writes of childhood with great understanding. As always the tenderest and most perceptive insights come in an understated prose describing apparently insignificant scenes. Take Anna's confrontation with the geese.

She made playmates of the creatures of the farmyard, talking to them, telling them the stories she had from her mother, counselling them and

74

correcting them. Brangwen found her at the gate leading to the paddock and to the duckpond. She was peering through the bars and shouting to the stately white geese, that stood in a curving line.

'You're not to call at people when they want to come. You must not do it.'

The heavy, balanced birds looked at the fierce little face and the fleece of keen hair thrust between the bars, and they raised their heads and swayed off, producing the long, can-canking, protesting noise of geese, rocking their ship-like beautiful white bodies in a line beyond the gate.

'You're naughty, you're naughty,' cried Anna, tears of dismay and vexation in her eyes. And she stamped her slipper.

'Why, what are they doing?' said Brangwen.

'They won't let me come in,' she said, turning her flushed little face to him.

'Yi, they will. You can go in if you want to,' and he pushed open the gate for her.

She stood irresolute, looking at the group of bluey-white geese standing monumental under the grey, cold day.

'Go on,' he said.

She marched valiantly a few steps in. Her little body started convulsively at the sudden, derisive Can-cank-ank of the geese. A blankness spread over her. The geese trailed away with uplifted heads under the low grey sky.

'They don't know you,' said Brangwen. 'You should tell them what your name is.'

'They're *naughty* to shout at me,' she flashed.

'They think you don't live here,' he said.

Later he found her at the gate calling shrilly and imperiously:

'My name is Anna, Anna Lensky, and I live here, because Mr Brangwen's my father now. He *is*, yes he *is*. And I live here.'

This pleased Brangwen very much.

(R, pp. 68–9)

The masterly simplicity of the episode contains many forewarnings of Anna's character. Her pleasures are self-contained: no one can intrude between her and her 'playmates'. Though she allows Tom into her private world, he must come as an assistant on her terms. Her will struggles to dominate the geese, first 'counselling them and correcting them', then stamping her feet in angry frustration when they ignore her. Lawrence observes the 'heavy, balanced birds' with the same trenchant accuracy, especially for details of sound and movement, which he shows in his animal verse; but the geese carry, too, their own representational value, as proud, wilful and independent as the girl who harangues them. That word 'balanced' matters: though the girl behind the gate (one of many

gates, entrances, doorways, archways, associated with the Brangwens; the image implies an opening out into the world which is
foreign, other, unknown) tries to interrupt them, the birds match
in colour and outline the setting they inhabit. Bird, horse, dog,
cow, rabbit also have their rôles in the symbolic patterning of *The
Rainbow* and *Women in Love*. Faced with their 'monumental' obstinacy Anna can only abuse the geese: the conflict of totally unlike
natures linked only by obstinacy cannot be resolved. Yet, as in the
battles with Will that dominate her early married life, she salvages
dignity from her intransigence. The imperious cries of the child are
only a step away from the Anna Victrix of a later chapter. Lawrence
chose the name Anna carefully; it is Roman, imperial, the queen
whom three realms obey. In this picture of the child we see the
authority as well as the shrillness of the natural woman. She
grandly declares to the geese, intending to be magnificent and
crushing, that she is not just a Lensky but a Brangwen too. She
acknowledges Tom and permits him access to her world, but if
they seem like lovers in their intimacy they remind us, too, of
priestess and acolyte.

The birth of a child to Tom and Lydia intensifies the communion
of soul between Tom and Anna. In the famous passage about the
night of the birth the pact between them is sealed. The scene
(R, pp. 78–81), beginning with Tom folding a shawl around the
child's shoulders as he carries her through the rain to the barn,
seems like an initiation rite for Anna. The barn is 'another world',
cocooned against the wild outside where 'one breathed darkness'.
A single light shines, casting shadows; 'a ladder rose to the dark
arch of a loft'. Like the inside of an egg, this world knows only
itself. Here, whilst Lydia struggles in the house to bring forth her
child, Anna too enters a new phase of her life. 'A new being was
created in her for the new conditions.' She watches the feeding of
the cows as if entranced – the stirrings of her own maternal instincts.
Peace descends between her and her adopted father, like the
sadness after love. They sink into a world of 'timeless stillness'.
Tom 'seemed to be listening for some sound a long way off, from
beyond life'. The child sleeps. In a sense Anna has found her life
here in the barn; as Tom fed the cattle she had looked on absorbed, as though seeing herself with the children who will one day
satisfy her almost totally. Tom comes out of his reverie and
returns to the house with the sleeping child. He goes to Lydia
as she continues the birth pains and then out again to the wet
dark night.

The swift, unseen threshing of the night upon him silenced him and he
was overcome. He turned away indoors, humbly. There was the infinite
world, eternal, unchanging, as well as the world of life.

(R, p. 81)

Two different kinds of awareness crystallize on the night Lydia
gives birth to her son. For Tom the reality of existence strikes like
the rain on his face, just as reassuring and life-nourishing. The
finite and the infinite worlds seem absolute. He belongs to them
both. Anna, on the other hand, has seen the finite world alone and
been glad of it. She closes herself to the other world of the infinite.
Her view denies wholeness as the end-possibility for man.

Anna's finite view of life becomes stronger as she grows older.
So does 'her passion for dominance' (R, p. 85). Together these
qualities appeal strongly to the finite side of Tom's own nature, and
so he determines to make a lady out of her. Like Mrs Morel, he
hopes to fulfil in the child the thwarted social ambitions in himself,
but Tom mistakes the importance of this part of himself which
needs fulfilment. By wanting 'to clamber out, to his visionary
polite world' (R, p. 90) – the world of Herbert Spencer that he
hears about at Mrs Forbes's house – Tom concentrates on the
social part of his being only; though much later, at Anna's wedding, when 'For the first time in his life, he must spread himself
wordily' (p. 137), he shows how uneasily he holds his instinctive
beliefs at bay. He seems inarticulate to his audience at the wedding,
but Lawrence makes him wholly credible as he dreams out loud
about the high possibilities of marriage and the value of his own.
Anna, by contrast, is happy with her more limited horizons. The
child who can feel no pity for the village cretin because 'He's a
*horrid* man' (R, p. 89) will not be much troubled in her life by
imagination.

It is worth asking at this point why Lawrence needed to create
an Anna Lensky at all. How does she fit the development of his
intentions for *The Sisters*? Could he not have altered the genealogy
so that Ursula, to whom all threads in the novel's fabric eventually
lead, became the daughter of Tom and Lydia, uniting just the same
the Brangwen and Lensky strains of character? Clearly Lawrence
thought that such a scheme would have entailed more than an
adjustment of the novel's social history (for, as it stands, Anna's
childhood is Victorian and Ursula's maturity is essentially part of
the post-war era). In his earliest references to *The Sisters* he talks of
Ella (as Ursula was first called) very much as the centrepiece of the
novel: there is no mention of her mother. Yet few readers of *The*

*Rainbow* would feel it anything but impoverished if Anna had no part in it. She suppresses any sense of infinite wonder in herself so effectively that she almost becomes a viable alternative to the virtually undefinable concept of humanity which Lawrence is still seeking to express at the end of *Women in Love*. She contentedly opts for a partial life, but in the end that is to live like a bird which cannot fly.

In 'Girlhood of Anna Brangwen' Lawrence explores the means by which the young girl hardens herself against her own curiosity or against any suspicion of mystery. She has princes and princesses in her life like any other child, and an exotic stranger like the absurd Skrebensky senior can seem 'a very wonderful person' (R, p. 99) to her as he might to many an impressionable girl. For Anna, however, the fairy tales affect her sense of reality, so that the natural sense of exclusiveness which she has inherited from her mother becomes a positive shrinking from anything commonplace: other little girls become 'bagatelle'. The way she handles her rosary says a lot about her: 'the string of moonlight and silver, when she had it between her fingers, filled her with strange passions'. Anna is attracted to the essence of the rosary but when she realizes what the words mean which she must utter when she uses it the sense of their feebleness is more important to her than the object in her hand and so she puts it away and does not use it. 'It was her instinct to put all these things away. It was her instinct to avoid thinking, to avoid it, to save herself' (R, p. 105). Avoidance becomes so much a part of Anna's nature that her inner responses eventually contract and she becomes hardened in her half-being, like the kernel of a nut where one half is wholesome and the other wasted into nothing. Her rejection of the words which must accompany the rosary typifies her rejection of language generally. 'She hated to hear things expressed, put into words' (R, p. 106). She cannot learn thirty lines of *As You Like It* (in contrast to her daughter, who gains from this same play 'a poignant sense of acquisition and enrichment' – R, p. 334). She despises articulation of feeling. Lawrence himself can be deeply suspicious of it. His severest scorn is always for cerebral, linguistic man. Anna, however, will not delight in language because she does not want to acknowledge the emotions or sentiments it seeks to express. Those elements of her personality which she can master she is happy to possess; those parts which she cannot understand she sends to the corners of her being where they shrivel and die. If Tom is a whole person cleft in twain. Anna's ideal is to be a contented half-person.

The greatest challenge to Anna's self-sufficiency comes both from outside and within herself. Will's entrance into her life arouses her sexual instincts in a way quite different from Lydia's entrance into Tom's life a generation earlier. Then Tom had been looking for a woman, and the woman herself already had a child and needed some kind of refuge. Will's attraction for Anna grows in her almost reluctantly. Like Shakespeare's Miranda, there has been only one man in her life, 'large, looming, a kind of Godhead' (R, p. 106). That emphasis on the Godhead matters, for as Will comes into her life he dethrones her settled gods. Lawrence insists on Will's darkness from the moment he enters the novel. He is like 'some mysterious animal that lived in the darkness under the leaves and never came out, but which lived vividly, swift and intense' (R, p. 106). Dark in colouring and often described as a black shadow, Will introduces 'a dark enriching influence she had not known before' (R, p. 110) into Anna's life. Lawrence uses this language of darkness and obscurity persistently and with a number of intentions. As a factor in Anna's life he represents a pagan force threatening her religion of self-containment. His blackness quickly takes a predatory form – a cat, a hawk; later, in marriage, he is a tiger and a leopard. Will creates in Tom 'a black gloom of anger, and a tenderness of self-effacement' (R, p. 118). Yet Will is hardly a demonic being. He has far more in common with Tom than either ever knows. Deep within him he has a fear of his own obscurity, a burning instinct to achieve and to express. Anna never fully perceives the flame within him, but when she glimpses it the excitement it arouses in her demands its extinction. She laughs at his powerful singing voice; she crushes his desire to carve. Lawrence embodies in the Anna–Will partnership his clearest example of creativity denied. In the two of them, drawn together by physical impulses out of a common environment, he gives us almost the mirror-opposite of Ursula and Birkin. Anna and Will draw back from the uncertainties of the deepest knowledge and communion, as though they had peered over the edge of a rim into a strange land and had cautiously withdrawn lest the new world claim them.

Lawrence's art at its height never converts his characters into props of doctrine, but because certain important passages in his narrative can effectively illustrate the means by which symbol and particularly rhythm counterpoint the themes, he has become over-anthologized in books of critical excerpts. A famous example would be the scene of sexual discovery at the time of the corn harvest, when the phallic stooks and the menstrual gold moon seem to correspond to the awakening lovers, Will and Anna. The sun–moon strand of symbolism in *The Rainbow* may be slightly portentous, but the rhythmic structure here is just right.

There was only the moving to and fro in the moonlight, engrossed, the swinging in the silence, that was marked only by the splash of sheaves, and silence, and a splash of sheaves. And ever the splash of his sheaves broke swifter, beating up to hers, and ever the splash of sheaves recurred monotonously, unchanging, and ever the splash of his sheaves beat nearer.

(R, pp. 123–4)

The language is perfectly controlled, though the repetitions have led to accusations of over-writing. The to and fro of the rhythm not only simulates a sexual rhythm but cross-refers to the ebb and flow of a tide or the wax and wane of the moon at other stages of the scene. The movement of the prose accompanies the action described within it, an aural representation of metaphor and image. The flow and recoil of life is matched by the means of expressing it. But the passage should not be a set-piece for the apprentice critic. Lawrence does not write in 'blocks' of prose but within a complex organization of character and philosophy. The rhythm of work done in unison yet suggests a broken movement where the fro must follow the to. For such will be the marriage of Will and Anna, not the steady curve of the arch but the jagged edge of the Gothic pinnacle, all points and recesses. In the same scene Will wonders, 'Why was there always a space between them, why were they apart' (R, p. 123), and he never finds an answer to the question.

The fertility of the harvest scene should not make us forget that the corn has also been ransacked and cut. Destruction has its place in the harvest gathering as well as ripeness, anticipating the destructive element in Anna's and Will's relationship. Significantly, Lawrence makes new use of the Eden image in the opening of his chapter 'Anna Victrix' where the young couple, now married, lie 'as if the heavens had fallen, and he were sitting with her among the ruins, in a new world, everybody else buried' (R, p. 144). They discover a new Eden for themselves. Though this new world is hardly the one that Lawrence aspires towards, being abandoned and self-absorbed, we ought not to be too moralistic in reacting to it. Lawrence is quite humorous here, after all, as he illustrates the happy laziness of the newly weds. The tacit denial of the world (p. 144) implicit in the opening lines of 'Anna Victrix' foreshadows the development of their partnership. Moments of total exclusiveness alternate with Will's sense of moral obligation to the outer world. This exclusiveness can be enriching; to the reader it can seem quite touching.

> 'I am dying with hunger.'
> 'So am I,' he said calmly, as if it were not of significance. And they relapsed into the warm, golden stillness. And the minutes flowed unheeded past the window outside.
> Then suddenly she stirred against him.
> 'My dear, I am dying of hunger,' she said.
> It was a slight pain to him to be brought to.
> 'We'll get up,' he said, unmoving.
> And she sank her head on to him again, and they lay still, lapsing. Half consciously, he heard the clock chime the hour. She did not hear.
> 'Do get up,' she murmured at length, 'and give me something to eat.'
> 'Yes,' he said, and he put his arm round her, and she lay with her face on him. They were faintly astonished that they did not move. The minutes rustled louder at the window.
>
> (R, p. 146)

Notice how many of the words here point to an other-worldliness in their bliss: 'relapsed', 'lapsing', 'half consciously'. The outer world 'flowed unheeded', then 'rustled louder'. Lawrence chooses a soft vocabulary to achieve real tenderness here. His humour appeals in a gentle way: like the tramps at the end of *Waiting for Godot* Will and Anna do not move, lest they break the seeming permanence of the moment.

> . . . it was as if they were at the very centre of all the slow wheeling of space and the rapid agitation of life, deep, deep inside them all, at the centre where there is utter radiance, and eternal being, and the silence absorbed in praise.
>
> (R, p. 145)

Lawrence endlessly selects images of beauty within deadness in these novels: the moon within the burr, the kernel within the nut, the husk or the rind or the rim which imprisons softness, fecundity, mystery or energy. Anna and Will know the inner reality within the outer, where 'time roared far off, forever far off' (R, p. 145), but they know it only in patches. Lawrence desired that this inner reality become the only one. Will's marriage tragically reveals to him the inner possibilities which the 'mechanical' man before had only guessed at, but the revelation only underlines the insufficiency of his daily life and the tantalizing unattainability of any alternative. His marriage gives him an awareness which pains him more than his earlier 'darkness of obscurity' (R, p. 116).

He surveyed the rind of the world: houses, factories, trams, the discarded rind; people scurrying about, work going on, all on the discarded surface. An earthquake had burst it all from inside. It was as if the surface of the world had been broken away entire: Ilkeston, streets, church, people, work, rule-of-the-day, all intact, and yet peeled away into unreality, leaving here exposed the inside, the reality: one's own being, strange feelings and passions and yearnings and beliefs and aspirations, suddenly become present, revealed, the permanent bedrock, knitted one rock with the woman one loved. It was confounding. Things are not what they seem! When he was a child, he had thought a woman was a woman merely by virtue of her skirts and petticoats. And now, lo, the whole world could be divested of its garment, the garment could lie there shed away, intact, and one could stand in a new world, a new earth, naked in a new naked universe. It was too astounding and miraculous. This then was marriage! The old things didn't matter any more.

(R, p. 150)

No wonder that, as he grows older, Will should retreat into his own private domain, unrelating to the social world and pathetically attempting through his organ-playing or his resumed carving to express the inner being, the reality in a sham world, which marriage has flashed before him. Before marriage Will had been a Christ or an Adam for Anna – 'Out of the rock of his form the very fountain of life flowed' (R, p. 130) – but now the rock of his being stands prepared for a new world, not a regeneration of the old. Only at the back of his mind lurks the fear that he will follow the archetype of the king for a day, the Cinderella who glimpses but cannot be confident of gaining the 'new naked universe'. His fear proves well justified.

Anna's capacity for vision, while no less intense or expectant than Will's, can more easily be subjugated. She, who from the heights of her personal Mount Pisgah stares Moses-like towards a shining rainbow as though it were the appearance of the Grail, settles for the rind. The point about the rainbow as a central image in the first novel is that it has no crust, no outer surface to be peeled off or diverted before the 'new world' can be seen. Anna rejects the rainbow, complete in its colour range though it is, because it lies too far away. 'Must she be moving thither? . . . She stood so safely on the Pisgah mountain' (R, p. 195). If, with Wordsworth, she knows that there has passed a glory from the earth, then let it go. 'All the love, the magnificent new order was going to be lost, she would forfeit it all for the outside things' (R, p. 151).

The struggle we have witnessed in Tom and Lydia resumes in Will and Anna, the conflict this time of eventual opposites. Anna is happier than Will: Lawrence accepts that much. The paradox of her freedom is that it must enslave her partner. She, who was the agent by which he saw, becomes the Delilah who blinds him. Anna Victrix is also Anna Destructrix, deriding Will's sense of the mystery in religion. The episode of the lamb in the stained-glass window illustrates this, and their battle over the credibility of the miracle at Cana. Theirs is a war between the infinite and the finite. Lawrence himself was hardly sure how such a conflict could end. Anna's victories are temporal, and in the end Lawrence believes the victory of intellect over mystery to be no victory at all. Anna 'believed in the omnipotence of the human mind' (R, p. 173), Will in the indefinable resources of the soul. As they battle they waste the passion that still flows between them. We must see that Lawrence is not writing a drama of matrimonial failure in the manner of Strindberg or Albee but an account of a perpetual human struggle which theologians call the conflict of the spirit and the flesh. Lawrence prefers to liberate the conflict from moral prejudice and see it only as a tragic division in man's nature which constantly separates his being as an amoeba chooses to split itself. But where the amoeba's action is planned and sexless, man's fragmentation causes pain and opposition.

Lawrence gives the practical victory to the woman, as a result of which she becomes the rock that originally Will had been for her. Life without her would be either extinction or 'the terror of the night of heaving, overwhelming flood' (R, p. 186). The apotheosis of their separation-within-bondage comes in chapter 7 of *The Rainbow*, 'The Cathedral'. Lawrence chooses his main image well. The apex of the cathedral, to which Will responds sublimely, enshrines all the arch and rainbow metaphors of the novel – with one exception. It has a roof. The eye and imagination soar upwards to the heavens, only to be excluded from the ultimate vision. The cathedral is seen, too, as seed, light, jewel, root and flower. Outside of time, like a world of reality within an outer chaos; succumbing to time, a side-show in the real world of life. The cathedral image serves dual and opposite purposes. Here Will is belittled by Anna and she glimpses something of the mystery to which he aspires. Yet neither is finally enlarged or consumed by the experience inside the cathedral. Will's deepest reaction has not been to 'the perfect surge of his Cathedral' (R, p. 205) but to a small face carved in stone which he takes to be the likeness of a monk and which Anna believes to be a man's representation of his shrewish wife. Will knows he is right, Anna hardly cares if she is or not, but their different views of the little face amply sum up the futility of their disagreement. Will yearns after the monk (wanting perhaps to have his single serenity), Anna scoffs at the malicious carver (perhaps fearing his criticism). They leave the cathedral almost glad to be away, but in their brief visit Will's spirit has been finally crushed. Anna has effectively removed his faith and barely knows she has done it. 'He ceased to fret about his life. He relaxed his will, and let everything go' (R, p. 207). Anna, by contrast, finds almost total fulfilment in the first children.

The Will we see hereafter veers between moody silence and inchoate rage, an imprisoned being who has accepted the mastery of his wife and who yet knows dimly of a lost world which he once nearly attained. The marriage of indifference which Lawrence shows us in the second half of *The Rainbow* and in the background of *Women in Love* is unlike any other that he wrote about. Detachment and dependency exist side by side. Will's brief forays out of his marital bondage seem stale substitutes for the relationship he never had. Typically we find some of Lawrence's most wayward writing in the moments of violent reconciliation which flare up between Will and Anna in almost as exhausting a way as their long bouts of hostility or tense neutrality:

He was obsessed. If he did not discover and make known to himself these delights, they might be lost for ever. He wished he had a hundred men's energies, with which to enjoy her. He wished he were a cat, to lick her with a rough, grating, lascivious tongue. He wanted to wallow in her, bury himself in her flesh, cover himself over with her flesh.

(R, p. 236)

The eroticism of a moment earlier, when Will thinks of the hollow under Anna's ankle and the thin blue vein which crosses it, almost collapses here into hysteria or pornography. In another context it would do so, but Will's fury of desire for Anna at this point must be set against the deadness of their connection at other times. It serves, too, to remind us of the misdirection of his creative energies. Outbursts of erotic fantasy are a diminished alternative to the fulfilment of the creative soul or the realization of the inner core which Will's daughter will also shortly be seeking. Lawrence goes on to depict Will's defeat in aesthetic terms. By exchanging the jagged imperfection of the Gothic for the 'supreme, immoral, Absolute Beauty, in the body of woman' (R, p. 237) Will replaces his search for inexpressible mystery with the contentments of sensuality. He and Anna become absorbed in each other again, but only in their bodies. Nothing more clearly contradicts the favourite mis-representation of Lawrence, that he was a writer who saw all the solutions to man's problems in sex. Will and Anna no longer meet at soul-level; spiritually they seek separate outlets, Will in a sense of public duty and Anna in rearing her family.

The harmony of mutual tolerance; the disharmony of opposing wills and souls: these lie at the centre of Lawrence's account of their marriage as he writes of its mature years. Perhaps because both partners claim the reader's attention equally, the Anna–Will rela-tionship gives an even greater sense of loss, of one being stifled and another only partially there, than the Tom and Lydia connection. The first marriage unites earth and shadow. In many ways Lawrence sees it as a success: it has elements of his own marriage, for Lydia, the foreign woman with a child, has something of Frieda in her. The marriage of Will and Anna shows a gradual reversal of the initial rôles, so that Will, who is rock, predator, devil, at the start, is made tame and conventional by his partner who herself becomes the keeper of her husband whilst being contentedly cow-like in her maternalism. Yet Will never quite loses the blind enquiry of the mole to whom he is likened when we first see him, and some remote light from the rainbow still finds its way into Anna's being. She finds, in the victory of the womb, her own kind of limited fulfilment, still with the impregnable will she had as a child. Taken together, Lawrence unites them in a special kind of tragedy, the key to which is their incompleteness as human beings. The abandoned wife in *The Trespasser*, the social and moral incom-patibility of the Morels, the bitterness of the Sissons in *Aaron's Rod*, the bickering of Richard and Harriet Somers in *Kangaroo*, the sterility of the Chatterleys – these have their tragic side, but in a way more fierce and less pathetic than the sense of possible absorp-tion in each other's being which lies unrecognized by either at the kernel of the Anna–Will marriage.

In *The Rainbow* Lawrence only rarely interrupts the movement of the novel to return to a character whom he has temporarily left out. In chapter 9, 'The Marsh and the Flood', Tom Brangwen dies. This death is given greater prominence than any other in either *The Rainbow* or *Women in Love*, unless the prolonged death-struggle of Gerald Crich's father matches it. Tom's demise has its symbolic value, for by this stage of the novel he has developed into a patriar-chal figure, embodying a distant world which dies with him. The new world no longer allows people to act as instinctively as he had always done. The epic nature of his death suggests something of the awe with which Lawrence acknowledged the passing of the old world. Furthermore, all the deaths in the novels betoken the author's obsession with mortality. It can hardly surprise us that Lawrence wrote so much about death. He grew up in a vulnerable community where the average life-expectancy, especially among men, was far lower than the national average. Later on, his mother's death affected him bitterly. He was himself constantly under medical observation and was already, at the time of writing *The Rainbow*, entering the first phase of the illness that killed him. Nor can we forget the war, in whose shadow both novels were written. Few important writers are unconcerned with death; for Lawrence to have been so at this time would have been sublimely unpitying.

Tom returns to the story only so that he may die. By this time he has matured into a gentleman farmer, prospering but rather lazy; this in contrast to his son-in-law who, in the bitterness of *his* failure, turns to the labour of church work and night school. Tom has become isolated and afraid, estranged not only from Lydia and Will but from his beloved Anna. His time to love is over and now is his time to die. The waters of the Marsh rise over him, then fall back as they did after Noah's flood. Lawrence makes the whole episode a parable of human isolation. Tom's death preserves him for ever in his separation from other men. To Anna he enshrines 'the majesty of the inaccessible male, the majesty of death' (R, p. 251), and to Lydia he 'was a majestic Abstraction' (R, p. 251), but to his sons he cannot be so readily converted into this kind of monumentalism. For them death shows the final disintegration of his being and the victory of nature over man.

Lawrence desperately seeks a *via media* between these two poles. If death renders a man 'abstract' and 'inhuman', as Anna and Lydia believe, then nothing has been made out of life, and if, like the sons, we can only see death as obscene and obstructive, then its victory seems cruel and purposeless. In Christian teaching death is in some ways the fulfilment of life, the fair mountain to which we climb after battening upon the moor. Lawrence could never accept that attitude, but, like Gerald Crich, he felt the attraction of death as the ultimate challenge to his senses and his understanding. When Gerald surfaces from the water after the drowning tragedy in chapter 14 of *Women in Love* he says, 'It's curious how much room there seems, a whole universe under there; and as cold as hell, you're as helpless as if your head was cut off' (W, p. 206). Lawrence half desired to explore that netherworld. Significantly he envisages death in both *The Rainbow* and *Women in Love* through images of water: Tom's flood, the drowning, Gerald's death in snow; even Mr Crich dies with the question on his lips, 'Is there much more water in Denley?' (R, p. 376). Death in these novels is liquid and insubstantial, distorting shape, size, colour and sound, all the properties of known reality. Death renders all human feeling, action and achievements impermanent, but not futile. In his essay 'On Human Destiny', written in the closing months of his own life, Lawrence writes:

I live and die. I ask no other. Whatever proceeds from me lives and dies. I am glad, too, God is eternal, but my idea of Him is my own, and perishable. Everything human, human knowledge, human faith, human emotions, all perishes. And that is very good; if it were not so, everything would turn to cast-iron. There is too much of this cast-iron of permanence today.

The themes here are taken up in many of the late poems, in 'The Man Who Died' and in *Apocalypse*. Death – which Lawrence usually apprehends as a conscious experience, though consciousness of what he cannot, of course, define – sharpens and almost sanctifies our life. The great religions maintain that life is of secondary importance to death, but Lawrence asserts their equilibrium and duality. The one intensifies the other in mutual dependency, the perceived and the unknown, the felt and the unrealized, the tangible and the liquid. The sacredness of life comes through the inevitability of death. 'The light shall never go out till the last day', he writes in 'On Human Destiny': "The light of the human adventure into consciousness, which is, essentially, the light of human God-knowledge.' Death conditions life: in that simple but far from banal understanding resides Lawrence's central humanity and his ability to reject either of the two attitudes he dramatizes in 'The Marsh and the Flood' – Lydia's sense of death as rendering life majestically irrelevant and the Brangwen sons believing (as does Gerald's mother, with even greater horror) that death contains the ultimate insult to man.

Ursula Brangwen may be the most life-enhancing character D. H. Lawrence ever created. As with Paul Morel, the conception and gestation of the child seems annunciatory and exalted, separating the mother, in her creative glory, from the husband, with his 'soul a black torment of unfulfilment' (R, p. 182). In *The Rainbow* Lawrence marries the archetypal and the ordinary, an eternal time-scale with the separate seconds of human change. Ursula's birth exemplifies this. Anna becomes the all-mother, urging herself to the crowning victory of a live child. At the moment the newborn baby suckles at her breast for the first time she cries her own plaudit, 'Anna Victrix' (R, p. 192), like a queen at a coronation. Yet in the moment of realization that she has produced a girl Anna betrays a disappointment that allows Will to 'claim' the child for himself: the vent of possession foreshadows not just the special intimacy of Will and Ursula but the girl's eventual resistance to being owned by anyone. Anna's fleeting moment of disappointment is often the instinctive response as the new-born creature is seen for the first time, and at this point one recognizes in Lawrence an unsentimental understanding of motherhood.

Both Anna and Will now live through Ursula, and later through their other children. Lawrence did not underestimate the richness of the parent–child relationship, but he saw that the birth of an infant not only separated the father and mother from each other but that both partners frequently dried up inside as a result. Anna's contentment in ministering to her children, and Will's sense that he can base his whole life on Ursula, 'on her support and her accord' (R, p. 220), suggest a denial of self in them both: denial of self, not selflessness, for the effect is constraint, not restraint. It also implies a claim, a demand on the child, which is to give the parents a satisfaction they have not managed themselves.

Lawrence's depiction of childhood is as understanding in Ursula's case as it is in Anna's. The scenes of potato-planting, diving into the canal, riding on a swing at the fair, in Lydia's bedroom after Tom's death – each incident adds tenderly yet acutely to the shape of Ursula's personality and helps to form her into the self-reliant, sensuous being of later chapters. Like her mother, she has an imaginative life which is more romantic than the drab reality of the common world, and so she develops the Brangwen–Lensky resentment of the mass world.

She lived a dual life, one where the facts of daily life encompassed everything, being legion, and the other wherein the facts of daily life were superseded by the eternal truth. So utterly did she desire the Sons of God should come to daughters of men; and she believed more in her desire and its fulfilment than in the obvious facts of life.

(R, pp. 276–7)

This remains true of Ursula throughout *The Rainbow* and *Women in Love*. By applying the religious metaphor of the last passage too literally we may find ourselves in the position which theorists of women's liberation have objected to: that Lawrence believes in the fulfilment, even the redemption, of women only by the higher power of men. I do not think he intended to say this. Ursula's whole being as she grows older scorns any notion of male superiority. She does not accept, however, the alternative extreme, that woman in herself has the capacity for complete satisfaction of her desires. Her sexual being requires the balance and complement of a male partner, just as Birkin knows that neither in himself nor in his love for Gerald can he find the completeness of his own being. Birkin's relationship with Gerald suggests a homosexual element in Lawrence's personality, but we must not think that he considered that only men should be permitted the possibility of such an intimacy. Ursula's friendships with Winifred Inger and Maggie Schofield are explicitly lesbian relationships. Lawrence wants neither sex to be exclusively bound by the opposite; he enquires about the need for affection, indeed love, between people of the same sex and suggests it is not just a need for homosexuals. He explores all the possibilities of self-fulfilment. To impose a single sexual theory or objection upon his constantly probing method reduces a series of hesitant questions to a set of didactic propositions. Lawrence does not work like that. His characters, Ursula chief among them, test possibilities, but their reactions are never final or doctrinaire. Lawrence died at the age of forty-five. He was only thirty when *The Rainbow* was published. We mistake his kind of writing if we ask from it a final balance-sheet of philosophical priorities or sexual ethics. The exploration of needs or possibilities can be more valuable than the arrival at settled conclusions, but critics who in recent years have brought their own notions of sexual justice to Lawrence's work have invariably disputed that. It was Lawrence's main belief that to rest inertly in a settled viewpoint is intellectual death.

Ursula's great task in life is nothing less than to make sense of the evolutionary process and her place within it. 'Out of nothingness and the undifferentiated mass, to make something of herself!' (R, p. 283). Ursula's concern to know herself would be vanity if it did not have a metaphysical justification. Lawrence sees the danger in the futile contemplation of one's own navel. Gudrun and Hermione, for example, live life for what self-gratification they can win from it, and so in the wrong way. They never feel with Ursula that 'Self was a oneness with the infinite. To be oneself was a supreme, gleaming triumph of infinity' (R, p. 441). Ursula aspires to that from her earliest years, first in her ideals of Tennysonian romance, then in her rhapsody of Christian faith, and eventually in sexual discovery as a manifestation of the greater mysteries of nature. We should remember, too, that she never rejects humanity entirely. Through her girl-friends, her relationship with Skrebensky, her determination in her first teaching post to live by her educational principles, through her ties with Gudrun even when in opposition to her, and in her own marriage to Birkin, she demonstrates her involvement with other people. Selective and exclusive though she is, Ursula never contracts into that perfection of life-denying isolation which is embodied in Gerald's glacial demise upon the mountainside.

Ursula's affair with Anton Skrebensky introduces a new kind of partnership to *The Rainbow*. Up to this point the main relationships of the book have led to marriage. Though Ursula contemplates marriage to Skrebensky, the reader remains unconvinced of its possibility; just as Jane Eyre rejects the chance of going to India with St John Rivers and of thus becoming a conventional Christian wife, so Ursula has to turn down a similar opportunity, for it would entail a denial of her being. Skrebensky has the blood of minor aristocracy within him, and Ursula seeks a kind of aristocracy for herself, but not on the terms he offers. Skrebensky comes to Ursula at the virginal stage in her sexual development. She loves him, but in the end she has to reject the imprisoning concept of his love and his merely social being. Here lies the shocking nature of *The Rainbow* rather than in the actual episodes (Anna's dance, naked and pregnant, and Ursula's swim with Miss Inger) which led to the book being suppressed on account of its 'immorality' and to questions about it in the British parliament. Ursula's frank wondering whether she may be carrying Skrebensky's child or her lesbian involvement with Miss Inger are conventional, compared with the kind of remark she makes in conversation with her friend Dorothy Russell.

'Love–love–love – what does it mean – what does it amount to? So much personal gratification. It doesn't lead anywhere.'

'It isn't supposed to lead anywhere, is it?' said Dorothy satirically. 'I thought it was the one thing which is an end in itself.'

'Then what does it matter to me,' cried Ursula. 'As an end in itself, I could love a hundred men, one after the other. Why should I end with a Skrebensky? Why should I not go on, and love all the types I fancy, one after another, if love is an end to itself? There are plenty of men who aren't Anton, whom I could love – whom I would like to love.'

(R, p. 475)

The official morality of England in 1915, though a host of personal memoirs have since shown it to be dubiously honest with itself, found this apparent recipe for promiscuity hard to take. Lawrence meant what he wrote, however. If a certain kind of romantic love. in Dorothy's words, is 'an end in itself', it cannot be more than a *cul-de-sac* in the evolution of feeling. Nowhere in either *The Rainbow* or *Women in Love* does Lawrence say love is pointless, but he rejected what he considered the romantic banality of believing there could be only one love and one kind of love for each type of person. For Ursula to marry Anton would be the right solution in a minor novel, but she cannot do so without invalidating her potential for self-discovery. With Tom and Will in mind, we easily see why the first novel must finish in its open-ended way. *Women in Love* became inevitable with the conversation quoted above. Indeed, it is almost repeated in that novel, with Ursula taking Dorothy's rôle this time. Birkin says, 'I don't believe in love at all ... It is just part of human relationships, no more', to which Ursula responds, 'Why do you bother about humanity?' Birkin's reply seems priggishly objectionable to Ursula – 'If I do love it ... it is my disease' (W. pp. 143–4) – but Lawrence intends by it a statement not just about relations with other people but on the central frailty in the purity of any artist's vision, his need to care individually.

Skrebensky is commonplace, as Birkin obviously is not. Nowhere else do we more evidently see what Lawrence meant by aristocracy: Skrebensky has the title, Birkin the blood-reality. Skrebensky's phrasing when he and Ursula talk of the war in the Sudan gives him away, a mixture of cliché ('It's about the most serious business there is, fighting' – R, p. 310) and jingoism ('I belong to the nation and must do my duty by the nation' – R, p. 311). For Lawrence, remarks like these are almost criminal, for they are self-abnegating, they express devotion to mere social and antlike ideals. No wonder that, for Ursula, Skrebensky is simply 'not there'. Even in their most intimate moments together Lawrence dwells on the hard separateness of their two souls.

So they danced four or five dances, always together, always his will becoming more tense, his body more subtle, playing upon her. And still he had not got her, she was hard and bright as ever, intact. But he must weave himself round her, enclose her, enclose her in a net of shadow, of darkness, so she would be like a bright creature gleaming in a net of shadows, caught. Then he would have her, he would enjoy her. How he would enjoy her, when she was caught.

(R, p. 320)

Like a sea-king with his captive, Skrebensky desires the victory of his will over Ursula's. The word 'intact', however, stands out from the sensuous rhythm of his prose, a clipped sharp word which emphasizes Ursula's refusal to be imprisoned. In the end he, the weaker of the two, becomes *her* conquest. 'So she held him there, the victim, consumed annihilated. She had triumphed: he was not any more' (R, p. 322). Her triumph in his submission satisfies her feminine pride, but she understands the hollowness of a victory that brings no fulfilment other than the thrill of proving her dominance. There is no equilibrium in conquest. The verbs of possession which prevail in all the scenes concerning Ursula and Skrebensky signify an imbalance in their connection. In the end, he has been no more than a stage in her sexual and emotional development, as incomplete for her as Rivers is for Jane Eyre.

In depicting Ursula as an unattached soul, Lawrence shows himself one of the first exponents of what has since become a major theme in twentieth-century fiction, non-commitment. The difficulty of finding an ideal or a faith or a cause in which to invest one's emotional being does not enter the English novel with Lawrence, but he may be the first major novelist to write of its positive advantages. He sees, too, the tragic sense of inner desiccation to which this inability to take root may lead. In Ursula's semi-doxology at the end of *The Rainbow* the glory and the waste come together.

I have no father nor mother nor lover, I have no allocated place in the world of things. I do not belong to Beldover nor to this world, they none of them exist, I am trammelled and entangled in them, but they are all unreal. I must break out of it, like a nut from its shell which is an unreality.

(R, p. 493)

We cannot point for point identify each of these statements with Lawrence in 1915, but the same fear of living only the husk or rind of life haunted him, too. Ursula comes close to believing that the unreality of things is more real than reality and that her inner spiritual world, and the fantasies that they have given rise to since childhood (compare Lettie in *The White Peacock*, Helena in *The Trespasser* or Miriam in *Sons and Lovers*), have more meaning than the world she inhabits physically and socially. 'If she could but get away to the clean, free moonlight' (R, p. 319): Lawrence saw in the moon not just a symbol of Ursula's feminine nature, as its cycle has traditionally made it in literature, but a means of expressing her yearning to be free, unattached, radiant, presiding, yet finally dependent on the powerful light of her partner, the sun. 'The man should come from the Infinite and she should hail him' (R, p. 494), she acknowledges at the end of *The Rainbow*. Independence, inter-dependence and dependence, each has its place in Ursula's composition.

The Ursula of *Women in Love* does not directly carry on from the Ursula of *The Rainbow*, and we mistake some essentially different characteristics in the second novel if we match the two Ursulas un-critically. The first Ursula expends much of her energy on trying to establish herself in 'The Man's World' (Lawrence uses the phrase as his heading for chapter 13 of *The Rainbow*) 'as a separate social individual' (R, p. 364). Many critics have, quite properly, invited us to see Ursula's battles in the classroom to assert her will over the recalcitrant children without sacrificing her liberal principles either as a comment upon the shortcomings of the educational world in 1915 or as an example of the male tactics which the emancipated female has to adopt if life is to be mastered. But the danger in Ursula's 'victory' is that she becomes, for a time, 'mechanical' (R, p. 401). Her hold over the children can be asserted only if she exchanges her innate sense of balance between people for the doc-trine of authority by one over another. Lawrence's next novels deal specifically with the nature of authority, but in *The Rainbow* he equivocates about it. Near the end of the book Ursula apprehends the imperfection of her form of authority, but only dimly so:

This lighted area, lit up by man's complacent consciousness, she thought was all the world: that here all was disclosed for ever. Yet all the time, within the darkness she had been aware of points of light . . .

(R, p. 437)

The gleam becomes brighter as she races naked on the southern downs, an innocent in Eden savouring a pre-industrial England before the day starts. Yet Lawrence's phrasing when he talks of this new day at the end of *The Rainbow* oversimplifies and condescends towards the working life of England. The 'blind, sordid, strenuous activity, all for nothing' (R, p. 466), grinding into motion for another mechanical day, has little reality to it. Similarly, Ursula's raising her eyes from the 'stiffened bodies of the colliers', from the 'dry, brittle, terrible corruption spreading over the face of the land' (R, p. 495) to the iridescent colouring of the revelatory rainbow itself, substitutes the symbolic pattern of the novel for truthful insight. In this respect the open-ended finish of *The Rainbow* illus-trates Lawrence's uncertainty of attitude towards the industrial life and the rôle of authority in society. The attempt to resolve these uncertainties lies at the core of *Women in Love*.

We do not need to know *The Rainbow* well in order to understand *Women in Love*, but as they are the two halves of one conception, some acquaintance with the first novel undoubtedly helps us to 'place' the Ursula Brangwen we meet at the start of the second. *Women in Love* opens with the two sisters discussing marriage. Gudrun no longer takes second place to her elder sister. 'She wanted to be quite definite' (W, p. 7), and in that assertiveness lie her strengths and her limitations. Ursula appears more diffident, answering 'I don't know' and 'It depends' and 'I'm not sure' to Gudrun's questions. Early in their conversation Ursula responds to her sister's 'You don't think one needs the *experience* of having been married?' with her first reasonably certain remark, that marriage is 'more likely to be the end of experience'. Ursula desires the knowledge of what life can provide just as fully as Gudrun, but she does not seek to restrict that knowledge to the social world about her. She holds the indisputable conviction that another kind of perceivable world exists, upon which the social world sits like an obscuring veil. The strength of this conviction distinguishes the Ursula of *Women in Love* from the Ursula of *The Rainbow*. In *The Rainbow* much of the battle within her centres on her attempt to take her place within the social world by moulding that world in her own image. Lawrence dramatizes the issue that traditionally faces the adolescent idealist, whose determination to change society nonetheless involves his wish to be a member of it. *Women in Love* advances beyond that, to a stage which possibly no English novel had reached before. Ursula still asks questions of the world – she will do so to the last page of the novel – but she no longer sees herself as a social being. During the course of the novel both she and Birkin abandon their professions. Only her own private soul, or any private relationship she can forge with someone of like kind, matters to her now. Ursula Brangwen in *The Rainbow* struggles to hold her place in the social world by cleansing it. Ursula Brangwen in *Women in Love*, despite all her urgency and insistence, is a more tranquil person for whom social merit means little. In attitude if not in fact, she has 'dropped out' from society already. The problem before her in the first novel was how to reconcile the reality of the world as it is with the reality it might become. In the second novel a recognition of the failure of the social world in any form has become instinctive to her, and Ursula's quest must now focus exclusively on her own being. The outer world of the husk and darkness must be shed if the inner light is to be released and realized. Chapter 26 of *Women in Love*, 'A Chair', makes this explicit. Helped but not directed by Birkin's tuition, Ursula freely exclaims, 'I don't want to inherit the earth.' Instead she will accept 'a whole other world' (W, p. 408), where 'things' and possessions are meaningless.

The ingenuity, if not actual paradox, of Lawrence's development of Ursula in *Women in Love* deserves comment. Having said that in this novel her knowledge of her private being virtually excludes her interest in the husk-world around her, we must admit that we actually see Ursula in company in this novel at least as often as we do in *The Rainbow*. It is a measure of Lawrence's narrative sophistication, which reaches its peak in *Women in Love*, that he can reveal the inner nature of Ursula in a social context. Whether with her sister or her lover, in a shop or a hotel, Ursula rarely appears alone, yet the sense remains strong of her solitariness or of her groping towards partnership with Birkin alone. In *The Rainbow* Lawrence normally conveys inner existence by descriptive analysis; in *Women in Love* he can more readily demonstrate it through incident or conversation. The opening of 'Class-Room' is an example. Scene, a botany lesson: a link with *The Rainbow* is established for the observant reader, since it was only in botany that Ursula had 'a glimpse of something working entirely apart from the purpose of the human world' (R, p. 436). The end of the school-day:

A heavy, copper-coloured beam of light came in at the west window, gilding the outlines of the children's heads with red gold, and falling on the wall opposite in a rich, ruddy illumination. Ursula, however, was scarcely conscious of it. She was busy, the end of the day was here, the work went on as a peaceful tide that is at flood, hushed to retire.

(W, p. 38)

A warm, creative, mellow light falls on the room. The scene Lawrence gives us has an innocent stillness, almost a monastic discipline, quite different from Brinsley Street school where she had practised her teaching. Ursula is instructing the children about catkins when Birkin enters.

She saw, in the shaft of ruddy, copper-coloured light near her, the face of a man. It was gleaming like fire, watching her, waiting for her to be aware.

95

Birkin appears to her like a vision, a face made from flames. His physical actuality counts for nothing. His fire warms her into life from a virtually catatonic trance (which has lasted years rather than a few sleepy moments at the end of a day in the classroom). '"It is so dark," he said. "Shall we have the light?"' Lawrence handles the symbolism explicitly and confidently here. Birkin – like Jane Eyre, with her candles when she returns to the stricken Rochester – brings literal and metaphysical light to Ursula. 'She looked like one who is suddenly wakened' (W, p. 39). Birkin now takes charge of the lesson, which, as an Inspector of Schools, he is entitled to do. He instructs the children on the pollination of the catkin. The children do not matter, though. A private dialogue goes on between Birkin and Ursula, on the subject of creative sexuality, until the harsh intrusion of Hermione Roddice. The episode lasts only two pages – yet it establishes the bond of fire and light between Birkin and Ursula. The imagery is positive throughout, no word is wasted, and, in a scene which defines their social positions, too, the inner beings of the two people have been lit up without sententiousness or rhapsody.

Birkin and Ursula come together at the same point in their personal evolution. 'Her spirit was active, her life like a shoot that is growing steadily, but which has not yet come above ground' (W, p. 57); 'his life seemed uncertain, without any definite rhythm, any organic meaning' (W, p. 58). The unregulated rhythm of their two lives never quite disappears, though even in the midst of their hectic battles they are linked by a tranquillity of disposition quite unlike the destructive struggle in which Gudrun and Gerald seem permanently locked. Indeed, the next occasion after the classroom meeting in which we see Ursula and Birkin confronting each other seriously is in chapter 11, 'An Island', where Lawrence, planning this novel with a confident symmetry, places the scene directly after a chapter of similar yet opposite confrontation between Gudrun and Gerald. He contrasts the 'diabolic freemasonry' (W, p. 135) of these two, and its talk of power and submission, with the debate between Birkin and Ursula about freedom, love and whether there is any hope for man's future.

We can easily misunderstand Lawrence if we take Birkin's vision in this chapter of 'a world empty of people, just uninterrupted grass, and a hare sitting up' (W, p. 142) as Lawrence's own. He raises it as an imaginative possibility, but not as an ideal. Ursula instantly counters it with her insistence that a world without man would be, in any conscious sense, a dead world. The philosophical veracity of her reply interests Lawrence as it does anyone who has thought about Plato's table, but the discussion does more than dramatize an intellectual problem or alternative points of view about man's right to survive the twentieth century. It shows that Birkin and Ursula seek answers to the same questions. Their approaches may sometimes differ – at one point Ursula finds herself agreeing with Hermione that Birkin is the kind of person who likes to take a bud apart 'to see what the flower will be like' (W, p. 158) – but they acknowledge the same priorities. Lawrence perhaps believed that to be the most vital part of a relationship. Means and ends may differ, but the question of what truly matters must be shared if there is to be any creative partnership. This accounts partly for the survival of his own marriage to Frieda. It explains the apparent contradiction in Birkin and Ursula, whose fights are productive while those of Gerald and Gudrun are not. Ursula 'was strictly hostile to him. But she was held to him by some bond, some deep principle. This at once irritated her and saved her' (W, p. 159). There exists no feasible salvation in the other couple.

In the Birkin and Ursula relationship, Lawrence was trying to come to an explanation of something which language, even the versatile English language used by a great novelist at the height of his powers, may not be able to express. He intimated this in the letter to Garnett speaking of his need to use 'another language almost' from that of all his previous work. Significantly, Birkin talks of knowing Ursula *finally* in a world 'where there is no speech' (W, p. 162), and she, we are told, 'was always frightened of words, because she knew that mere word-force could always make her believe what she did not believe' (W, p. 492). Lawrence rejected purely cerebral man, but was bound by his best art to find articulate verbal expression for felt perceptions. He struggled in the last five years of his life to be a painter, because there he could dispense with language and make statements from pure intuition.

It is to me the most exciting moment – when you have a blank canvas and a big brush full of wet colour, and you plunge. It is just like diving into a pond – then you start frantically to swim. So far as I am concerned, it is like swimming in a baffling current and being rather frightened and very thrilled, gasping and striking out for all you're worth. The living eye watches sharp as a needle; but the picture comes clean out of instinct, intuition and sheer physical action. Once the instinct and intuition gets into the brush-tip, the picture *happens*, if it is to be a picture at all.

The act of painting here in Lawrence's essay 'Making Pictures' more or less describes what Birkin wants from his partnership with Ursula, something towards which one struggles as if swimming against a strong current, in which the 'living eye' of intelligence does not go blind, and from which a spontaneous creative achievement evolves 'clean out of instinct, intuition and sheer physical action'. Ursula shares this vision as long as it does not either dispense with the centrality of sex or deny the humanity of man. She saves Birkin from pompous etherealism as he saves her from virtual death, 'a life that is a repetition of repetitions' (W, p. 215).

Ursula Brangwen, from childhood to marriage and after, provides the most positive evidence in his work that Lawrence was on the side of life. Each quarrel ends in reconciliation and a restored, not an impaired, harmony. Ursula, 'new and frail like a flower just unfolded' (W, p. 416), embodies Lawrence's vision of the new woman. That phrase had a special meaning for the aware women of Ursula Brangwen's generation, reading Shaw, demanding their first vote, experiencing an emancipation which their forebears, the Brangwen women of the opening pages of *The Rainbow*, had only glimpsed as a far-off light. Ursula – Gudrun, too, in this respect – is a new woman socially. She has claimed her independence. That particular rainbow is realized through her. But in claiming the free status which her Brangwen ancestors had desired, and towards which the heroine of almost every nineteenth-century novel aspires, Ursula willingly gives up one portion of it for the greater consolation of shared partnership. Lawrence understood the need for the feminist struggles of his own day, though in the essays on modern womanhood collected in *Phoenix II* he can be gently ironic: 'Women, women everywhere, and all of them on the warpath!' The point is that Lawrence believed that the target at which women should be aiming ought not to be just an electoral vote or the right to be a mother without being a wife or equal pay or easier divorce – in truth, he was not passionately interested in any of these – but the attainment of 'the new superfine bliss, a peace superseding knowledge':

'How can I say "I love you" when I have ceased to be, and you have ceased to be: we are both caught up and transcended into a new oneness where everything is silent, because there is nothing to answer, all is perfect and at one.'

(W, p. 417)

Maybe that silent existence cannot happen except through death. If so, then, as the closing conversation of *Women in Love* affirms, we need not despair at the prospect of death. Perhaps Ursula's yearning to obliterate the whole past, her own and the human race's, so that 'the pain of evolution' may be forgotten and 'only the achievement' (W, p. 460) remain, attempts to jump across the gulf of the next few centuries in too visionary and unscientific a way. Lawrence could not know any more than we can. He could only try, by his creation of Ursula Brangwen, to demonstrate his rich concern that mankind *should* have a future and that love and its beyond are feasible goals for man to work towards.

> Ursula quivered.
> 'I don't know a bit what is going to happen,' she said. 'I only know we are going somewhere.'
> Gudrun waited.
> 'And you are glad?' she asked.
> Ursula meditated for a moment.
> 'I believe I am *very* glad,' she replied.
>
> (W, p. 492)

During the early part of the First World War, Lawrence, John Middleton Murry and Katherine Mansfield (calling herself Matilda Berry) briefly ran a magazine entitled *The Signature*. It survived for only three issues, but in each number Lawrence contributed a portion of his essay 'The Crown'. In this essay, an adjunct to *The Rainbow*, he spoke of the conflict between the two sides of man's nature, the flesh-darkness versus the spirit-light; he emblematized this as the struggle between the lion and the unicorn for possession of the crown. *The Signature* had been started, Lawrence said, in response to Murry's urge to 'do something', but in his Note to 'The Crown' Lawrence makes it clear that 'I knew then, and I know now, it is no use trying to do anything – I speak only for myself – publicly.' The charge that Lawrence moaned about the awful state of modern society but resisted doing anything about it has to be met seriously. Bertrand Russell, after all, who broke with Lawrence at about the time *The Signature* came out, after what he calls in his autobiography a 'brief and hectic' acquaintance in which 'it was only gradually that we discovered that we differed from each other more than either differed from the Kaiser', was a rampant critic of the government and the war, and acting chairman of the No Conscription Fellowship, and was already proposing his experimental school. Russell did something; Lawrence only shook his head in bitterness – that, at any rate, was Russell's view fifty years later when he wrote that Lawrence 'had no real wish to make the world better, but only to indulge in eloquent soliloquy about how bad it was'. There was some truth in this, though Russell utterly misunderstands the tragedy in Lawrence's position. It was not that he was a poseur or a prophet of doom but that he seriously doubted if Russell's habit of tinkering with reform or writing solemn letters to international statesmen would have any significant effect. 'It is no use trying merely to modify present forms', he writes in 'The Crown': 'The whole great form of our era will have to go.' Russell, motivated by a patriotism just as mis-represented in subsequent decades as Lawrence's, could at least write in a letter dated 29 October 1915, 'The more England goes down and down, the more profoundly I want to help.' Lawrence, spurred on a little by the insensitive way in which he was treated in the war (as we see in the chapter in *Kangaroo* where he describes it), did not really want to help in the improvement of a society which he believed to be inherently rotten morally and to be foun-ded on the misconception that man's social ease was a more signifi-cant standard at which to aim than his inner fulfilment.

When first talking about *The Sisters* back in April 1913 Lawrence had written to Garnett, 'I can only write what I feel pretty strongly about.' At the time his strongest feelings were, he went on to say, for 'the establishment of a new relation, or the readjustment of the old one, between men and women'. As the work evolved it became a work on evolution itself. The relation between the sexes remained at its centre but in the necessary context of a discussion about the function of contemporary society. Lawrence's revulsion at the im-poverished lives bred in an industrial community is explicit only in parts of *The Rainbow*; it becomes central in *Women in Love*. Of course, in the first novel the episode of Ursula's battle to survive her teach-ing job amply illustrates the kind of demand a mechanically organ-ized society imposes upon the individual. The social system which the school helps to perpetuate can be seen in the scarred landscape around Cossethay and in the Wiggiston miners 'subjected in slavery to that symmetrical monster of the colliery' (R, p. 350). Lawrence imparts to the Ursula of *The Rainbow* some of the reform-ing zeal of a Mrs Pankhurst or a Marie Stopes – 'No more would she subscribe . . . to the great machine which has taken us all cap-tives' (R, p. 350) – but in *Women in Love* her rage at the social tyranny of industry has changed almost to indifference. She has advanced beyond a belief in the reform of society to a sense of its irrelevance for her. The same can be said of Lawrence, for whom England by 1915 seemed dead and insupportable.

Lawrence's indictment of industrial society in *Women in Love* resulted partly from the natural evolution of his metaphysics, but also from his familiarity with the collieries and his horror at mechanical warfare. Thus, in a novel which, unlike *The Rainbow*, gives as much prominence to non-Brangwens as to Brangwens, the spirit of individualism finds dramatic personification in two characters, Gerald Crich and his father. The Crich men embody an unenriching side of human nature in opposition to the potential of Birkin. They can be traced back to Pentheus and Dionysus in *The Bacchae* of Euripides, the repressive but prurient king and the god of natural fertility. Lawrence's pity for the wracked Gerald Crich, so much more interesting and less contemptible a capitalist than Clifford Chatterley, says much about the author's state of mind during the war. He knew he would have to abandon England, but he still felt a great compassion for the country of his upbringing. He realized that England would not welcome his pity, yet he had a sad regard for the fate she was willing upon herself. Gerald represents not just the capitalist rationale ('. . . you can't do away with the spirit of emulation', he tells Birkin. 'It is one of the necessary incentives to production and improvement') but something of the soul of England itself.

Gerald's physical magnificence is apparent from the start; he is a natural patrician with whom Lawrence associates certain primary words: 'magnetized', 'northern', 'glisten', 'crystal', 'ice', 'arctic', 'wolf' (W, all p. 15). All are hard, male, somehow north European words, matching Gerald's fair hair, blue eyes and masterful aspect: an opposite blood-type to Tom and Will Brangwen or to the Latin sexuality of Cicio in *The Lost Girl*. Gerald Crich embodies upstanding Aryan purity and white Anglo-Saxon manliness – a true son of England. It might have been easy for Lawrence to resort to the obvious irony of making Gerald's physical stature a mask for an acquisitive, speculative capitalist greed underneath. This he avoids. Gerald cares, in his own way, about the state of England: he would like a new leader to rise up and regenerate it. He fails, however, to look beyond the structure of class, money, education and bureaucracy which holds his concept of England together. When Birkin asks him '. . . wherein does life centre for you?' he can only answer hopelessly, 'As far as I can make out, it doesn't centre at all. It is artificially held *together* by the social mechanism' (W, pp. 63–4). The tragedy of modern England, Lawrence believed, was this identification of the soul of England with its institutions. How far we are from that earliest Brangwen generation at the opening of *The Rainbow*, living 'full and surcharged, their senses full fed' with their mere knowledge of 'the intercourse between heaven and earth'!

Gerald's inability to perceive a life beyond the social mechanism leaves him with a dark inner awareness of something lacking. When not presiding over his industrial empire, he finds his natural habitat, before Birkin and Gudrun enter his life, in the vulgarly self-conscious bohemianism of the Café Pompadour. No doubt Lawrence enjoyed himself with his parodies of Middleton Murry, Russell, George Santayana, Philip Heseltine and the other literary or society notables of the day. Certainly the mood of that café-and-country-house fraternity, a mixture of silliness, pretension and *gravitas*, comes across as brutally in *Women in Love* as in any novel by Aldous Huxley, who also shared in it. Gerald, however, desires more truthful experience than the Café Pompadour can give him. Had Lawrence wanted us merely to despise Gerald, he would not have shown him resisting the fashionable attractions of London or pondering more upon life than art. Lawrence expressed in Gerald as well as in Birkin his own distaste for café attitudes and for the type of house-gathering which Ottoline Morrell invited him to at Garsington. If Gerald is in part a portrait of England, then Lawrence pays England some kind of compliment. The fashionable display of post-Edwardian high society remains firmly on the perimeter of *Women in Love*, an object of satire but not of debate. Gerald represents the working soul of England, atrophied and misdirected, perhaps, but serious, energetic and neither trivial nor ridiculous.

The central ethic of Victorian England, the means by which imperialism abroad could be vindicated in economic theory and culture at home prevented from toppling into anarchy, was that society held together only if everyone worked together with a shared conception of the common good. That principle survived the First War. It did not, perhaps, survive the 1920s when economic collapse and a recognition that the war had solved nothing contributed towards a revaluation of traditional social morality, a greater emphasis on leisure, and the separation of society into those desiring to preserve the old system and those seeking to consummate their vision of a new society. Gerald, nearly twenty years after Queen Victoria's death, represents the apex of the Victorian ethic:

every man was fit for his own little bit of a task – let him do that, and then please himself. The unifying principle was the work in hand. Only work, the business of production, held man together. It was mechanical, but then society *was* a mechanism. Apart from work they were isolated, free to do as they wished.

(W, p. 114)

So common was this point of view in the England of 1920 that Lawrence may partly have written *Women in Love* to justify *to himself*, by reasoned discussion, the counter-argument, though it is a failing of the novel that he makes Gerald the only representative, apart from his father, of the traditional order. What freedom is left, we would have to ask Gerald, when the unifying principle is 'the work in hand'? What end does 'the work in hand' hope to achieve, if not the perfection of the present state and the confirmation of the class system upon which it thrives? Gerald's belief in a natural order where, for example, if a man is master of his horse and not its equal partner or its servant then so must he be of those who work for him, cannot be easily dismissed. Almost everyone willingly participated in that order. Only the privileged, or the talented like Lawrence himself, could evade being part of it. Hence the writer's pity extends not only to the miners, 'thousands of blackened, slightly distorted human beings' (W, p. 250), but to the father Crich, permanently dying like the society he manifests, his wife, 'cut off from all purpose or continuity' (W, p. 247) and his son, 'inheriting his own destruction' (W, p. 248).

The effect of his compassion, however, may be to weaken the social criticism in the novel, which Lawrence allows to be too general, too implicit. The Crich mentality is founded on two misapprehensions – that society is a mechanism held together only by work and that work itself is merely mechanical. In *Women in Love* Lawrence debates these notions in such a way as to make explicit the partially self-defeating nature of the Criches, but he does not fully point out the inadequacies of their social creed. At times he almost endorses their mechanistic view of society, and by the end of the novel it is clear that any personal freedom which Birkin and Ursula may attain will be without the social context and will involve working and sharing only between themselves. Since such a possibility is not open to most of us, we may legitimately regret the absence in *Women in Love* of any more rounded concept of society than that which Gerald offers. Lawrence here says nothing of the stimulus of work or the comradeship and pride it can give rise to even in an industrial situation, as Walter Morel's life testifies in *Sons and Lovers*. Lawrence, in the later novel, hardly considers the human element in the way society runs itself. Yet his sense of man's enduring humanity, and of the value of this, is an essential part of Lawrence's interest for us in so much of his other writing.

In some ways Gerald personifies Lawrence's view of western man, elevating the machine to the status of a godhead, seeking conquest of his environment rather than absorption into it. At the same time Gerald's philosophy of the pure instrumentality of man (i.e. 'As a man as of a knife: does it cut well? Nothing else mattered' – W, p. 251) betrays certain pivotal tenets of modern western culture. It minimizes the individuality of men and, in Lawrence's words, substitutes 'the mechanical principle for the organic' (W, p. 260). Gerald virtually sets up a religion of efficiency in which he views the miners as 'sporadic little unimportant phenomena' (W, p. 260) and the 'white-collar' workers as 'so much lumber' (W, p. 250). Christian humanism must be dethroned, nature subjugated, the harmony of things exchanged for their organization. Gerald's is the programme of an anti-God or a Lord of Misrule. Hence the terrified warning that Lawrence urges on his readers in his presentation of Gerald Crich: 'This is the first and finest state of chaos' (W, p. 260).

Gerald's creed is founded on a central avoidance, a fear of the dark abyss into which he must sink if his will should prove too weak to resist it. His father's death is seen as a dragging down into a great darkness. Gerald strives with primitive ferocity to avoid the same eclipse. Lawrence evokes in him the stuff of elemental tragedy, for by creating his own anti-religion Gerald confirms his fate rather than evades it. He remains dull to the inner life which Birkin and Ursula seek to release from within themselves. All his relationships are described in images of power or industry. With Gudrun, under the bridge where so many of the young colliers have stood with their sweethearts, 'the master of them all pressed her to himself . . . as if he were soft iron . . . everything in her was melted down' (W, pp. 372, 374). His life seems lived in darkness or underground. He only climbs upwards towards the heavens at the end of the novel, but then it is to die amid rock and ice, just missing, as he has all his life, the southern road to the sun.

Birkin presents Gerald with the one creative possibility that might save him from his pagan doom. We know from the Prologue of *Women in Love* that Lawrence envisaged a more physically explicit relationship between the two men that even the chapter 'Gladiatorial' suggests. He suppressed that Prologue, though it can now be read in *Phoenix II*. We may suspect Lawrence of indulging

himself in a vivid personal fantasy as he wrote this rather frenzied
prose; his refusal to publish it was probably less because he feared
it might give offence than because he realized it lacked discipline
either in its passion or its language. The piece outlines Birkin's
failed relationship with Hermione, whose all-spiritual, all-conscious
love denies the sensual in him. Birkin knows that true fulfilment
can come only in the union of the separate halves of oneself – the
desire for wholeness being central to Lawrence's conception of the
novel. Hoping for this internal harmony is not the same as effecting
it. 'The will can destroy, but it cannot create',˙Lawrence observes
in a phrase that could serve later on for Gerald's epitaph. There
follow a few pages in which Birkin acknowledges, with guilt, the
physical passion he has felt for other men.

He wanted to cast out these desires, he wanted not to know them. Yet a
man can no more slay a living desire in him, than he can prevent his body
from feeling heat and cold. He can put himself into bondage, to prevent
the fulfilment of the desire, that is all. But the desire is there, as the
travelling of the blood itself is there, until it is fulfilled or until the body
is dead.

Lawrence believed that every person should acknowledge to himself the inherent nature of his desires and not try to suppress them.
That could have been another explanation why the Prologue was
dropped. In it Birkin tries to escape from his bisexual instincts as
though they are a cause for shame. In the novel proper the specific
detail of his feelings for men may be more restrained, but his freedom to love how and whom he will is entirely without guilt.
Indeed, his final comment on the last page of *Women in Love* affirms
his belief (which we may take to be Lawrence's, too) in the possibility of brotherhood between men coexisting with love of women.

Lawrence's presentation of Gerald and Birkin should probably
less be read as frankly homosexual than as an appeal for affection
and rapport between men. Touch would be important in such a
relationship – hence the famous wrestling scene – but Lawrence
never indicates an approval of sexual intercourse between men.
The debate about his own possibly homosexual tendencies will
never be finally resolved, though Frieda admitted that his feelings
for William Hocking (a farmer friend in Cornwall who was the
model for John Thomas in *Kangaroo*) were partly physical. In almost
all his novels Lawrence writes about intimacy, both spiritual and
tactile, between men, but he never does so in a homo-erotic way.
The nearest he comes to that is in a brief passage between Don

Ramón and Don Cipriano in *The Plumed Serpent*, but there it forms part of an exotic ritual that distances it from explicit sexuality. Similarly, in that rejected Prologue to *Women in Love* the homosexuality seems remarkably chaste. Lawrence only mentions Gerald in the Prologue in two paragraphs which he tacked on at a later date in order to forge a bridge to the opening chapter. The sentences emphasize the mutuality of feeling between Crich and Birkin. 'In both men were the seeds of a strong, inflammable affinity.' Two central Lawrentian images, the seed and the flame, encourage us to view their relationship positively. Their physical affinity unites them while their values tend to pull them apart. Gerald and Birkin exist as moral opposites, but Lawrence so powerfully emphasizes Gerald's capacity for mastery and even for glamour that the reader is obliged by the comparison to judge Birkin's with the utmost rigour. In the end, however, Birkin's verdict upon humanity, a brilliant variant on the rind or husk image, must be taken as Lawrence's particular view of Gerald and the social system for which he stands: it 'never gets beyond the caterpillar stage – it rots in the chrysalis, it never will have wings. It is anti-creation, like monkeys and baboons' (W, p. 143).

If in *The Rainbow* the marriages of Tom and Lydia and Anna and Will are, to some extent, the pairings of opposites, then by contrast the pairings in *Women in Love* often explore the companionship of like kinds. The drama of opposition still happens, as much between Birkin and Ursula or between Gerald and Gudrun as between more obvious opposites like Birkin and Hermione or Ursula and Loerke. Lawrence is as interested now, however, in investigating affinities between people. We have seen something of Birkin's dual affinities, with Ursula and with Gerald; but Gudrun, too, is the subject of two relationships, with Gerald and with Loerke. She and Hermione embody types of womanhood alternative to Ursula. Lawrence intended a measure of parody in both cases, putting aspects of Katherine Mansfield into Gudrun and Ottoline Morrell into Hermione, but it would be wrong to see either of them as mere satirical vignettes. Hermione responds to the 'mental thrill' (W, p. 45) of experience and Gudrun suffers 'from a sense of her own negation' (W, p. 185), but whereas there is an eventual banality in Hermione's view of life, Gudrun possesses exactly what Gerald recognizes in her when she dances the rôle of Ruth, a 'mocking weight' and 'dangerous power' (W, p. 102). Lawrence presented many versions of Hermione in his novels and stories, most of them less fantastic or less predatory than this one, but all manifesting a cerebral or aesthetic view of human relations. Gudrun is a more original creation. Lawrence does not investigate sexual detachment through her but the destructive wilful possibilities of sexual potency.

Gudrun is not attracted to Gerald for social reasons, though she values social status. She flaunts her unorthodoxy in dress and manners – her patterns and colours tend to be harsh and mixed where Ursula's are soft and natural. She recognizes, however, an affinity between herself and Gerald in which 'he would be helpless in the association with her' (W, p. 135). Her will demands mastery over the object of its desire. There can be no interest in a whole world when the emotions and mind of a person are directed to one end, the conquest and humiliation of another individual through sexual domination. Thus we have many examples of Gudrun's lack of interest in the natural or even the social world around her. It is true that when she contemplates the miners she senses 'a glamorous thickness of labour and maleness, surcharged in the air . . . the voluptuous resonance of darkness' (W, p. 128), but these emotions, like Alvina Houghton's when she visits her father's colliery in *The Lost Girl*, are entirely self-regarding. The miners as people mean nothing to her. For her, 'They belonged to another world' (W, p. 129), not the world of living experience but of some netherworld in which she would like to trespass with Faustian curiosity and lust. Constantly in the novel Lawrence emphasizes Gudrun's lack of compassion for other people, whether it be the Cockney boys on the Thames pleasure-trip (W, p. 180) or her lover on the night he steals into her bedroom at home. 'She seemed to look at him as at a pebble far away under clear dark water . . . Ah, this awful, inhuman distance which would always be interposed between her and the other being' (W, p. 390). She establishes real connection only with Gerald's dying father and with Loerke, both witnesses to dead creeds.

Chapter 18, 'Rabbit', mirrors Gudrun's personality. As a section it reads like a short story. Gudrun arrives at the Crich home in order to instruct the little girl in drawing and modelling, two pastimes that perhaps encourage detachment from the natural world. Her 'insatiable curiosity to see and to know everything' (W, p. 263) has brought her to Shortlands, ironic phrasing when we think of how little knowledge could ever be found among the Criches. Immediate sympathy springs up between Gudrun and the child, whose remoteness resembles her own. Lawrence observes the details of the scene wittily and shrewdly – the French governess, the absurd pekinese, the precocity of the child – but its seriousness lies in the revelations of character. When Gudrun and Gerald admire a flower neither can name it and neither is really interested in it. Their sexual tension governs everything. Gudrun strikes attitudes to tantalize Gerald. She is like a macaw and later a seagull, for Lawrence sustains a network of bird imagery in this novel, applying it to each main character. The climax of the episode centres on the pet rabbit, which Gudrun releases from its cage. Her manner changes from sardonic amusement to 'heavy rage' and 'heavy cruelty' (W, p. 270) as the rabbit struggles for freedom while Gudrun holds on to it. Gerald takes over and the battle for mastery continues. The rabbit has no existence for either adult beyond its brute animation which must be subdued. The phrases of the chapter are uncompromising: 'The scream of the rabbit . . . seemed to have torn the veil of her consciousness', 'She was revealed', 'she seemed like a soft recipient of his magical, hideous white fire' (W, pp. 271–2). The scene ends with the rabbit's renewed frenzy, this time a crippled mad energy as if it 'were obeying some un-known incantation' (W, p. 273). A kind of pact has been sealed be-tween Gudrun and Gerald, an initiation which justifies Lawrence's adjective 'obscene'. Conquest through self-debasement: the chap-ter brilliantly encapsulates the unnatural union of the two lovers. Lawrence frequently uses an animal as the evidence for human action – Gudrun's indifference to the cuttlefish or exultation in Gerald's treatment of his mare are earlier examples in *Women in Love* – but the illustration of human cruelty in 'Rabbit' shocks more deeply than most.

Only a force more concentrated and more single-minded could destroy the bondage of Gerald to Gudrun. Loerke supplies that force. Like most characters in *Women in Love*, he was probably suggested by a real person. Mark Gertler, the Bloomsbury Group painter whom Lawrence met in 1914 and with whom he regularly corresponded while working on *The Sisters*, was drawn to subjects similar to Loerke's and was evidently some kind of model for the character. Not too much should be made of the resemblance, however, for Lawrence liked Gertler and, since they were both tubercular, sought his advice on health matters. Though Gertler eventually killed himself, eight years after Lawrence's death, Lawrence may have found in the friendship a rare opportunity to boost someone else's morale. The troll-like Loerke, who enters *Women in Love* less than a hundred pages from the end, entirely lacks Gertler's self-awareness. 'He seemed to be the very stuff of the underworld of life. There was no going beyond him' (W, p. 480).

For Gudrun, Loerke consummates her passion for the undiluted perfection of a being dedicated only to work and to the kind of art which has little to do with life, being all self-absorbed and self-justifying, though willing to be used by industry or the state. For Ursula he has the attraction of a primeval reptile: it is less a question of there being 'no going beyond him' as there being nothing more primitive. The polar differences between the two sisters could not be more clearly represented than by their attitude to Loerke. Gudrun sees in him the culmination of civilization and experience, Ursula the root depravity and anti-living of past human history. In Lawrence's view the two are much the same, modern sophistication of the Loerkean sort being connected to primitive forces. Both sisters want knowledge of the maximum scope which existence can offer, but whereas Ursula will always try to go forward to new worlds Gudrun finds her ultimate reality here. She goes backwards in her search for the new world, to where 'there were no more men, there were only creatures, little, ultimate *creatures* like Loerke' (W, p. 508). Hers is a return to a before-Eden, to the riot of unsorted creation, a movement against the flow of natural evolution, though it takes her to the apex of social evolution. Loerke crystallizes a central motif in *The Rainbow* and *Women in Love*: man's progress towards what he terms 'civilization' has been against the current of natural progression. Like Hardy, Lawrence perceived the incompatibility of man's order and the natural order but does not believe that this is irredeemable. Ursula's denial of what Loerke stands for shows that vigorous life-affirming counter-forces can exist and develop, too.

Is there a hint of prophecy in Gudrun and Loerke at the end of this novel, taking the wind that blows them towards Germany? Bertrand Russell believed the road that Lawrence trod 'led straight to Auschwitz', but the absurdity of this notion must strike every reader of the last chapters in *Women in Love*. Loerke, who venerates labour and the machine and the pure divorce of art from life, who denies sensibility and knows 'fearful central secrets, that the world dared not know' (W, p. 504), has something in common with the Nazi ethic. Lawrence dissociates himself from all that Loerke says, so he would surely have dissociated himself from the fascism of the 1930s. Certainly Loerke's views lead more directly to Auschwitz than the *Blutbrüderschaft* of Gerald and Birkin does, though it was of Lawrence's 'blood-knowing' in this and later works like *The*

*Plumed Serpent* that Russell was thinking when he made his denunciation.

Lawrence named his characters in *Women in Love* with particular care. One ought not to overstress the schematic planning of the novel or its representational qualities, but the names Gudrun and Ursula must surely connote the two motifs in western culture, the pagan–mythic and the Christian–spiritual. There are several Gudruns in northern European lore, all of them tending to bring woe upon those who know them and all of them presented in pagan contexts. Ursula, on the other hand, was a British saint and the daughter of a Christian king. Though she was reputedly martyred in a massacre of Christian virgins, St Ursula can in fact be traced back to the Swabian moon-goddess Horsel and to Isis, the Egyptian goddess of nature. The moon and nature images which Lawrence associated with his Ursula suggest that he knew this. The Ursuline Order of nuns, incidentally, was founded to teach and to sanctify womanhood, so Ursula's name seems doubly appropriate. Gerald's name derives from a Germanic root denoting a warrior, and, like Sigurd, Gudrun's lover in the *Volsunga Saga*, he dies young. As for Birkin, the word exists in English only as a north-country form of 'birch', an appropriate outdoor association with the Lawrence character, since its slender white hardiness matches his physical appearance. However, the adjective 'birkie' indicates self-assertion or 'having a mind of one's own' – a secondary association which may have crossed Lawrence's mind. He was certainly interested in regional vocabularies. Loerke's name may hint at the evil one among the Norse gods, Loki, who schemes for the destruction of the idealist Balder as Loerke gloatingly manoeuvres Gudrun away from Gerald.

These name associations suggest that Lawrence intended *Women in Love*, and, indeed, the whole concept of *The Sisters*, to remind us of our cultural origins. By drawing on saga and legend, upon the pagan and the Christian, the Norse and the Latin constituents in the English national character, he related his contemporary society with its past. Allusions proliferate in both novels, not just in the arguments but in the language which so often reverberates with biblical emphasis or gleams with Revelation images.

Sometimes, however, the language loses its tautness and suggestiveness, collapsing into high-sounding but ultimately vague and unsatisfying rhetoric. At such moments Lawrence seems to value resonance more than sense. We can explain this in a passage of Birkin's which demonstrates both the character of Lawrence's loosest writing and the futility of one strand of thinking in *Women in Love*.

'Well, if man is destroyed, if our race is destroyed like Sodom, and there is this beautiful evening with the luminous land and trees, I am satisfied. That which informs it all is there, and can never be lost. After all, what is mankind but just one expression of the incomprehensible. And if mankind passes away, it will only mean that this particular expression is completed and done. That which is expressed, and that which is to be expressed, cannot be diminished. There it is, in the shining evening. Let mankind pass away – time it did. The creative utterances will not cease, they will only be there. Humanity doesn't embody the utterance of the incomprehensible any more. Humanity is a dead letter. There will be a new embodiment, in a new way. Let humanity disappear as quick as possible.'

(W, p. 65)

Lawrence tries to point here to the soul of the universe. 'That which informs it all is there, and can never be lost.' The creative source continues, even if the eruption of which we are all small bits should cease. This source is a mystery only to man, but it 'informs' all things, whole and eternal like Wordsworth's 'primal sympathy – which having been must ever be'. This is not quite a philosophy of despair unless, like Gerald, one's creed only acknowledges man as on the perimeter of all things. Certainly Lawrence cannot be accused of being without feeling for the past, for the passage insists upon the continuity of existence. But in doubting the necessity of the human consciousness as the fulcrum of creation, Birkin preaches at us wildly and perhaps even uselessly. He substitutes vague rhetorical gestures for reasoning: 'that which is expressed, and that which is to be expressed, cannot be diminished'. We can accept 'There it is, in the shining evening' as a gasp of half-articulated appreciation, but hard statements like 'Humanity is a dead letter' and 'Let mankind pass away' take us nowhere. They are mean phrases: worse, they deny the whole purpose of *Women in Love*, which affirms the worthiness of human living. If Birkin's speech were to be the final word of the novel we would be left with a celebration of the unknowable. 'There will be a new embodiment, in a new way' is hardly the prose of a visionary who can barely wait to see the realization of his own anticipation but the prophecy of someone who does not really see into the future at all. If Lawrence speaks through Birkin here, as to some extent he surely does, then we have to admit that the ending of his major fiction is unsatisfactory because it offers no consolation and no method for living life now. But Birkin's is not the only voice at the end of the novel.

Ursula's existence becomes especially important because in her we see a guarantee of human continuity, of practical vision and of a check on rhetoric.

Without *The Rainbow* and *Women in Love* D. H. Lawrence's reputation could not possibly stand as high as it does, though it must be remembered that only a few lone voices like F. R. Leavis's were prepared to champion him in the 1930s and 1940s. Amongst the great autobiographical novels *Sons and Lovers* would always now win a place, but it is unlikely that it alone could have secured Lawrence's fame as a novelist of social, moral, metaphysical, sexual and psychological importance. *The Sisters* demonstrates Lawrence's mind at its most enquiring, his art in complex refinement, and his sympathies enlarged by a compassion, wisdom and pity which, the honest reader must confess, he never wholly found again. His masterwork, the *Brangwensaga* – as some commentators have called it – has produced every kind of reaction from the prosecution which greeted the publication of *The Rainbow* to the self-indulgence of the Ken Russell film of *Women in Love*, but no one would dispute its major status among the novels of the twentieth century.

What, then, is the achievement of *The Rainbow* and *Women in Love*? They brought back to the English novel a sense of discovery and wonder about the nature of mankind. By using the form of a family saga Lawrence maintained his links with a main tradition in the novel but managed to rescue that form from the atrophy and desiccation into which Galsworthy and others had led it. He could do so only by reviving the theory that the individual soul of each man is unique and special and yet gives evidence of the creative power from which all life has its being. Without the advances in psychology made in his generation Lawrence might not have expressed himself as he did, but essentially his work at this period was the product of deep intuition rather than scientific understanding. He needed the questioning atmosphere of the age as much as he contributed to it, for *The Rainbow* and *Women in Love* raise all the issues about the nature of society and the nation which concerned thinking people at the time and since.

Above all, he asked questions to which he could not give the total answer. Human history is open-ended unless one believes that the irrevocable destiny of science is to destroy man. Lawrence appears not to have believed that, however depraved he reckoned the scientific mentality to be. He suggests that man *may* have served his purpose as other species, long extinct, have served theirs, but he does not write as though this must be so: and should it come about that mankind must cease, then a cosmic radiance will continue to flow through the universe eternally even though this will be no comfort to the dead species. Man of the present generation cannot know what his future is and cannot yet understand the nature of this radiance. His intuited knowledge that it exists, however, should lead him, as it leads Birkin by the power of will, to the edge of discovering the ultimate truth. There are blind alleys, down which the Brangwens and the Criches have frequently gone, but the forward movement of the human race, like the current of the universe, is possible. Birkin and particularly Ursula are the products of their past, absorbing the best and sloughing the worst. Their certainty that the ultimate mysteries, once attained, could release and consummate man testifies to a measure of optimism in Lawrence. But it is a nervous, tentative optimism, beseeching courage in man but offering no specific hopes. Lawrence planned *The Sisters* to be a study of the checkered state in which man exists, both as an individual and in society. He moves from Eden to the new heaven and the new earth, from the Marsh to the infinite, but his evolutionary view of life ought not to be reduced to a straightforwardly linear account of human progress. Both parts, especially *Women in Love*, work exploratively, probingly, always testing and questioning but rarely giving final comprehensive judgements. Lawrence sustained this scheme, possibly the grandest conception in English fiction, whilst being constantly provocative in every area of social and moral perception.

# 6

## *The Lost Girl*

The immense creative effort that lay behind the two great novels we have just considered obviously contributes to the feeling of imaginative exhaustion which so many critics have noticed in almost all Lawrence's subsequent work. So automatically is the assumption sometimes made that the later Lawrence alternates mystic obscurity in some writings with prosaic didacticism in others that we need to remind ourselves in the next few chapters that no great artist ever contents himself with repetition of his past achievements. Lawrence seldom stayed in one place for long, either in his life or in his work. He did not want to write *Women in Love* twice over, but in searching for the new direction that his writing might take no clear avenues opened before him. In moments of such uncertainty Lawrence invariably returned to his roots. Over half of *The Lost Girl* has an industrial English setting. Here Lawrence examines, for the first time in a novel, the social attitudes of the *petite bourgeoisie*, in particular their effect on a young girl awakening to her own sexuality. He contrasts small-town morality with the instinctual behaviour of the non-industrial man.

In looking for a new way to write, the Lawrence of 1917–19 saw two possibilities: to abandon fiction altogether or to write as every other novelist seemed to be doing in England at the time: less spiritually, less enquiringly than was his gift. The abandonment of fiction was a real temptation. Neither of the principal prose works in this period, *Movements in European History* and *Studies in Classic American Literature*, was a novel. A lot of poetry, including *Look! We Have Come Through* in 1917 and *Bay* in 1919, an attempt at a play, some travelogues and essays, these occupied Lawrence's writing hours far more often than his fiction. The tone of his correspondence, when he refers to his fiction in this period, lacks enthusiasm or wit:

Philosophy interests me most now – not novels or stories. I find people ultimately boring: and you can't have fiction without people. So fiction does not, at the bottom, interest me any more. I am weary of humanity and human things.

(Letter to John Middleton Murry, 23 May 1917)

Aimlessness and defiance predominate in his feelings about ordinary life.

One keeps some sort of a superficial wits, but I think it would be wrong to assume that one is quite sane just now. But I think it is a crisis – the storm is at its height – it will break soon. But the afterwards one can't contemplate. There seems no afterwards, in known terms. What will be will be, however, and I don't care. We'll come through by a gap in the hedge, if not by the gate.

(Letter to Catherine Carswell, April 1918)

Feeling the strains of the last war years, and always conscious of the irretrievably shattered society around him, Lawrence surprises us in summoning up even the guarded optimism of this letter. We should not be surprised that he turned to history, foreign literature and philosophy in an attempt to make theoretical sense of the abysmal horrors into which his generation was plunged. He did not completely neglect fiction but wrote it only sporadically and lethargically, sometimes questioning whether any sort of intellectual or imaginative endeavour was really worth it.

I am very restless and at the end of *everything*. I don't work – don't try to – only just endure the days. There will either have to come a break outside or inside – in the world or in oneself.

(Letter to Mark Gertler, 26 June 1918)

When the war was over and Lawrence was living again in Italy, he appears to have taken stock of himself. Eventually, in *Kangaroo* (1923), he came to grips with the effect that the war had had upon him and wrote what is, apart from *Sons and Lovers*, his most thoroughly personal book. Even so, all his post-war novels are coloured by his horror at what had been allowed to happen.

If we were to look at the bookshelves of the average intelligent novel-reader in 1918 we would be much more likely to find on them works by H. G. Wells, John Galsworthy and Arnold Bennett than by D. H. Lawrence. Their particular kind of social realism, explicit rather than allusive, liberally class-conscious, concerned more with the conduct of characters than with instincts, always articulate and seldom stressed by the dark mysteries of personality, ought not to be scorned. Lawrence himself never took a simplistically dismissive line on these writers, though he was fully alive to their limitations. In his essay on John Galsworthy he distinguishes between 'a really vivid human being' and 'social beings'. The Forsytes are, of course, the latter. The essay on Galsworthy was not written until 1928, nine years after Lawrence had himself played with that kind of fiction in *The Lost Girl*, but in truth it is hard to find evidence that he ever admired what these contemporaries were writing. After reading Arnold Bennett's *Anna of the Five Towns* for the first time on a wet October Friday in 1912 he wrote to A. W. McLeod. 'I hate it. I want to wash again quickly, wash off England, the oldness and grubbiness and despair.' To McLeod again he wrote of Wells, 'He always seems to be looking at life as a cold and hungry little boy in the street stares at a shop where there is hot pork' (26 April 1913). Of Shaw, who comes in for a few chirpy knocks in *The Lost Girl*, he simply writes, 'Too much gas-bag.' On occasions Lawrence can show all the qualities he deplores in these other authors, but only in *The Lost Girl* did he approach the kind of novel which they might have wished for their own. Their conception of character in fiction led more often than not to sub-Dickensian near-eccentrics or to literally described exponents of 'normal' life. Lawrence presents several such characters in *The Lost Girl* – Mr Houghton, Mr May, Miss Pinnegar, for example. Usually in his work he did not try to emulate Galsworthy or Arnold Bennett, but the strongly personalized, physically detailed characters who surrounded the main character in the 'English' chapters of *The Lost Girl* show how effectively Lawrence could write in the Galsworthian (or, in ancestry, Dickensian) manner when he wanted to. Significantly, however, these chapters were written before the war: Lawrence had embarked on a new novel in Germany, the manuscript of which he had to leave behind when hostilities were threatened. The last chapters, set in Italy and written after the war, show him less and less interested in viewing character externally. The tone becomes more insistently typical of his other work as the novel goes on.

We have plenty of evidence, not just in the Italian chapters at the end but in the current of the novel, that Lawrence did not value writing like Galsworthy's about the Change, or Bennett's about the Five Towns. Like Alvina herself, he was concerned with the interiors of things – by which he certainly did not mean the drawing-room or the parlour but the heart and soul of human beings. Before starting work again on *The Lost Girl* Lawrence wrote to Mark Gertler of 'some mystic quality inside a few of us' which made him yearn to be 'houseless and placeless and homeless and landless'. He ended the letter by insisting that 'I *hate* and *abhor* being stuck on to any form of society.' Alvina's cautious rejection of her own conventional upbringing demonstrates this abhorrence. Yet despite this disavowal of orthodoxy, Lawrence is often thought in *The Lost Girl* to have demeaned himself by imitating masters who, in the field of social description, were supreme. Graham Hough's verdict in *The Dark Sun* is not untypical: 'the dullest and least characteristic Lawrence, the nearest thing to a pot-boiler that he ever wrote' (p. 90). If we recall Lawrence's modest advice about this 'queer book' it may help to test our reaction to it: 'Somehow it depends what centre of oneself one reads it from.'

*The Lost Girl* concerns Alvina Houghton, her 'insurrection', her 'mixed marriage' and her eventual 'perdition'. Lawrence proposed all three of these phrases as possible titles, and any would have done; all three invoke Alvina's reaction against a restricting kind of English social respectability; by her protest within the social conventions, by her marriage outside them, by her willing acceptance of their power to ostracize her totally. The period of the novel is 1913–14, contemporary with Lawrence when he embarked on it but a lost world when he returned to it after the war.

Alvina is the only child of James Houghton, draper. A man of poetic regard for the fabrics he sells, with 'a taste for elegant conversation and elegant literature and elegant Christianity' (p. 13), James Houghton is the author of his own irretrievable decline. He leaps like a grasshopper from one disastrous enterprise to another while his establishment declines into a seedy corner store and finally disappears. He dabbles with a mine, a private hotel, a music hall, each project more elaborate and more foolhardy than the one before. Yet from this commercial suicide Alvina inherits his stubbornness and a certain inclination to romance. Like her father, she rejects the sensible, and dreams instead of what might be. Her invalid mother, her governess, the housekeeper, all are bastions of social convention and on each she lavishes a certain devotion, but her spirit constantly yearns for the sort of fulfilment which Woodhouse will never be able to provide and which the mind cannot properly envisage, a commitment of the flesh and the soul. She flits from one experience to another, rather as her father does: a proposal of marriage is refused, she trains as a nurse in London, she flirts, she attends church, she does not take her expected place in Woodhouse society. Only in the last period of her father's ostentatious dwindling, when he is managing Houghton's Endeavour (a seedy theatre at the wrong end of the town), is Alvina confronted by an actual possibility for escape. A group of continental troupers, reminiscent of Sleary's circus troupe in Charles Dickens's *Hard Times*, visit the theatre, ruled by their Madame and united by mock rituals which retain off-stage some of the Red Indian splendour they hope to present in performances. The Natcha-Kee-

Tawaras include among their number Francesco Marasca, called Cicio for short, the inarticulate but magnetic Italian to whom Alvina is quickly drawn. The relationship between them does not immediately prosper, though eventually Alvina loses her virginity to him and joins the Natcha group with the new name Allaye. A period of frostiness follows between the aloof English Alvina and her volatile companions. She leaves the group to take up a nursing position in Lancaster. Once again a life of spinsterhood and worthiness seems to face her, from which a middle-aged Scottish doctor offers to rescue her with a proposal of marriage and sleek security. The return of Cicio confronts her with the crucial choice of her life, and unlike Ibsen's Lady from the Sea she rejects the certainty of proffered love and material ease for the ambiguous tenderness and wild southerliness of her Italian lover. The last chapters of the book show Alvina as Cicio's wife, her rejection of England, her journey through Europe to the most secret barren part of the Neapolitan *campagna*, her months of solitariness and physical discomfort, her pregnancy, her determination to survive and, if Cicio returns from the war he must reluctantly fight, her possible future in America.

It sounds like the scenario of a sentimental romance, and certainly there are passages of the novel where not even Lawrence can overcome the silliness of a second-hand situation. Cicio's return in chapter 12 is one example. Alvina has befriended the self-willed, hysterical Mrs Tuke, who is about to give birth to a child she does not want. Suddenly the sound of an Italian mandoline is heard from the moonlit garden below. Lawrence half knows that the scene is too theatrical. Mrs Tuke tosses a white rose from her room – 'ineffectually, of course'. Her husband splutters about 'emotional Italian music. Perfectly nauseating' (p. 327). The ironies do not save the scene from cliché at just the point where the superior animal attraction of Cicio must be felt at its strongest. As a result, Alvina's unresisting acceptance of him seems schematically rather than compulsively necessary.

In *The Lost Girl* Lawrence is much concerned with gradations of society: not just with the English class system, but with types of provinciality, with the human disposition to suspect foreigners, with the disharmony of societies and geography, so that Cicio seems an exotic animal in Woodhouse but a sad small man in his own territory, while Mr Houghton fails to sell lengths of cloth in his home town which would be the rage of the London season. In none of these points does Lawrence have much in common with Galsworthy, unless it be in the recognition that class distinctions are ultimately based on money. As Mr Houghton's fortunes decline, so proportionally does his standing in the community. Links which more obviously suggest themselves are with Thomas Hardy and Charles Dickens. Both authors understand, like Lawrence, the incorrigible association of provincial snobbery and material gain; both show the effect of a stranger upon the inmates of an enclosed self-sufficient society; and both write of the disjunction between what we are capable of theoretically and what may be expected of us actually, given the social circumstances we are foredoomed to occupy. Alvina shares with several of Hardy's heroines the determination not to go under, and in the end she probably succeeds. She can be traced back at least to Louisa Gradgrind, the daughter of an industrialist, who is the heroine of Dickens's *Hard Times*. Both women determine to assert the truth of their own feelings over social requirements.

In the first paragraph of the novel Lawrence establishes the newness of Woodhouse society, 'a mining townlet . . . with a population of ten thousand people, and three generations behind it'. To the people of Woodhouse three generations are sufficient to be 'well-established' and to have forgotten the enormous disruption of landscape and antiquity which their own existence there must have entailed almost within living memory. Lawrence does not spell out ironies like these, but they are implicit in the deceptively straightforward prose with which Woodhouse is described. 'Woodhouse wanted a gently graduated progress in mediocrity, a mediocrity so stale and flat that it fell outside the imagination of any sensitive mortal' (p. 16). Physically Woodhouse appears very much like Bestwood in *Sons and Lovers*, and both are admitted to be modelled on Lawrence's home town of Eastwood. However, the author has undergone a great change of attitude towards the town between the writing of the two novels. In *Sons and Lovers* life may be cheapened or brutalized by the economic realities of a mining society, but it is never undignified. Lawrence avoids sentimentalizing the people with whom he grew up. Walter Morel's most positive quality is a vigorous determination to take his natural part in the work and pleasures of the community, however depressed, an instinct to belong that he shares with most of the people around him. His wife's gentility and puritanism mark her out as the exception, not the rule; though when she returns home to die of cancer and is greeted by a streetful of neighbours we feel at last that even she has become part of the community she has half fought to resist. Woodhouse society appears wholly different, mostly because we only see its middle-class stratum. Its tribute to Mr Houghton at his funeral is much more formal than the welcome accorded to the dying Mrs Morel. It is a close-knit, resentful and constantly judging society: judging by the standards of 'respectability'. Houghton's decline results not just from his own foolishness but from the town's philistinism and ignorance. Alvina's 'disgrace' is a subject for gleeful gossip and whispering innuendo. This world corresponds more to the malice-corroded Barbie of George Douglas Brown's *The House with the Green Shutters* than to that of *Sons and Lovers*. Lawrence sees nothing life-enhancing about Woodhouse: always the adjectives describing it evoke blankness, complacency, tawdriness and claustrophobia. Its working-class equivalent is, perhaps, Tevershall in *Lady Chatterley's Lover*.

At the centre of this unoriginal town lies the Houghtons' home, Manchester House, the name of which suggests the heart and self-assurance of Victorian industrial expansion, though in reality it combines a permeating gloom with a forbidding sense of doom. Lawrence was less acquainted with the trading classes than with mining folk, but he manages to capture in his representation of Manchester House the emotional vacuity which he felt to be at the core of English commercial life. James Houghton differs from many of his class in that he does not do well. When he sells his stuff he is too much 'like an author on his first night in the theatre' (p. 15). Lawrence knows that the soul of an artist, even a second-rate one, does not square with the necessary canniness of a merchant. Manchester House, Houghton's 'commercial poem' (p. 13), is a monument to its owner's taste and showmanship, but like many monuments it never serves a function. It quickly becomes a mausoleum for the souls buried within it. Mrs Houghton wastes away in self-pitying maladies whilst the omnicompetent Miss Frost and the pinched Miss Pinnegar make sure that nothing unusual will ever disturb the proper dullness of the house.

Lawrence could easily have made these watchdogs of Manchester House into twin gorgons of respectability, tyrants of moral scrupulosity. Indeed, had he done so, Alvina's rejection of her home would have fallen into sharper relief and the reader's sympathy for her might have been more specifically engaged. That he does not create an 'opposition' of this kind testifies to his refusal to fall in with the easy cliché. From *Jane Eyre* onwards the English novel is full of the justified rebellion of young people against the imprisoning self-righteousness of their guardians. The reader firmly aligns himself with Jane Eyre and Oliver Twist. Alvina Houghton exists in a more equivocal world, for Lawrence creates neither ogres nor wardresses in the Misses Frost and Pinnegar. If he had, the social criticism implicit in the novel would probably have been lost. Alvina's revolt would have been the only course open to her in a monstrous world: as it is, she defies the values upon which, in the end, the English middle class profoundly congratulates itself. The ordinary reader does not like to think of himself as a Brocklehurst or a Bumble (the tormentors of Jane and Oliver), but if he is honest he will see something of himself in the unadventurous women of Manchester House.

Miss Frost fades out of *The Lost Girl* fairly early on, but she affects the course of the novel, if only because she represents the sort of being Alvina yearns not to be like and the kind of thwarted unfulfilled life she is unconsciously determined not to have. Alvina (and Lawrence through her) does not pass any moral criticism upon this blameless and devoted woman; indeed, Miss Frost is a woman with kindness and depth of feeling, and the love of the two women for each other is intense. Yet Miss Frost embodies spinsterhood. She discourages visitors so that her charge can be protected from the dreadful possibilities of the outside world. She imparts trivial priorities to Alvina, 'including the drawing of flowers in water-colour, and the translation of a Lamartine poem'. Miss Frost is aptly named: not that she is cold or sudden, but she unconsciously nips in the bud the aspirations of her young Vina. Only occasionally does 'the lamb open a wolf's mouth, the dove utter the wild cackle of a daw' (p. 34), awful moments when Miss Frost's career of instilling decency and gentleness seems exploded by the girl's strange subterranean lewdness.

In *The Lost Girl* one of Lawrence's main strengths lies in the solid realization of subsidiary characters. We have smaller examples than Miss Frost: the fussy, ebullient, rather 'camp' Mr May, the vain Dr Mitchell, the petulant Mrs Tuke. On a slightly grander scale we have Madame, jealous of her ascendancy over her young men and spiteful towards Alvina when Cicio claims her, mean and haughty where Alvina is giving and amenable. In Miss Frost, Lawrence invests a quantity of pain and emotional waste which he only hints at in these other characters.

The terrible poignancy of the woman of fifty-two, who now at last had broken down, silenced the girl of twenty-three, and roused all her passionate tenderness. The terrible sound of 'Never now, never now – it is too late,' which seemed to ring in the curious, indrawn cries of the elder woman, filled the girl with a deep wisdom. She knew the same would ring in her mother's dying cry. Married or unmarried, it was the same – the same anguish, realized in all its pain after the age of fifty – the loss in never having been able to relax, to submit.

(p. 40)

The tensions and frustrations here are frankly and unsentimentally expressed. Within a convincingly pathetic character sketch the writer draws an archetype, the old maid, the principle of whose life serves as a brutal warning to Alvina of what she will become if she does not save herself. Lawrence stays very close to his characters in this novel, for that is part of the Bennett-like realism, but occasionally he darts back from individual scrutiny to raise a general principle. Miss Frost will do again. After Mrs Houghton's demise,

Miss Frost wept in anguish, and saw nothing but another woman betrayed to sorrow and a slow death. Sorrow and a slow death, because a man had married her. Miss Frost wept also for herself, for her own sorrow and slow death, because a man had *not* married her. Wretched man, what is he to do with these exigent and never-to-be-satisfied women? Our mothers pined because our fathers drank and were rakes. Our wives pine because we are virtuous but inadequate. Who is this sphinx, this woman? Where is the Oedipus that will solve her riddle of happiness, and then strangle her? – only to marry his own mother!

(p. 60)

A touch facetious at first sight; but shrewd – showing how Lawrence has extended the range of his prose since *Sons and Lovers*, and proving, as Bennett or Galsworthy seldom can, that the author is constantly aware of human behaviour as a whole. The individual's pain is theirs alone: yet the same kind of pain is endured by many others. Miss Frost's plight, which is Alvina's potential plight (and the fate which, paradoxically, would make her respectable in the eyes of her Woodhouse fellows), becomes a state-of-being recognized by Lawrence as typical of multitudes of tormented women.

Lawrence's authority resides in this capacity to create people who both seem credible psychologically and yet serve as specimens for an idea of human behaviour which he wishes to put across in the particular novel. I do not intend this to sound too clinical, for Lawrence is usually in far greater danger of over-commitment to a character (even one like Gerald Crich, whom he does not much care for 'emotionally') than of cynical dissection. Look at that repetition of 'sorrow and slow death' in the last passage quoted: it stops just short of pummelling us into a poignant regard for Miss Frost. In each novel, however, he takes as part of his subject matter a kind of human existence which he believes to be profoundly life-denying. Often the 'mechanical' nature of many jobs is his target: soulless or impotent marriage, dreary motherhood, poverty, wealth. In *The Lost Girl* he writes about spinsterhood and how society views it. The theme occupied him in many short stories too: 'The Horse Dealer's Daughter' and 'Daughters of the Vicar', for example. He can be disconcertingly direct about the subject, as we find very early in the first chapter of *The Lost Girl*:

Perhaps these unmarried women of the middle-classes are the famous sexless-workers of our ant-industrial society, of which we hear so much. Perhaps all they lack is an occupation: in short, a job. But perhaps we might hear their own opinion, before we lay the law down.  (p. 12)

This must be placed in its topical context – the women munitions-workers of the First World War and the suffragettes, for example. But Lawrence may really have at the back of his mind the plight of many women in 1919 who had said goodbye to their fiancés as they left for the Front and who were now doomed to be a generation of old maids. Perhaps that war altered attitudes to the figure of the unmarried woman more emphatically than any amount of emancipatory propaganda, for it left so many more in its wake.

Isolation and unfulfilled yearning are central concerns in all Lawrence's work. He tries to sense the inner tragedy of the Frosts and Pinnegars of the English provinces as they grow towards middle life, as their sexual energies drain away unused, and as the knowledge of elderly loneliness confronts them. Alvina seems born to be such a woman. If the novel twists abruptly in a new direction in the last chapters and becomes more conventionally 'Lawrentian' it is because Alvina, having escaped the fate of an old maid, has taken on a freshness and vigour reflected in the prose. In this she resembles two of E. M. Forster's characters, Harriet in *Where Angels Fear to Tread* and Miss Bartlett in *A Room with a View*. Before their 'conversions', society has cast them in a rôle which outwardly they show all the signs of fulfilling. In Alvina's case, she provides for her future by learning to be a nurse. It would seem clear that her destiny is to be 'planked upon the shelf among the old maids' (p. 76). As Lawrence observes, the panic which overcomes her at this prospect is the same 'terrible and deadly panic which overcomes so many unmarried women at about the age of thirty' (pp. 80–1).

Alvina's difference from the others, as the novel implies from the start, is that she has inherited her father's inner sense of his own superiority and something of his buccaneering concern less with what people think of him than with what he thinks of himself. Alvina simply knows she is worth more than Woodhouse.

> Ordinary people, ordinary fates. But extraordinary people, extraordinary fates. Or else no fate at all. The all-to-one-pattern modern system is too much for most extraordinary individuals. It just kills them off or throws them disused aside.
>
> (p. 107)

Lawrence was ten when Oscar Wilde was sentenced. Now that he was in his middle thirties he could not feel that the governing influences in the country were any more sympathetic to the non-conformist. Certainly every 'unorthodox' gesture which either Mr Houghton or his daughter makes earns the frowns (or giggles) of a local community which mistrusts anything with which it is not already familiar.

Indeed, the townsfolk can react more open-mindedly to the absurd pageant of the mock Red Indian troupers as they march down Lumley main street than they can to Alvina's erratic love affairs. Fantasy is acceptable; unusual reality offends. Lawrence dwells on this near-paradox, for he always cares deeply about the spiritual state of the society in which he sets a novel. A small strand of *The Lost Girl* concerns the rising popularity of the cinema, which Lawrence records not just for the sake of background detail or even as a means of pointing the folly of Mr Houghton's old fashioned music-hall, but as an image of a generation brought up in this 'all-to-one-pattern modern system' to sit gaping at the canned impressions and blown-up fantasies on the screen. Even the 'reality', or actuality, of grease-painted actors on a stage has become too difficult to contemplate. Alvina tries to explain the reason for this to Mr May.

> The film is only pictures, like pictures in the *Daily Mirror*. And pictures don't have any feelings apart from their own feelings. I mean the feelings of the people who watch them. Pictures don't have any life except in the people who watch them. And that's why they like them. Because they make them feel that they are everything.
>
> (p. 144)

Alvina is not speaking very clearly here, but it is interesting to see Lawrence concerned with the massive potential of the picture industry as early as 1919. His particular point about films being a cushion from reality and a means of confirming one's sense of one's own value still seems penetrating. Once again we find that the general observation connects with the particular: the people of Woodhouse possess such self-assurance where their standards of morality are concerned that Alvina need only step out of line to the extent of playing the piano in an orchestra pit or cards on a Sunday to be pronounced irrevocably lost.

In writing a novel about a heroine who does not endorse the precepts of the society that has reared her, Lawrence hardly embarks upon a new theme in the English novel. As he notes in his 'Study', Thomas Hardy deals obsessively with those who have 'escaped for free action, after having left the walled security, and the comparative imprisonment, of the established convention'. Alvina is just such a case. Lawrence introduces Hardy thus:

This is the theme of novel after novel: remain quite within the convention, and you are good, safe and happy in the long run, though you never have the vivid pang of sympathy on your side: or, on the other hand, be passionate, individual, wilful, you will find the security of the convention a walled prison, you will escape, and you will die, either of your own lack of strength to bear the isolation and the exposure, or by direct revenge from the community, or from both. This is the tragedy, and only this: it is nothing more metaphysical than the division of a man against himself in such a way: first, that he is a member of the community, and must, upon his honour, in no way move to disintegrate the community, either in its moral or its practical form; second, that the convention of the community is a prison to his natural, individual desire, a desire that compels him, whether he feels justified or not, to break the bounds of the community, lands him outside the pale, there to stand alone, and say: 'I was right, my desire was real and inevitable; if I was to be myself I must fulfil it, convention or no convention,' or else, there to stand alone, doubting, and saying, 'Was I right, was I wrong? If I was wrong, oh, let me die!' – in which case he courts death.

The passage may help us to recognize that the likely ancestor of *The Lost Girl* is not so much *Anna of the Five Towns* but novels like *Far from the Madding Crowd* or *The Return of the Native*. Is not Alvina the most Hardyesque name of all Lawrence's heroines, the companion to Bathsheba and Eustacia? Lawrence cannot bring himself to the same pitch of agnostic desolation that Hardy often conveys, but certainly at the end of the novel we are in even more doubt than we are with Rupert and Ursula about the future course of the marriage. A child is to be born and Cicio may return from the war, but the first months of marriage have been far from easy. When we finish with Alvina we do not question that she was right to fulfil her desires, 'convention or no convention', but we cannot be sure that she will not be saying before long, 'Oh, let me die!' Lawrence's novels almost always end with this kind of doubt.

Hardy suggests himself in another major way, for in *The Lost Girl* Lawrence talks a great deal about fate. His own life, at the time when he revised the novel, was particularly uncertain. His tuberculosis had declared itself; England, he felt, had spurned him; his marriage was not going well; he questioned whether he should write fiction at all. What *could* he believe in? He refused the rationalist arguments for Christianity, was hostile to modern science, yet felt intuitively convinced that life ought not – must not – be nihilistic; he wondered if there was not a dark mysterious force, an instinct, an urge, a potency, which lay within all naturally created things. Rejecting the intellect, he could accept that the dark god of his imagination intended that there should be a pattern within the cosmos. The struggle to perceive that pattern, to see revealed the organic effulgence with which all nature is informed, became the meaning of his life in the post-war years. If a mystery lies within the chaos, then the force of that mystery must touch every part of existence, the aware and the unaware, the Ruperts and Alvinas, the Geralds and the Miss Frosts, D. H. Lawrence himself. To believe in the operation of fate was no more than to admit the strength of the unknown centrifugal darkness which created us.

Early in *The Lost Girl* Lawrence asks, 'What is one's own real self? It certainly is not what we think we are and ought to be' (p. 48). Alvina recognizes this. 'Now Alvina decided to accept the decision of her fate. Or rather, being sufficiently a woman, she didn't decide anything. She *was* her own fate' (p. 49). The slightly ironic inflection must not prevent us from recognizing the kind of person Lawrence intends Alvina to be. She will not plan her life 'sensibly' as her relations and companions in Woodhouse think she should, but allows the current of her fortune to sweep her along as it will. 'Fate' and 'fortune' recur many times as crucial words in this novel. A quality which draws Alvina to Cicio is 'the beauty of old fatality, and ultimate indifference to fate' (p. 265). Essentially, though, we cannot afford such indifference, for 'every individual has his own, or her own fate, and her own sphinx' (p. 290). Lawrence suggests that to immobilize oneself by resisting this fate is an impertinence to nature, an act of Oedipal folly whereby one blinds oneself in the act of averting one's gaze from the dark forces. Lawrence is not being predestinarian here; such logic is far from what he intends. The instinctive forces burning in the dark centres of ourselves and our surroundings are sensual and mystic.

Alvina's descent into her father's coalmine at Throttle Ha'penny is possibly Lawrence's clearest equation in the novel of symbol and mystery. He is scarcely interested in the mine as a place of actual work or social life. 'The miners were competent enough', he says, and we hear a snatch of dialect from one of them, but little else suggests their working existence. The focus is exclusively Freudian.

> The roof and the timbered sides of the way seemed to press on you. It was as if she were in her tomb forever, like the dead and everlasting Egyptians.
>
> (p. 64)

The mine evokes feelings in Alvina of an obviously sexual nature, but the association of sex and doom should not go unremarked. Throughout his work Lawrence speaks of two kinds of death, the sterile and the creative. Woodhouse is death-in-life, a constricted, stultifying place, like Bestwood in *Sons and Lovers*, in which the instincts and possibilities of human nature cannot flourish. The bowels of the earth into which Alvina now descends suggest another kind of death which obliterates material awareness. Alvina impels herself towards this sense of being overwhelmed rather as the Woman Who Rode Away in the story of that name summons her own sacrificial murder. 'There was a thickness in the air, a sense of dark, fluid presence in the thick atmosphere.' Alvina desires to be swamped by that dark fluid, to have destroyed her identity as Alvina Houghton. It is no coincidence that her late association with Cicio leads to a change of name: she becomes Allaye, and has a new identity. Her visit to her father's mine allows her to glimpse the sensual currents flowing beneath the surface of her ordinary life. The mine can exactly express this image of another life beating darkly below the crust of normal society: Lawrence was fortunate to be able to use it with the intimacy of close personal knowledge.

So she emerges from the mine fundamentally changed, with, as Lawrence puts it, 'a new vision'. The surface world has altered. It is now

> a velvet surface. A velvet surface of golden light, velvet-pile of gold and pale luminosity, and strange beautiful elevations of houses and trees, and depressions of fields and roads, all golden and floating like atmospheric majolica.
>
> (p. 65)

Later, when she succumbs to Cicio, the same images of dark, destructive doom that Alvina experiences in the mine are evoked again.

But the spell was on her, of his darkness and unfathomed handsomeness. And he killed her. He simply took her and assassinated her. How she suffered no one can tell. Yet all the time, this lustrous dark beauty, unbearable.

(p. 244)

Alvina had seen the colliers as 'slaves of the underworld'; now she realizes that Cicio 'intended her to be his slave'. The new 'velvet' world she perceives around her on coming to the surface of the mine denotes a transfiguration, partly sexual and partly spiritual. It is the equivalent of the social shock she receives on first going to London. By comparison to either experience the aftermath of sleeping with Cicio is more restrained, a scene of his male indifference, the landlady's rough coyness and Alvina's sense of betrayal. Cicio hardly ever releases in her the total identification of selfhood and mysterious nature which the mine scene asserts as possible.

Cicio is, in fact, one of the problems of the novel. As the instrument of Alvina's release he must possess animal qualities. He is the magnet or the flame to which she responds. Yet Lawrence creates a more guarded portrait of sensual potency than we see in Annable, Siegmund or Mellors. He comes late into the novel. Alvina is already established in our minds as *déclassée*; she has shocked Woodhouse and Miss Pinnegar by not marrying the obvious candidate, by training as a nurse in London, and by 'drumming out flea-pit waltzes' at the Endeavour. She already seems half lost. Cicio weaves the threads which are already upon the loom.

Francesco Marasca: his surname is also the name of a cherry. Lawrence hints, none too subtly, at the passion and bloodconsciousness with which he invariably associates the colour red. Cicio, though, has 'yellow tawny eyes', and the colour yellow predominates over the red. At all stages of the novel Lawrence deliberately raises questions about the fullness of Alvina's release. Her life with Cicio will involve adventure and many moments of mutual fulfilment, but is he, in the end, worthy of her? Exactly the same problem confronts us in *The Plumed Serpent* when Kate decides to stay with Don Cipriano. If we speak of 'animal' qualities in one of Lawrence's characters we inevitably wonder what kind of animal is being invoked. Cicio is feline, with the athletic coordination and sensuous beauty of the cat but also its independent nature, its indifference to affection, its furtiveness and its cruelty. The yellow-tawny eyes denote something cunning and predatory. Lawrence never dispels this sense of Cicio's untrustworthiness, however frequently he may write conventionally of 'the brown, slender Mediterranean hand' (p. 157) or, in sexual matters, of 'a certain finesse of knowledge' (p. 212). He approaches the Italian male in a much more cautious manner than Forster, who sees him as charming, sensual and gaily Latin, but never as threatening or inscrutable. Lawrence is here emphasizing, or overemphasizing, that the person one loves is 'other', is totally different. He makes the point emphatically by portraying Cicio as so 'other' that he scarcely seems human. He is certainly not one of Forster's jolly, warm Italians, who conform to a stereotype, and so are known, not 'other' – are a cliché. But he carries it so far that one wonders what there is in Cicio sufficiently stable to rest a marriage on. Alvina partly recognizes this. 'Cicio's muscular slouch made her feel she would not trust him for one single moment' (p. 167). His savagery and primitivism are constantly emphasized: 'Makes your blood run cold', as a Lumley woman observes. Among the Natcha-Kee-Tawaras, Cicio is the most like the traditional vagabond, a wanderer who flits into the night and emerges when least expected. In the elaborate dance with Kishwegin which forms the centrepiece of his act with Madame and the other Natchas, Cicio's rôle is that of hunter, torturer and killer. Though Lawrence's description of the dance falls flatly between the comic and the pastoral, conjuring up in the modern reader's mind ideas of a provincial *Rose Marie*, he clearly intended the scene to bear witness to the destructive, brutal, essentially catlike qualities of his hero. Even Cicio's silence – he says very little in the novel and is noticeably more graceful in movement than in words – suggests the cat in his nature. The cruel remoteness of which he is capable prefigures the captors in 'The Woman Who Rode Away'. From *The Lost Girl* onwards Lawrence set the majority of his fiction in hot exotic settings. He was not interested in exploring them for the charm of their foreignness but for their genuine strangeness. Cicio starts the process. Is what Alvina sees in him really there, or is he something altogether more dangerous, unreliable and different (in the blood) from what she thinks? Lawrence means us to ask this question, and at the end of the novel he leaves the answer open.

Whenever she is in his arms Alvina feels herself 'dead', like trapped prey. In marrying him, as Madame points out, Alvina will become under Italian law Cicio's property. That fate she partly avoids because of the strength of her will and the ordinariness of Cicio once he returns to his own country. Most of the novel, however, is set in England, and Lawrence emphasizes Cicio's foreignness there by deliberately leaving it equivocal whether he is a cunning fortune-hunter, sexually alive but emotionally indifferent to Alvina, or a peasant aristocrat whose contempt for English society ('Uncouth, they seemed to him, all raw angles and harshness, like their own weather' – p. 228) is akin to his own. Early in the novel, when tramping through a derelict area behind Lumley, Alvina had met a white woman married to a Negro. She recalls the moment when she becomes Cicio's mistress and glories in the sense of being an outcast. 'She clung to Cicio's dark, despised foreign nature. She loved it, worshipped it, she defied all the other world' (p. 258). This sense of being 'outside the pale of her own people' magnificently affirms Lawrence's admiration of the person who has the courage to reject society's opinion of him, but he has not made in Cicio a character quite strong enough to sustain the rôle in which he is cast, a character who can single-handedly counterpoint the conventional world. There is little strong or impressive about him when, in 'reclaiming' Alvina, Cicio 'did not want to see her looking at him, and ran from side to side like a caged weasel, avoiding her blank, glaucous look' (p. 323).

Lawrence emphasizes the weakness in Cicio in the Italian chapters of the novel. On the eve of their departure for Italy, Cicio's sexual glamour is at its height. He mesmerizes Alvina as a cat can still a bird – his 'spell', 'aura', 'presence', the sense of 'extinction' under his influence, these are the words Lawrence insists upon. 'There was a dark leopard-like pride in the air about him, something that the English people watched' (p. 342). In Italy he sinks unidentifiably into his own people and sheds the exotic plumage he wore in England by virtue of being a southerner.

The last section of the novel reflects Lawrence's sentiments about Italy. He stresses the grim remoteness of the south. When he speaks now of 'the darkness of the savage little mountain town' (p. 360) the words carry a force different from their force when applied to a human being.

It seems there are places which resist us, which have the power to overthrow our psychic being. It seems as if every country had its potent negative centres, localities which savagely and triumphantly refuse our living culture. And Alvina had struck one of these, here on the edge of the Abruzzi.

(pp. 370–1)

The model for Pescocalascio, Cicio's home, was 'the God-lost village of Picinisco', a remote hamlet near Caserta where, in a house just like that described in the novel, the Lawrences spent a short time late in 1919. They abandoned it quickly, principally because of the winter cold, and moved to Capri and then to Taormina. *The Lost Girl* was completed in Sicily. Lawrence remained in Italy for some months and in late 1921 published in New York his travel book *Sea and Sardinia*. His next novel, *Aaron's Rod* (1922), contained some tumultuous political scenes set in Italy. The country exercised a constant fascination for him, but the politics and the social life, even in the comparative isolation of the south, became oppressive. Perhaps his close sympathy for Italian culture – he was engaged for some months on translating the Sicilian novelist Giovanni Verga, who died in January 1921 – itself became a burden, for Lawrence's sense of responsibility to the little-known or the underestimated artist was always strong. A combination of factors led Lawrence to abandon Italy, and he and Frieda sailed for Ceylon at the end of February 1922. They were to return to Italy on more than one occasion but for the moment they were disenchanted. Some of their hostility comes across in the last part of *The Lost Girl*.

Alvina almost literally goes off the map by settling in Pesco-calascio. The full force of the word 'lost' in the novel's title now becomes apparent. She has moved worlds away from all her previous experience and far from the 'decent' values by which many readers of the novel will still define western civilization. All the references to Cicio as 'prehensile' and 'primitive' fall into place in this 'old eternity' (p. 372). Lawrence does not sentimental-ize this obscure place, remote 'from the world's actuality'. If it is a 'pre-world', it is not pre-lapsarian: the hill-peasants are 'watchful, venomous, dangerous' (p. 282). The women have sunk not into the dark extinction of sexual mysteries but into a weary acceptance of subjugation. Lawrence implies that, in this one respect, Pesco-calascio may not be so much different from Woodhouse, equally suspicious and enclosed. Alvina, to survive, 'must avoid the *inside* of it' (p. 393), just as she avoided being sucked into the centre of her own town. In the last pages of the novel Lawrence evokes the days of the gladioli harvest and spring sunshine: a more affec-tionate picture of Italy, though one shadowed by the coming of war. The details here are ill assorted. What, for example, does Lawrence intend by Pancrazio, with his memories of being a model for the Victorian artist Alma Tadema? Perhaps he wishes to stress the masculine orientation of this society, as earlier in the novel he highlights the special affection of Cicio and Geoffrey, but the handling of the subject seems diversionary. Giving shape to the end of the novel, fate re-emerges as part of its subject matter. Though we abandon Alvina and Cicio at the first crisis of their marriage – she resistant to the emotional rôle that peasant society expects of her, he faced by the uncertainties of the war – we can at least recall Alvina's assurance on the last page that 'We have our fate in our hands . . . I know it' and Cicio's implied corroboration.

The Lawrence of these last chapters may have been wary of southern Italy as a possible Eden, but his view of England as Alvina and Cicio depart from it is unambiguously mordant. England, in his mind, was finished – exhausted by what he thought had been an ignoble war, riddled by indestructible class values, given over intellectually to the effeteness of Bloomsbury or the philistinism of everyone else. The 'ash-grey coffin' of England (p. 347) sinking into the sea will be mentioned again in *Kangaroo*. In these years, 1919–23, Lawrence felt himself sick of England as he believed the country was sick of him. *The Lost Girl* was completed in this mood of despair, for there can be no more bitter emotion for a man of deepest commitment to his roots than that of patriotic disillusionment.

Lawrence goes far beyond the kind of Galsworthian model he may have set out to imitate. Nowhere else in his fiction does he scrutinize provincial morality so closely, but his analysis of its effect upon his heroine soon leads him into the sexual and metaphysical psychology of personality in a way Galsworthy and Bennett were not interested in exploring. Alvina's name must be related to the Italian *alvo*, which can be used to mean 'the womb'. Galsworthy, one suspects, would have blenched at such an allusion.

# 7

## *Aaron's Rod*

*The Lost Girl* had taken Lawrence a long time to write, partly for the sound practical reason that he had left the manuscript of the first part in Germany, where it had to remain until the war was over. It was followed by *Aaron's Rod*, which, of all his novels, most evidently shows the creative tiredness and emotional debility into which he was sinking by 1917, the year he began the book. He wrote the first part, pushed it to one side, then took it up again three years later to add the 'travel' chapters of the second half. It resembles *The Lost Girl* in a few respects. The main character of *Aaron's Rod*, Aaron Sisson, shares with Alvina Houghton an instinct to know another life apart from the imprisoning conventionality of a small town. Like *The Lost Girl*, the story starts in a midlands industrial setting, some of the place-names being familiar from earlier Lawrence novels; it then opens out to the broader perspectives of Italy. The Italy of *Aaron's Rod* is more 'sophisticated', more 'arty', even more 'touristy' than Cicio's Pescocalascio. It is the Italy of the expatriate rather than the native. Lawrence responded to it with the keen eye he brought to all his travel descriptions, but as the expatriate often cultivates detachment from his adopted country so Lawrence meanders from episode to episode with a certain lack of spirit. However, the novel has its moments of real gaiety as well.

The heart of *Aaron's Rod* is usually said to be Aaron's relationship with Rawdon Lilly, though this occupies only two sections. These are Aaron's life in London where he is first fêted by fashionable young moderns and then, on falling gravely ill, is nursed back to health by Lilly, who has literally picked him up from the gutter; and the last part of the novel when the two men are reunited in Florence ('Nel Paradiso' is the chapter heading). Aaron has deserted his wife and family to come to London where his talent as a flautist wins him a place in the orchestra of the Royal Opera House. His gesture of defiance in abandoning his home ought to convey the same shock as Nora Helmer's decision to do the same at the end of Ibsen's *A Doll's House*: both of them put duty to self before duty to kin. In Nora's case, however, we have during three acts seen her grow towards liberation. Aaron, by contrast, is resentful from the start; his wife is embittered, and the children, seen struggling over the Christmas decorations, are assertive and grasping. So Aaron's flight hardly ruffles us, though his wife's sourness towards him on the single occasion that he returns home seems more reasonable than perhaps the author intended. In the years since writing *The Trespasser* and *Sons and Lovers* Lawrence had become oddly unsympathetic to the beleaguered plight of a mother obliged to rear her family virtually alone, constrained by poverty to demand that the husband be mere loyal breadwinner. Comparison with *The Trespasser* can be especially helpful, since the abandonment of family is central to that novel as well as to *Aaron's Rod*. In both cases the hero is a musician; but, where the 'adultery' in the early book is conventionally sexual, in the later work the break with home precedes the forming of an extra-marital relationship which, when it occurs, is a spiritual and moral force, not primarily a sexual one. Aaron therefore breaks his domestic mould because it is rigid and constricting, not because he is in love with someone else.

The domestic scene at the start of *Aaron's Rod* gives some of Lawrence's most stringent writing, full of chilling lovelessness. The opening chapter, 'The Blue Ball', reads almost like a self-contained short story. This passage, from the start of the novel, shows how Lawrence's prose, at its sparest, can quickly point to the essentials of a character and to the tension in a domestic setting.

He strode over a stile, crossed two fields, strode another stile, and was in the long road of colliers' dwellings. Just across was his own house: he had built it himself. He went through the little gate, up past the side of the house to the back. There he hung a moment, glancing down the dark, wintry garden.

'My father – my father's come!' cried a child's excited voice, and two little girls in white pinafores ran out in front of his legs.

'Father, shall you set the Christmas Tree?' they cried. 'We've got one!'

'Afore I have my dinner?' he answered amiably.

'Set it now. Set it now. We got it through Fred Alton.'

'Where is it?'

The little girls were dragging a rough, dark object out of a corner of the passage into the light of the kitchen door.

'It's a beauty!' exclaimed Millicent.

'Yes it is,' said Marjory.

'I should think so,' he replied, striding over the dark bough. He went to the back kitchen to take off his coat.

'Set it now, father. Set it now,' clamoured the girls.

'You might as well. You've left your dinner so long, you might as well do it now before you have it,' came a woman's plangent voice, out of the brilliant light of the middle room.

(pp. 11–12)

The phrasing is direct and functional, like the lives of the people it describes. It emphasizes the separation of the people from each other: there is little conjoining of interests. The house has no atmosphere of sharing: 'he had built it himself'. 'My father – my father's come', one child cries possessively, and together they assert ownership of the tree: 'We've got one.' The mother refers to her husband as 'you' all the time, and she seems to loom 'out of the brilliant light' as a separate yet central feature of Aaron's life. Lawrence describes with great acuteness the bleak deadlock into which this family has drifted. The denied passion between Aaron and his wife allows Lawrence to be stark and uncompromising in his language: the subject matter of the rest of the novel requires him to be more exploratory. While a similar demand had led him a few years earlier to the high art of *Women in Love* and was still to lead him to the absorbingly personal *Kangaroo*, in *Aaron's Rod* the tentativeness can often seem more like diffidence, or even fecklessness.

The first intimation of this can be seen when Aaron leaves home and goes to London. Lawrence so loathed London himself that little of its vibrant life enters his descriptions of the city in *Aaron's Rod*. He makes plain his view of the capital city through the silliness of the people who inhabit it and the boring nature of their social diversions. He expanded on these feelings about London in an essay written a few years later:

The strange, the grey and uncanny, almost deathly sense of *dullness* is overwhelming. Of course, you get over it after a while, and admit that you exaggerated. You get into the rhythm of London again, and you tell yourself that it is *not* dull. And yet you are haunted, all the time, sleeping or waking, with the uncanny feeling: It is dull! It is dull! This life here is one vast complex of dullness! I am dull! I am being dulled! My spirit is being dulled! My life is dulling down to London dullness.

('Dull London', *Phoenix II*)

The same dullness permeates the London of this novel. Lawrence could not resolve the problem of how to make interesting to the reader the dullness of people like Josephine Ford (or is she Josephine Hay? – the tired writing shows even in minor details).

In Aaron's success with these shallow London types Lawrence may be recalling his own engagement with the social scene in 1915, though none of the brash people who chatter their way through Verdi's *Aïda* have an ounce of Bloomsbury intellect or Garsington charm. Certainly in February 1915 Lawrence helped John Middleton Murry return to health after a serious bout of influenza, an event which became the basis for Lilly's nursing Aaron. Most of the incidents in *Aaron's Rod*, in London or Italy, have their origin in Lawrence's own life, but, whereas he had been able in his earlier fiction to make an imaginative transformation of his personal experience, in this novel it can seem like thin satire or mere caricature.

Murry, who was later one of the few reviewers to give whole-hearted applause to the publication of *Aaron's Rod* – 'the most important thing', he wrote in 1922, 'that has happened in English literature since the war . . . much more important than [James Joyce's] *Ulysses*' – was the friend in whom Lawrence saw at this time some possibility of *Blutbrüderschaft*: the model for that aspect of Rupert Birkin and Gerald Crich. The friendship between Lawrence and Murry was intense but often quarrelsome. Probably they approached it differently, for Lawrence seems to have sought in it a spiritual kinship, whereas Murry wanted a more literary and intellectually productive relationship. The Lilly–Sisson attraction reflects Lawrence and Murry only in the most general outline. Essentially, it falters on two main counts. First, unlike Lawrence and Murry in real life or Rupert and Gerald in the earlier novel, the two men in *Aaron's Rod* are not sufficiently distinguished from each other. At times they seem to merge into each other by advocating the same principles. Aaron's letter to Sir William Franks declaiming against love (pp. 307–8) is hardly different in its aggressiveness from Lilly's denunciation of the 'love-urge' in the closing pages of the novel. Lawrence intended that a deep affinity should clearly exist between the two men: they 'had an almost uncanny understanding of one another – like brothers . . . Like brothers, there was a profound hostility between them. But hostility is not antipathy' (p. 129). This affinity is stated but not as delicately explored as that between Rupert and Gerald. Secondly, Lilly has no apparent charisma to justify his influence on Aaron. Since his appeal does not appear to be physical like that of Gerald for Rupert, we look for some distinguished quality of intellect or soul in Lilly to make credible Aaron's pursuit across Europe, and the implied decision at the end that Aaron will accept the need for 'the deep, fathomless submission to the heroic soul in a greater man' (p. 347).

Because of this theme of submission, *Aaron's Rod* is invariably grouped with the two novels that succeeded it, *Kangaroo* and *The Plumed Serpent*, though the nature of the submission differs in each novel: primarily emotional in Aaron's case, primarily political in *Kangaroo*, political and religious in the Mexican book. Other resemblances include the foreign setting of some chapters (but Lawrence had also 'moved abroad' in *Women in Love* and *The Lost Girl*) and the bitterness of the war memories. *Aaron's Rod* lacks, however, the kind of positive enquiry we find in the next novels: it is almost entirely negative. *Kangaroo*, the most spontaneous and discursive of the 'submission' novels, demands re-evaluation more than *The Plumed Serpent*, with its tighter formal structure and its alienating neo-theology; but both books seek for the establishment of a new society and explore possible programmes of action. Lawrence had pointed in *The Rainbow* and *Women in Love* to the failures of the old world, developing the thesis that a regenerated social and moral system must develop through individual revelation. *The Lost Girl* carries on this theme of independent self-discovery. In *Kangaroo* Lawrence examines the feasibility of a new society wrought directly through political action and social comradeship. His conclusions are negative, but at least he deals, in the Australian novel, with real or practical possibilities. In *The Plumed Serpent* he abandons a merely political programme, or rather converts it into an aspect of religious revival. *Aaron's Rod* has no practical thesis or plan of action to debate, and thus seems not just more abstract than *Kangaroo* and *The Plumed Serpent*, but more arbitrary. Rawdon Lilly does not embody any kind of formulated creed, as Willie Struthers in *Kangaroo* and Don Ramón in *The Plumed Serpent* do. For Aaron to 'submit', he must have something to submit to: submission entails faith. Lilly does not sustain that kind of importance. He *claims* leadership but lacks either the philosophical interest or the physical aura to justify it.

It has been suggested that Lawrence based Lilly less on himself than on the young Mussolini. His rise to power may be in the background of *Aaron's Rod*, giving the riots and explosions which occur in the novel, but by no stretch of interpretation can Lilly be equated with Mussolini. He has no popular following, no policy for reform and no explanation of how the 'power-urge' he advocates could be harnessed to the world's good or even to his own salvation. Lilly, whatever Lawrence wanted him to represent, is merely an individual whose personality impresses Aaron. His description of marriage as 'Egoisme à deux . . . Two people, one egoism' (p. 122) would serve as well for their own relationship when the novel ends.

Talk of Aaron's Rod as a novel about submission diverts the reader from some of its other concerns. Lilly, after all, plays quite a minor part in the tale, whereas the mood of weary disenchant-ment with modern shallowness pervades every page. The novel's intrinsic interest surely lies in its implicit commentary upon the Lawrence of 1917–21, bored with fiction, doubtful about his marriage, uncertain where to live, and wholly out of tune with the chaos of attitudes he encountered both in England and abroad. The peculiar unrootedness of Aaron's Rod reflects his own unsettled life in these years. Lawrence was always at his best in depicting settled communities, but Aaron lives by wandering among wan-derers. His drifting takes him to no community of ancient social culture. If this sounds absurd, remembering that the last part of the novel occurs in Florence, high peak of European culture, then we should notice how Lawrence's eye there dwells much more on buildings than on people. Just as the Josephines, Julias and Jims of the London chapters are peripatetic, not people actually belonging to the city, so the American Marchesa del Torre typifies the Florentines we meet. In Kangaroo Lawrence may deplore the suburban philistinism of his characters, but in their instant way they do attempt to drop anchor in a community of their own creation. The Plumed Serpent offers in Sayula richer evidence of settlement, with the pent-up fire of its ancient energies merely awaiting release into a renewed vitality. Aaron's Rod, once Lawrence abandons the industrial setting at the beginning, has no such social roots: a novel about itinerants which offers no explanation of why most of them are adrift is bound to seem more concerned with the flotsam of existence than with the destiny of man.

Lawrence's way of dealing with the purposelessness of the world, as he saw it at this period, can loosely be termed satirical, though satire so little edged as to have scant practical use. 'For even satire is a form of sympathy', he writes in Lady Chatterley's Lover (p. 104), but Aaron's Rod hardly bears this out. In it he strays into territory which Evelyn Waugh and Aldous Huxley were to explore much more acutely, the bored (to Lawrence, boring) ethos of the socialite twenties.

'I say', said Jim, from the remote depths of his sprawling. 'Isn't there something we could do to while the time away?'

(p.40)

To treat life as a diversion was for Lawrence not just contemptible: it was virtually sacrilegious. Yet almost all the characters whom Aaron meets in London or Italy approach life with this butterfly mentality. Most of them are based on actual people whom Lawrence had recently met (he models Jimmy Argyle, for example, on the novelist and essayist Norman Douglas). Their names often have the same literary affectation as Waugh's characters: Lady Artemis Hooper, Manfredi Del Torre, Algy Constable, Mr ffrench. They were types for whom he could have no love. It is rare to find him bothering with so many worthless people. Characters like Mr Crich or Clifford Chatterley may embody social principles he urgently desires to refute, but he sees them as victims of these forces, too, worth his attention and worth some of his sympathy. Angus and Francis and the rest of the effete pleasure-seekers in *Aaron's Rod* do not embody any principle, either of work or art, so Lawrence has nothing to attack except their dilettantism. They inhabit an idle, vaguely homosexual world which has always existed on the fringes of cultured society, but in themselves they have neither talent nor a sound philosophical rationale for their hedonism.

Waugh made people like these poignant representatives of their generation. Lawrence lacked the special kind of wit or poise needed to do that – his portrait is merely venomous. There are exceptions in the novel – Sir William Franks, as his surname suggests, makes a bold defence of self-aggrandizing capitalism which Lawrence can at least respect as a considered approach to life; the little Hindu doctor in the second chapter is precisely sketched, perhaps because he, too, at least possesses a point of view (that India should be allowed to rule herself because people can only be responsible to themselves); the wives Lottie and Tanny come alive because they are independent and resistant. Moreover, both Aaron and Lilly believe in the enduring bond of marriage, even if their relationship with their wives is a struggle. Lottie and Tanny matter as people if Aaron and Lilly matter, for the two women are inalienable factors in the existence of their husbands.

*Aaron's Rod* displays more narrative unease than Lawrence's other novels. We see some indication of this in Lawrence's uncharacteristic use of Victorian addresses to the reader:

Don't grumble at me then, gentle reader, and swear at me that this damned fellow wasn't half clever enough to think all these smart things, and realize all these fine-drawn-out subtleties. You are quite right, he wasn't, yet it all resolved itself in him as I say, and it is for you to prove that it didn't.
(p. 199)

Who is this 'I' who has suddenly been introduced? Why should a reader in 1922 be flattered for his gentleness? The novel has many similar touches: Aaron often becomes 'our hero' and 'our friend'. Lawrence goes up narrative *culs-de-sac* too readily. Jim Bricknell's visit to the Lilly home in chapter 8, for example, hardly advances the story, for Jim is never heard of again, and it stretches our credulity that he should come to Lilly because of a sudden vision that 'if ever there was a man in England could save me, it was you' (p. 91). The writing is very 'contemporary', with its references to Queen Mary and Lloyd George, yet it wastes time on anecdotes like the one explaining how Queen Victoria came to say, 'We are not amused' (p. 138). More centrally, there is little to account for the sudden resumption of the Aaron–Lilly relationship after their acrimonious quarrel in London, beyond the vague claim about the affinity between them.

Though there is nothing in *Aaron's Rod* to match the vivid bitterness of the chapter in *Kangaroo* called 'Nightmare', there can be no doubt that the horror of the First World War colours this novel just as much. Lawrence sees that Europe still suffers from its prolonged shell-shock and that 'It was too soon after the war for life to be flowing very fast' (p. 184). Because of the international disaster that lingers on, each individual is thrown back into himself even more strongly than before. As the Hindu doctor says at the start of the book, 'People should always be responsible for themselves' (p. 34). *Aaron's Rod* insists upon the solitariness of the individual. Aaron and Lilly have both existed in ultimate detachment from their wives, however inextricable the ties with them, each declaring through the pattern of his life that

By the innermost isolation and singleness of his own soul he would abide though the skies fell on top of one another, and seven heavens collapsed.
(p. 197)

Lawrence believed that even the profoundest partnership could be no closer than two halves of a globe: the crack between them might hardly show, but it was irrevocably there and always likely to reveal itself in open fracture. For this reason, the thesis of submission by one person to his more potent superior, of Aaron to

Lilly, seems inconsistent. The self-responsibility of each individual must conflict with any potential bond.

In giving Aaron his name, Lawrence perhaps wished to imply between him and Lilly the relationship between priest and prophet: between Aaron and Moses. There is no biblical source, however, for the doctrine of the power-urge with which *Aaron's Rod* ends. ......

I told you [Lilly says] there were two urges – two great life-urges, didn't I? There may be more. But it comes on me so strongly, now, that there are two: love, and power. And we've been trying to work ourselves, at least as individuals, from the love-urge exclusively, hating the power-urge and repressing it. And now I find we've got to accept the very thing we've hated.

(p. 345)

Power ought not to be defined only as a political strength. That kind of power, after all, produces the mob demonstrations and the anarchist bomb outrage which are attacked as bullying in the novel. 'The will-to-power – but not in Nietzsche's sense' (p. 345), Lawrence insists. He meant something much closer to what we now call 'charisma': a central instinct for leadership which gathers disciples around itself. Mussolini had it; in recent times Chè Guevara has had it; but in any historical example we may cite there are the complications and prejudices of real history. Lawrence spoke of a metaphysical power which would reveal itself almost through its own glamour. Christ might seem to be the exemplar of what Lilly–Lawrence is talking about, but he wilfully resists naming anyone who can specifically embody the power-urge. 'I think Love and your Christ detestable' (p. 96), says Lilly. Lawrence fails in the closing pages of *Aaron's Rod* to define what this power-for-life is, or to state what kind of person (other than Lilly himself, whom we have already seen to be inadequate) might manifest its force.

In *Women in Love* Lawrence had started to show, through the interest in African carved figures, an awareness of other civilizations than his own, and we can see a continuation of this in Rawdon Lilly's reading of the anthropologist Leo Frobenius. One passing reflection of Lilly's, though it explains little about *Aaron's Rod*, may help us to move naturally on to *The Plumed Serpent*:

I would have loved the Aztecs and the Red Indians. I *know* they hold the element in life which I am looking for – they had living pride.

(p. 119)

Before examining this living pride among the Aztecs and the Indians, Lawrence was to spend several months in Australia, during which he wrote most of *Kangaroo*. In the next two novels Lawrence explored alternatives to western European values. *Aaron's Rod*, by contrast, is a novel without a context, a minor work which tells us a lot about the dispirited Lawrence of the years in which he wrote the book, but which, in the perceptive phrase that Leavis uses of the way the Sisson family is evoked, cannot escape 'the prevailing undersense of grudge'. The only novel he wrote without a main female character, it attacks women with little moderation; obsessed with masculine society, it nevertheless portrays it as 'acrid', 'vicious' and 'derisive' (p. 220); embittered with England, it examines only the effete alternative of expatriate Italy. 'That Rod', he said, referring to this novel in a letter to Catherine Carswell (24 January 1922), 'I'm afraid it is gentian root or wormwood stem. But they've got to swallow it sooner or later: miserable tonicless lot.' If we have difficulty in digesting it, however, it is hardly because the message is too bitter for us but because it is not quite sharp enough.

# 8

## *Kangaroo*

Perhaps because it was written with extraordinary rapidity and hence shows some of the imperfections of hasty construction and nervously eager leaps of thought, *Kangaroo* has tended to have a bad press from its critics. Lawrence wrote the book whilst wandering the globe. Though he flirted with the possibility of staying in Australia, we know from the correspondence of the period (May to August 1922) and from the edginess even of the opening pages of the novel that Lawrence had no intention of stopping in the Antipodes and little compulsion to go there at all.

> We are going to Australia – Heaven knows why: because it will be cooler, and the sea is wide . . . Don't know what we'll do in Australia – don't care.
>
> > (Letter to Lady Cynthia Asquith, 30 April 1922)

> We shall probably go on from Sydney across the Pacific, and I want to stop in the South Sea Islands a bit, if I can: and ultimately land in Taos, New Mexico – where I was going first.
>
> It's queer here: wonderful sky and sun and air – new and clean and untouched – and endless hoary 'bush' with no people – all feels strange and empty and *unready*. I suppose it will have its day, this place. But its day won't be our day.
>
> > (Letter to Curtis Brown, 15 May 1922)

> And I shan't be able to leave till July – the *Marama*, July 6th at the earliest – and a pokey little steamer. God, how I hate new countries.
>
> > (Letter to Mrs A. L. Jenkins, 28 May 1922)

His attitude mellowed, became more ambiguous, and finally he was almost idolatrous, at least about the beauty of the landscape, though Australia never captivated his whole heart. He remained a visitor in transit, with Taos always on the horizon. Nor was the visit to Australia of Lawrence and his wife a holiday interlude in which the cares of the world could be suspended. The quest which Birkin and Ursula embark upon at the end of *Women in Love* was in essence Lawrence's quest too. His soul was perhaps more agitated now than it had ever been, his conscience more perturbed, his mind more provoked. To look on the balmy Pacific days described in *Kangaroo* as quietening and restful is only half the truth:

Lawrence's deepest instincts had been outraged by the humiliations of the First World War years, and a violent inner eruption constantly threatened the tranquil appearances. He was literally at sea; but metaphorically, too, he was uncertain in which direction his ideas, his instincts or even his marriage were leading him. It is no coincidence that two of the dominant images in *Kangaroo* are of volcanoes and of ships. A third image is the flower which wakens from the sleeping bud, as Lawrence hoped to find the dawn of a new life wherever he finally landed.

Critics have pounced on the apparent waywardness with which this novel is constructed, citing the chapter entitled 'Bits' as the microcosm of a fragmented whole. My defence of Lawrence's book cannot be total, for it has its abrupt changes of direction and its occasional irrelevances, but *Kangaroo* is not randomly disordered. The central images, in Australia, forge a more unified work of art than I believe is normally recognized. It was hastily written – begun on 3 June 1922, finished but for the last chapter on 27 July the same year – but the 'bittiness' which is usually attributed to this speed of composition reflects more on the state of Lawrence's personality at this transitional stage of his existence. His last glimpse of England, 'like a grey, dreary-grey coffin sinking in the sea' (p. 286), had been as a mourner at a funeral. Though passages of *Kangaroo* suggest a wake for the deceased life of the once-loved country, Lawrence writes as though England were irretrievably of the past. The future has still to be discovered. Australia, in the interim, acts like an anxious relative, giving consolation to the mourner and yet offending by its total incapacity to make up for the past or to serve as an adequate next stage. The emotions of *Kangaroo* are by turns restless and benumbed, bitter and nostalgic; the prose oscillates with similar unease. All this suggests to me less a novelist unable to handle his great themes, or too rushed for time to try, than a writer too shocked, too confused and too searching to write in any other way than he does here. *Kangaroo* is not a failed novel that could have been brushed into shape. It is as it is because it could not be otherwise. To 'improve' it by revision would have been to destroy the hectic uncertainty which gives it life. The form of the novel matches the mind of its creator as he writes.

Lawrence wrote *Kangaroo* as he experienced Australia. The experiences of the day are sifted in prose sometimes written on the same day. This is not to deny the imaginative parts of the novel or the place of incidents, especially political ones, which Lawrence knew of only by hearsay, but perhaps no other novel he wrote so thoroughly matches current moods with current sensations. The Lawrence who looks back even through the perspective of only a few months is missing in all but the last chapter of *Kangaroo*. Australia springs before the reader with the freshness of an eye seeing it here and now. Distaste, mockery, anger – Lawrence displays each in turn in relation to the human face of Australia – but his awareness of the ancient land upon which the new country is being seeded never deserts him. Early in the first chapter Somers walks alone into the bush at night and senses a pervasive terror which haunts the surrounding emptiness: 'the roused spirit of the bush' (p. 19), he calls it. 'It was biding its time with a terrible ageless watchfulness, waiting for a far-off end, watching the myriad intruding white men.' A social attitude is implied even here: the *colon* intrudes, he does not pioneer. What strikes us, though, is the life within the bush, the pulse which Lawrence feels each time he leaves the tidy villas or the lit city. Even Sydney 'seemed to be sprinkled on the surface of a darkness into which it never penetrated' (p. 18). The massive Australian continent lies dark and imponderable behind the human action of the novel, seldom insisted upon but always present. No major Australian novelist from Marcus Clarke to Patrick White has been without this sense of a dark, breathing flesh upon which the towns of Australia seem like a pin-scratch. What astonishes us now is how powerfully Lawrence detected the living force of this landscape, seldom judging Australia as the Australians he met seemed invariably to do – a land of opportunity, of human possibility – but as a continent whose physical authority rendered human enterprise nearly irrelevant. Somers's refusal to join with Kangaroo in his great plan for humanity or to enter a political affiliation with Willie Struthers reflects what Lawrence felt about Australia itself: all human effort seemed trivial beside the ageless certainty of the bush. The dark god for whom Somers searches in the novel surely has his physical home in the 'lonely, unbreakable silence and loneliness that seemed to him the real bush' (pp. 196–7).

The plot of *Kangaroo* scarcely exists. A volatile couple, Richard Lovat Somers and his wife, Harriet, come to Australia filled with despair at the spiritual state of the England they have abandoned. Lawrence makes no attempt to 'fictionalize' himself or Frieda: they are merely rechristened. Their retreat from Europe, especially on Somers's part, suggests a desire to turn away from people to find total companionship in each other. The motto of the novel, quoted within it more than once, might be *Noli me tangere* – do not touch me. Ironically they encounter the overt robust matiness of the Australian personality before they have time to set up any barriers. Jack and Victoria Callcott inflict their friendship – for that is how Somers sees it – upon the newcomers, and though ripples of mistrust and philistinism on one side conflict with disdain and resentment on the other, a quartet of feeling is established. Through Jack, Somers is introduced to the political other-world which exists beside the complacent suburbia. Ben Cooley, the Kangaroo of the novel's title, is the authoritarian leader of a right-wing movement called the Diggers. Kangaroo preaches love and fatherhood but presides over a sinister gang of militarists. His rival, Willie Struthers, from the left wing advocates reform through socialist revolution led by trade-union activists. The two leaders fairly accurately reflect the political possibilities in Australia (and much of Europe) for anyone seriously interested in political change in the early 1920s, what one might broadly call the authoritarian right and the trade-union-based left. Both desire the support of Richard Somers, but he finds that neither leader, charismatic though they both are, represents the dark god who alone will satisfy him. The novel is often speculative and didactic, taking up the social and political issues of contemporary Australia only to lead off into disturbed realms of metaphysical self-enquiry.

At the core of the novel is the famous section 'The Nightmare', in which Lawrence sorts out his feelings about the way in which he and Frieda were treated in the war years. It is sometimes dismissed as an irrelevant intrusion, but the whole novel takes its tone from this centrally formative chapter which fundamentally explains Lawrence's heartbroken rejection of England and there-fore his presence in Australia: also – for that matter – his earlier inspection of Italy and his fetching up in Mexico. There follows a fairly rapid series of actions and reflections which chart the process of Somers's non-commitment. The open battle which bursts out between the Diggers and the socialists near the end of the novel justifies his withholding himself. Vulgar and criminal, it shows a terrifyingly brutal side of Jack's character (Somers 'realized the depths of the other man's malevolence, and was aghast' – p. 321) and leads to Kangaroo's own death. Somers feels unable to compromise himself even to the extent of professing love for the dying man. This express refusal, and the clear horror at Jack's blood-lust, is to be borne in mind in arguments about whether Lawrence was a 'fascist' or not. Here Lawrence rejects right-wing politics of the European kind. Somers retreats from Australia in awe at its physical antiquity and climatic loveliness, but outraged by its social imperfections, which are essentially those of Europe. Harriet, whose tragedy the novel nearly seems to be, has to face the exclusiveness of male comradeship and the necessary separation which sexual difference brings about even in the most intimate marriage. Ursula faces the same situation in *Women in Love*, but she seems a less abandoned figure than Harriet.

To summarize thus is to lose the novel, for it is not essentially in action but in debate and enquiry that it has its life. 'The Nightmare', for example, does not advance the story of *Kangaroo* one jot, but it focusses and clarifies the mood of Richard Somers during his Australian sojourn. The critic could do worse than follow Lewis Carroll's logic and start at the middle until he comes on to the beginning. 'The Nightmare' chronicles the life of Richard and Harriet during those 'Awful years – '16, '17, '18, '19 – the years when the damage was done. The years when the world lost its real manhood' (p. 237). Lawrence, now three years away from the humiliations of that period, was only now able to articulate the feelings he had towards the harassments and misery of the war years. The 'manhood' he believed the world to have lost was not so much the flower of its youth, though he had a human grief for the Rupert Brooke generation sent as lambs to the slaughter-house, but the right of each individual to believe in his or her own worth, his individuality, without being brutalized into mob patriotism. 'The deepest part of a man', Lawrence writes at the start of the chapter on the war, 'is his sense of essential truth, essential honour, essential justice. This deepest self makes him abide by his own feelings, come what may' (p. 236). Wars are fought for the sacred freedom of the individual, but they can be won only by the denial of the same freedoms. Emile Delavenay rightly notes that the irritations and suspicions which the Lawrences endured in the war were not wholly unjustified. His 'outraged protestations of innocence in *Kangaroo* and in his letters reveal not only his complete failure to understand the impression he might have made on anyone responsible for security, but also a distinct propensity for provocation. Despite his great gift for plumbing the depths of the subconscious, he failed signally to perceive the immediate and natural reactions of his own neighbours' (*D. H. Lawrence: The Man and His Work*, p. 246). Lawrence, however, could not tolerate the uniformity of feeling which the war demanded. He did not wish to see the Kaiser waving from the balcony of Buckingham Palace but neither could he honestly endorse 'the stay-at-home bullies who governed the country' (p. 235). Perhaps the basic horror of the war was not the day-to-day checking up on his and Frieda's movements or even the physical degradation of the army medicals he was forced to endure but the knowledge that he could not share in the national unity. Lawrence yearned for mateship and kinship: what greater bond than the corporate struggle of a whole nation to defend its liberties? To such rhetoric he could only reply with despair, and eventually with the anger of the crucial chapter in *Kangaroo*. Society, he felt, had branded him as its Cain, and this he would never forgive.

The problem for Lawrence, dramatized with particular poignancy in *Kangaroo* but evident on many other occasions, was that he wanted the mateship and community sense which only work in a congenial group of people can give. Once he had left Eastwood and had given up his teaching job at Croydon, Lawrence never again belonged to a profession or to a settled society. The fraternity of writers who tried to enlist him in their number when he first became noticeable were a motley group held together more by aesthetic pretensions than by any natural community of being. Yet the kind of comradeship Lawrence wanted can exist only in a working community. For this reason the affinity between Lilly and Sisson in *Aaron's Rod* does not ring completely true: neither has shared in a great task. What Lawrence sought for probably existed most explicitly in the mining community he had left behind: 'This physical awareness and intimate *togetherness* was at its strongest down the pit', he says in his essay 'Nottingham and the Mining Country'. The war seemed to him like a grotesque parody of this bond of companionship in the pit. The national unity that the war created certainly existed, but it was a union of subjection, a monstrous perversion of the work ethic.

It may help us to understand Lawrence's attitude to the war if we recall a letter he wrote to Lady Cynthia Asquith on 15 November 1916 when he was staying in Cornwall, scene of several abject humiliations reported in 'The Nightmare':

For me, the war is wrong, and nothing, neither life nor death, can make it right . . . Believe me, I am infinitely hurt by being thus torn off from the body of mankind, but so it is, and it is right. And believe me that I have wept tears enough, over the dead men and the unhappy women who were once with me. Now, one can only submit, they are they, you are you, I am I – there is a separation, a separate isolated fate. And never again will I say, generally, 'the war'; only 'the war to me'.

Indeed, he echoes the theme of this letter when he laments the absence of 'courage in any man to face his own isolated soul, and abide by its decision' (p. 237). It may be easier now to contemplate non-service in wartime than it was between 1914 and 1918, but even then the pacifist or conscientious objector was reluctantly admitted to have some moral vindication. Lawrence pleaded neither cause. Though he loathed the militant camaraderie of army life, despised the politicians and the generals alike, and did not support the perpetuation of the social system that the war was fought to maintain, he nonetheless presented himself for medical examination at army centres on more than one occasion. He was rejected, on legitimate physical grounds. His wife was German. He was an intellectual known for his unconventional views. On all accounts society conspired to make him feel its most useless member. When the war was over, he left England with a bitterness that cloaked sadness and hurt. 'It is just hopeless, me trying to live here – I can't . . . I dread it horribly, but must go', he wrote to Edward Marsh in July 1919. Not until the writing of *Kangaroo* in 1922 did he sort out on paper exactly why he had to go.

Passages of 'The Nightmare' possess a strange beauty. Lawrence is not often grouped with the war writers whose verse and prose caught a pagan splendour in the daily horrors of 1914–18, but his picture of London at this time has a fine impressionism which few of his contemporaries on leave or in the sanatoria surpassed.

In 1915, autumn, Hampstead Heath, leaves burning in heaps, in the blue air, London still almost pre-war London: but by the pond on the Spaniards Road, blue soldiers, wounded soldiers in their bright hospital blue and red, always there: and earth-coloured recruits with pale faces drilling near Parliament Hill. The pre-war world still lingering, and some vivid strangeness, glamour thrown in. At night all the great beams of the search-lights, in great straight bars, feeling across the London sky, feeling the clouds, feeling the body of the dark overhead. And then Zeppelin raids: the awful noise and the excitement. Somers was never afraid then. One evening he and Harriet walked from Platts Lane to the Spaniards Road, across the Heath: and there, in the sky, like some god vision, a Zeppelin, and the searchlights catching it, so that it gleamed like a manifestation in the heavens, then losing it, so that only the strange drumming came down out of the sky where the searchlights tangled their feelers. There it was again, high, high, high, tiny, pale, as one might imagine the Holy Ghost far, far above. And the crashes of guns, and the awful hoarseness of shells burst-ing in the city. Then gradually quiet. And from Parliament Hill, a great red glare below, near St Paul's. Something ablaze in the city. Harriet was horribly afraid. Yet as she looked up at the far-off Zeppelin she said to Somers:

'Think, some of the boys I played with when I was a child are probably in it.'

And he looked up at the far, luminous thing, like a moon. Were there men in it? Just men, with two vulnerable legs and warm mouths. The imagination could not go so far.

(p. 239–40)

Lawrence quivers at the heightened tension in the air and picks out the colouring and the light. London arouses his senses at their most alive. That word 'feeling' applied to the searchlights (later, 'the searchlights tangled their feelers') suggests a giant octopus or a net encompassing the sky above the city. The deities (of death? of war?) preside majestically: the Zeppelin, 'like some god vision', a *deus ex machina* of wonderful impersonality. Yet Lawrence cannot long forget the human agony involved. His picture is not callously aesthetic. The human scale is restored – ' "Think, some of the boys I played with when I was a child are probably in it." . . . Just men, with two vulnerable legs and warm mouths.' Wilfred Owen's pity lives within Lawrence's prose.

The network of searchlights in the night sky imprisons those beneath it. Lawrence sincerely believed that envy of their non-commitment caused the harassment he and Frieda suffered in the war years. 'They hated him', he writes in 'The Nightmare', 'because he was free, because of his different, unafraid face. They hated him because he wasn't cowed, as they were all cowed' (pp. 252–3). Like Rudyard Kipling, he saw that belonging to a group easily turns into bullying the outsider or the person who won't conform. Whether he is speaking of the 'mechanical' strain in modern life, or the 'Bottomleyism' of the politicians who ruled England at the time, or the mindless group-brutality of the Diggers, Lawrence despairs of that instinct in so many men to merge themselves into anonymous mobs. At times he seems almost to contradict his own sense of the possible physical mateship and blood-partnership which can exist between men, especially working men. He did not intend this contradiction, for there is a great difference between the generosity and alerted senses that natural harmony among men may give rise to and the numb regimentation of a nation drilled into conformity. In *Kangaroo* he deplores the songs of the First World War ('the wail of a dying humanity' – p. 255), the mindless faith in John Bull as an ideal worth fighting for, and the wretchedness of a system that sets one man to spy upon another. There is scant compensation in the little jokes he is able to play upon the 'jackals' or in the humorous absurdity of the bungling official who mistakes a packet of salt for a camera. On Armistice night Somers and Harriet sit alone in their cottage singing German songs, a moment of half-intentional comedy which yet highlights the difficulty of meaningful protest.

Constantly Somers–Lawrence is thrown back on his own isolated self. The twilight communing with the Celtic spirits of old Cornwall presages the same solitary mood in the Australian bush. 'The moors looking primeval, and the huge granite boulders bulging out of the earth like presences' (p. 252) have much in common with 'the age-unbroken silence of the Australian bush' (p. 390). For a moment in 'The Nightmare' we seem to be reading a novella within a novel, for Lawrence in the Cornish passages explores an area on the edge of time and culture, just as he felt the bush to be. The war had led to a catastrophic loss of faith in humanity, but in Cornwall he could find a splendid confirmation of life by studying the sea, the rocks and the sky. In one of the press cuttings quoted in *Kangaroo* Lawrence remembers that 'We know nothing whatever of the awful forces at work beneath the crust of the earth, and nothing of the internal fires' (p. 185), but in Cornwall, as in the bush, he glimpses this inner demonic energy, thrilled by its force. Lest we think of Lawrence as wandering away to a natural solitude of Wagnerian intensity we must ask what human outlets were still available to him: other, of course, than Frieda, whom, anyway, he half neglected at this period. The answer lies in a young Cornish farmer, William Hocking, whom Lawrence befriended in 1917. Hocking possessed dark Celtic looks and clearly attracted Lawrence as a physical type. In *Kangaroo* he becomes John Thomas (the name even hints at a sexual rapport between the men). Not much is made of the relationship either in the novel or in the correspondence, but its existence shows Lawrence's need for male companionship and respect. Through John Thomas's pride in Richard Lovat Somers's courage (p. 257) he reminds himself that there were still people who did not consider him at this time a social pariah.

What relevance has 'The Nightmare' to *Kangaroo* as a whole? Without this chapter the rest of the novel might seem negative and confused. In charting the intense disillusionment, those 'serious deaths in belief' (p. 274), which drove him out of England, Lawrence gives the reasons for Somers's rejection of both Kangaroo and Struthers in Australia. The war years crystallized his hatred of mob feeling, whether it manifested itself in the blind patriotism of the trenches or in the wild violence of radical revolution. He had felt hunted throughout the war: the authorities were 'jackals' or 'like hyenas just going to bite'. So, like Coriolanus, he became the lonely dragon who haughtily turned his back on those who cast him out. All this Lawrence records in Richard Somers.

He took his stand absolutely on his own judgement of himself. Then, the mongrel-mouthed world would say and do what it liked.

(p. 278)

Never again would Somers be at the disposal of society. He can resist the half-temptation which Kangaroo embodies because he has made this great vow of principle not to be a part of any social movement. Perhaps Lawrence never understood the anarchism implicit in his decision to remain 'apart from mankind, a Cain, or worse' (p. 276), but his rejection of the *canaille*, the contemptible leaders (as he saw them) who had run the affairs of England throughout the war, suggests that had he lived into the 1930s he would have despised even more the fascist governments of Europe. In his novels he could admire the blood-strength of one masterful imagined individual, but in political terms Lawrence flirted with authoritarianism only to abhor it. He outlawed from his own ethics anything which reduced the human capacity for wholeness and fulfilment. When, for example, he revisited the Eastwood of his youth, Lawrence found virtually nothing left with which to identify himself. The nation seemed no longer to spend its leisure hours walking the woods; it had chopped them down for trench props. The old England was chopped down in the process: the politicians were the foremen while the people wielded the axe. Lawrence returned to this theme of national disintegration in *Lady Chatterley's Lover*, where the process has virtually gone out of control.

'The Nightmare' elaborates what is hinted at throughout the early part of the novel: dead Europe must be exchanged for the virgin freshness of new continents. When the Somerses come to Australia they are struck by its physical brilliance and freshness. A strange discrepancy between the land and the people becomes a dominant motif in *Kangaroo*, however. This continent of bright confident flowers and animals amazes Harriet especially. The dahlias are like chrysanthemums, the birds have no fear, the sea itself seems deeper and more dynamic than it does elsewhere. Yet the flowers are called 'extraneous' (p. 16), the birds emphasize in their flight the stranded human society, and Somers wishes that the sea 'would send a wave about fifty feet high round the whole coast of Australia' (p. 31). This last touch typifies Somers's half-amused, half-bitter response to the people he encounters. Lawrence even finds comedy in his Christ imagery, normally among the grander moments of his prose. 'Three months in which to get used to this land of the Southern Cross. Cross indeed! A new crucifixion. And then away, homewards!' (p. 26).

Lawrence's attitude to colonial society has not been much discussed, but as the reaction of a major novelist to a white dominion of the 1920s *Kangaroo* has a special place in the canon of imperial literature. His view shares much with that of a writer who, in our own time, has interpreted colonialism with especial penetration, V. S. Naipaul. Both detect an essential fraudulence at the heart of it, an element of mimicry and even puppetry. The commercial life of the country, for example, 'goes on full speed: but only because it is the other end of English and American business' (p. 13). Of Sydney, Lawrence writes,

It was all London without being London. Without any of the lovely old glamour that invests London. The London of the Southern hemisphere was all, as it were, made in five minutes, a substitute for the real thing.

(p. 25)

It is amusing to find Lawrence extolling lovely old London when he is well away from it – a different view of the city from the London chapters in *Aaron's Rod* or in the essay 'Dull London'. His feelings towards Europe blow hot and cold from page to page, perhaps reflecting Lawrence's own mood on the day he happened to be writing. Towards the Australian people, who define the character of the colonial atmosphere, he remains less equivocal. A colony, Somers asserts, is perhaps even older than its parent country, 'one step further gone' (p. 57). Traditions which feed the life-blood of one country become degenerate copies in the other. Lawrence extracts some fun from this situation. Victoria's mounted bullet, once lodged in Jack's jaw and now adorning the mantelpiece, obviously amuses him. Australian taste parodies European, so that the tastelessness of English suburbia reappears magnified in countless homes such as Coo-ee and Torestin. In this wry view of Australian suburbia, Lawrence looks forward to the early novels and stories of Patrick White, where Sarsaparilla has the same combination of newness, self-assurance and vulgarity.

Throughout *Kangaroo* Lawrence explores the nature of colonial society more fully than he was to do at any other time. From the remarks of the Hindu doctor at the beginning of *Aaron's Rod* and from the presentation of the expatriates early in *The Plumed Serpent*, who import food at great expense rather than use local produce, we can pick up Lawrence's observations upon imperialism in fits and starts, but *Kangaroo* deals with the subject at first hand. The reader who has never visited Australia obviously can speak with no first-hand knowledge of his perception, but as Lawrence feels his way towards understanding the people we may recognize a steadiness of vision which lends him credibility. He bluntly refuses to compromise in his idea of the Australian personality.

The bulk of Australians don't care about Australia – that is, you say they don't. And why don't they? Because they care about nothing at all, neither in earth below or heaven above. They just blankly don't care about anything, and they live in defiance, a sort of slovenly defiance of care of any sort, human or inhuman, good or bad. If they've got one belief left, now the war's safely over, it's a dull, rock-bottom belief in obstinately not caring, not caring about anything. It seems to me they think it manly, the only manliness, not to care, not to think, not to attend to life at all, but just to tramp blankly on from moment to moment, and over the edge of death without caring a straw. The final manliness.

(p. 72)

A kernel of envy lies embedded in this aggressive prose. Lawrence does not totally reject the uncerebral way of life, with its emphasis on manly self-confidence. He perceives in the people surrounding him all the qualities of assurance, toughness and certainty about the whys and wherefores of existence which he lacks himself as he writes the novel. Intellectually he rejects 'the profound Australian indifference' (p. 379), but a society of men that places high emphasis on its maleness undoubtedly attracts him. The mental blankness which Somers finds amongst everyone except Kangaroo, Struthers and William James appeals to him rather in the way that the Eastwood colliers moved Lawrence: living, as he writes in the essay entitled 'Nottingham and the Mining Country', 'almost entirely by instinct . . . not intellectually interested . . . but in a flow'.

Jack and Victoria Callcott, who are based on actual neighbours of the Lawrences when they were staying at 'Wyewurk', Thirroul, New South Wales, embody Lawrence's view of the archetypal suburban Australian. Lawrence limited his account of Australia to this stratum of society, the only one he had seen first-hand. He does not speak of the aborigine, the gold-digger or the outback sheep-farmer. The novel sticks to Jack Callcott's world and to the dangerous cabals it can breed. The keynote of this world is its aggressive masculinity. 'Jack . . . was the manly man, the con-sciously manly man' (p. 45). He reveres hard work only when it involves physical toughness. He has no understanding of Somers's life, although the two men share a theoretical socialism and Jack assumes that there must be a common bond between them on account of the working-class background that they share. The relationship between the two men is a paler version of that which Kangaroo would like with Somers, filled with 'a strange light of purpose and of passion' (p. 65). This passion seems oddly negative, however. Jack's view of life holds little hope for the future, despite his hectic talk of what will be done 'when the time is ready'. He wholly lacks imagination. When he offers Somers a form of comradeship so total that he would be prepared to lay down his life for him, Somers resists partly because Jack is so exclusive. Somers 'had all his life had this craving for an absolute friend, a David to his Jonathan, Pylades to his Orestes: a blood-brother . . . And now at last, when it really offered . . . he didn't want it, and he realized that in his innermost soul he had never wanted it' (p. 120). Jack, one almost feels, has no innermost soul and little insight into Somers's paradoxical nature which yearns for soul-union on the one hand while standing aloof on the other. Even Jack's political horizons seem narrow – 'leave us Australians to ourselves, we shall manage' (p. 208) – and at the end of the novel his exultation at taking life ('Having a woman's something, isn't it? But it's a flea-bite, nothing, compared to killing your man when your blood comes up!' – p. 352) reveals within the man a hideously distorted set of values. It is worth comparing him with Gerald Crich, in whom there lurk the same seeds of brutality, but, whereas in *Women in Love* it was Gerald who drew back from the total commitment of 'absolute friendship', in *Kangaroo* it is the Birkin-like Somers who resists. Lawrence has shifted his ground in this novel, away from an ultimate conviction in the bond between man and man. *Kangaroo*, in fact, adjusts the stance adopted towards male comradeship in *Women in Love* and *Aaron's Rod*. Lawrence took up the theme again in *The Plumed Serpent* but presented it there more in intellectual than emotional terms.

Victoria, like her husband, has an impoverished response to life, though she is more vulnerable than he. Lawrence occasionally milks her for a little social comedy at the expense of Australian provincialism. We find her, for example, peeping 'through her lashes to see how Harriet behaved. As Harriet behaved in the vaguest manner possible, and ate her sweets with her fish-fork and her soup with her pudding spoon, a study of her table manners was not particularly profitable' (p. 41). Victoria and Somers attract each other but deny the bacchic urges within themselves. Both wife and husband have therefore offered themselves, the one in body, the other in soul, to the visiting Englishman. Innocence and tranquillity colour Victoria's nature, however, and she it is who waves goodbye to Richard and Harriet when they finally depart from Australia.

Through Jack, Somers meets Ben Cooley, the 'Kangaroo' of the novel's title. Why did Lawrence give this nickname to the enigmatic political agitator? When in Sydney he wrote a poem about the kangaroo, a small part of which reads:

> Wistfully watching, with wonderful liquid eyes.
> And all her weight, all her blood, dripping sack-wise
>   down towards the earth's centre,
> And the live little one taking in its paw at the door
>   of her belly.
>
> Leap then, and come down on the line that draws to the
>   earth's deep, heavy centre.

Unlike the swift, light, small animals of the north, the kangaroo seems solid, weighty, as though married to the gravity of the earth. Lawrence's kangaroo is at one with the landscape. He stresses the motherhood of the kangaroo, its most distinctive feature; he senses the warmth and humour of the mother–child intimacy without sentimentality. He suggests, too, a keenness in the animal and an immeasurable sadness.

> She watches with insatiable wistfulness.
> Untold centuries of watching for something to come,
> For a new signal from life, in that silent lost land
>   of the South.

The silent continent lies waiting, the kangaroo its sentinel. Ben Cooley is such a man in such a land.

We are well into the novel before Lawrence mentions Kangaroo. '"Who is he?" asks Somers. "He's the First," replied Jack slowly' (p. 116). An air of godlikeness surrounds Kangaroo all the time – a Christ, a saint, a phoenix. Yet, like Don Ramón in *The Plumed*

*Serpent*, the god-rôle is played in an often very domestic setting. When we see him for the first time he is presiding over a lunch table in bourgeois splendour.

> The luncheon was almost impressive: a round table with a huge bunch of violets in a queer old copper bowl, Queen Anne silver, a tablecloth with heavy point edging, Venetian wine-glasses, red and white wine in Venetian wine-jugs, a Chinaman waiting at table, offering first a silver dish of hors d'oeuvres and a handsome crayfish with mayonnaise.

> (p. 121)

Kangaroo's revolution entails few sacrifices of comfort or style. The Digger movement he has founded, with its neo-masonic rites and its veneration of spartan self-discipline (when Jack first talks about it he says, 'We go in chiefly for athletics' – p. 104), proves élitist not only in its ideology but also in its behaviour. Lawrence does not, however, have a merely condemnatory attitude to Kangaroo's advocacy of a form of benevolent despotism in the opening confrontation between Somers and Cooley. Kangaroo, enigmatically and rather artificially described by Jack as 'a glass finger-bowl with a violet floating in it . . . so transparent' (p. 121), presents himself to the reader as a repository of innocence. 'And he was almost purely *kind*, essential kindliness, embodied in an ancient, unscrupulous shrewdness' (p. 123). Lawrence offers us the loving side of the kangaroo of his poem. Is he not hinting at Christ-likeness, too? He associates Kangaroo with flowers throughout the novel; he emphasizes his Jewishness; he makes him not only 'the First' but 'the highest'; and in Kangaroo's eyes there shines 'a queer, holy light' amid the features of 'the kangaroo face' (p. 127). Yet in the end the novel does not endorse Kangaroo's values, so that the Christ parallels act as a critique of the Christian kind of love.

Lawrence sees the dangers of sentimentalizing Kangaroo. The man has failed in his relationships with other people: marriage, for example, has broken down. *Kangaroo*, written hurriedly, is full of crucial details of this kind which are not fully woven into the fabric of the novel but which pick out important areas of suggestion. His protestations of love sound an occasionally strident note – 'But the fire that is in my heart is God, and I will not forswear it, no, not if you offer me all the world' (p. 136) – and Kangaroo's physical presence can embody menace as well as god-beauty. Most seriously, the reader is bound to ask what *kind* of love it is which Kangaroo exhorts for the world.

I believe in the one fire of love. I believe it is the one inspiration of all creative activity. I trust myself entirely to the fire of love. This I do with my reason also. I don't discard my reason. I use it at the service of love, like a sharp weapon. I try to keep it very sharp – and very dangerous. Where I don't love, I use only my will and my wits. Where I love, I trust to love alone.

(p. 148)

Lawrence puts into Kangaroo's words his own sense of love as an energy, flaming and creative like the force at the earth's centre. 'Leap then, and come down on the line that draws to the earth's deep, heavy centre', he says at the end of the poem: acknowledge, and be moved by, not just the gravity but the demonic burning which lies at the core of existence. Yet Kangaroo's affirmation of this life-force threatens as much as it exhilarates. He will use dangerous reason in the service of love: thereupon he denies instinct and substitutes policy. He destroys individuality, for there can be no exceptions to the all-embracing compass of his doctrine, if it is to succeed in the way he wants it to.

As Somers feels drawn physically and spiritually to Kangaroo, only to discover something repellent at the man's centre, so Lawrence tests himself in the doctrines he gives to Kangaroo. We can easily see how Somers incorporates Lawrence's own self, but Kangaroo is another form of his *alter ego*. Important, too, as the social nature of Australia is to the novel, Lawrence uses the country 'Rousseauistically', a virgin landscape in which to try out his theories about love in human behaviour. Kangaroo often speaks with the authentic Lawrentian tone.

Well then, all that man ever has created or ever will create, while he remains man, has been created in the inspiration and by the force of love. And not only man – all the living creatures are swayed to creation, to new creation, to the creation of song and beauty and lovely gesture, by love.

(p. 149)

Lawrence only partly believes this; he believes that the inability to recognize the truth in what Kangaroo says has led to the crippled state in which most men live; yet he is also at this stage of his life deeply suspicious of the claims of 'love', as a demand and a discipline. Kangaroo goes on:

The earth and sun, on their plane, have discovered a perfect equilibrium. But man has not yet begun. His lesson is so much harder. His consciousness is at once so complicated and so cruelly limited. This is the lesson before us. Man has loved the beloved for the sake of love, so far, but rarely, rarely

158

has he *consciously* known that he could only love her for her own separate, strange self: forever strange and a joyful mystery to him. Lovers henceforth have got to *know* one another.

(p. 149)

This too is a give-away: the other person cannot, in Lawrence's view, be 'known'. There is an element of classicism in this view of the correspondence of the universe unmatched by man's own state. We, Kangaroo suggests, have converted the force of love, which is magnetic and harmonizing, into a mere ethic. We substitute a social ideal for the essence of creation. Lawrence's passion for the mystery of existence sounds in Kangaroo's words and gives the man himself a 'sort of magnetic effusion' to which 'Richard's hand was almost drawn in spite of himself' (p. 152). Yet though Lawrence writes with sustained intensity (even a kind of desperate rhapsody) in this scene between Somers and Kangaroo, the other part of himself stands relentlessly aside. 'I don't quite believe that love is the one and only exclusive force or mystery of living inspiration', Somers says (p. 150). Lawrence continues to find irreconcilable the Rupert and the Gerald in his nature, and he goes on finding a demand, a possessiveness, an attack on the uniqueness of the individual, in the claims of 'love'.

In writing of the inevitable conflict which arises between Somers and Kangaroo, Lawrence objectifies a dilemma that existed within himself at the time. It is no coincidence that 'The Nightmare' follows immediately after the clinching quarrel between the two men, when Kangaroo – the saint and leader now changed into a clown and enemy – implores Somers to leave Australia. Lawrence saw in men like Cooley the decisive single-mindedness which a part of him would have liked to enjoy. A stock response to Lawrence's books is that he harangues the reader with his own extraordinary views; but though no one could deny the urgency of tone with which he often speaks, it is less usual to find it accompanied by exclusive conviction. Lawrence has been accused of many sins ranging from dangerous radicalism to arch-fascism, from pornography to puritan rectitude, but the truth resides uncertainly between these extremes, often unclear even to the writer himself. We are accustomed with many of the great novelists to seek out moral definites. Critics may argue about the art or the social purpose of a Jane Austen or a Dickens, but they will probably agree about which side the author is on, or where the moral priorities of the novel lie. Sometimes the same is true of Lawrence – virtually the whole of *Lady Chatterley's Lover* is a case in point – but often a mixture of intelligence, arrogance and an awareness of conflicting passions within himself leads naturally to non-commitment, to the dramatization of alternative views. *Kangaroo* illustrates this perfectly. The ideals of its title character excite Lawrence ('excitement' is a key word in the novel); he responds to his principle of love and to his hope for the future. Intellectually he knows that these values are likely to be brought into being only through the social and political action of the many. And there's the rub. When the herd instinct takes over from the love instinct, barbarism follows. Love conceived as 'knowledge' is possessive and restrictive, and leads to tribalism. So Lawrence retreats into the intellectually untenable, though emotionally consoling, position of believing that the new Eden will come about only through each individual's own effort. He may be assisted by his mate, though she or he will probably suck away as much vitality as is given, but essentially the salvation of man will come only as one by one we break with social uniformity and insist on being ourselves. Lawrence was far too alert not to perceive the anarchy, the wilfulness and the death of love to which this might give rise, and so at different stages of his writing he tries to find alternatives to social action. Sex, one of the strongest urges in humanity and a natural source of harmony; mysticism, transcending reality; pantheism, linking man and nature; all these powerfully influence him and seem at moments in his writing to be the force to which he can totally subscribe. Yet each in turn disappoints Lawrence, for none exists without its cancerous element. This sense of disappointment does not drive him into despair or melancholy or bitterness, though he displays each of these by turn; rather, he feels driven to further exploration of the layers of human experience and feeling. Inevitably, then, there are inconsistencies and contradictions as he discovers new areas and raises the standard of discovery there, only to see it buffeted by counter-winds. Exhilaration in the search, tragedy in its consequent disappointment, exist side by side in Lawrence's work.

Somers's rejection of Kangaroo demonstrates this inability to be committed. Recalling Wilde, Lawrence writes, 'Each man *does* kill the thing he loves, by sheer dint of loving it' (p. 220). A few lines later he counterpoints this remark by insisting that 'the human heart must have an absolute'. Kangaroo is too flawed a god, part-ghoul, part-clown, to be the absolute that Somers is looking for. He draws away from the man's charisma and in the end refuses Kangaroo consolation; when the assassinated leader lies on his death-bed, Somers will not utter the untruth of saying he loves him. Lawrence writes here in a way which is opposite to the way he describes Mrs Morel's protracted death in *Sons and Lovers*. Steeliness and chill honesty predominate in Somers. The vaguely holy associations surrounding Kangaroo – his words 'like some far-off voice of annunciation' and his 'wonderful smile' (p. 238) – lack tenderness, and the final image of 'the vague yellow mass of the face . . . sunk half visible under a shadow, as a dusky cuttlefish under a pool' (p. 370) denote only ugliness and threat. Almost as though to justify to himself his own incapacity to be the kind of man he creates in Kangaroo, Lawrence emphasizes the hideousness of the dead man. Somers, too, seems diminished by it. Kangaroo was dangerous; he had to die; but his death leaves Somers empty and once more searching. For the rest of the novel he is almost always alone. Lawrence has traced, through Somers's relationship with Cooley, his own temptation towards group solidarity, political involvement and social idealism. In rejecting it because of the loss of spiritual independence it would entail he seems to recognize a consequent impoverishment in himself.

The increased solitariness of Richard Somers in the last pages adds further poignancy to the other central relationship in the novel, that of Somers and his wife. Harriet Somers closely resembles Frieda Lawrence. Ostracized in the war because of her German nationality, she has in peace largely withdrawn from society to find fulfilment in her marriage, her crafts and the wild beauties of nature. Her love for Australia is immediate; her husband's is gradual, reluctant and never total. Yet the continent serves almost as a metaphor for their marriage. Full of promise, and capable at times of yielding the most profound intimacy between man and nature, Australia yet withholds a part of itself. The primeval mystery cannot be fully understood. So it is in Lawrence's evocation of the Somerses' marriage. Indeed, words applied earlier in the novel to the Callcotts could by now work as well for Richard and Harriet:

Where their two personalities met and joined, they were one, and pledged to permanent fidelity. But that part in each of them which did not belong to the other was free from all inquiry or even from knowledge. Each silently consented to leave the other in large part unknown, unknown in word and deed and very being. They didn't *want* to know – too much knowledge would be like shackles.

(p. 40)

The scale of that part which is left 'unknown in word and deed and very being' becomes a source of conflict between them, for Somers's involvement with Kangaroo and the Diggers necessarily entails Harriet's exclusion: or rather, it seems necessary to Somers, though he cannot explain it to her. Cooley's chivalry in sending violets to Harriet and her courtesy and the sympathy with his aims in her reply cannot cover up the degree of separation between herself and her husband that she believes the 'Kaiser Kangaroo' to have brought about.

Initially Lawrence seems almost to write the novel as a tribute to his wife. When Somers recognizes in Harriet 'her gay, undying courage, her wonderful fresh zest in front of life' (p. 75) we see at once that Frieda is in his mind. The tension evoked between them must reflect what the Lawrences were going through as the novel was written. She cannot understand his desire 'to move with men and get men to move with me before I die' (p. 77). She values their mutual self-sufficiency. Lawrence perhaps fails to give us the Frieda whom others sometimes saw – many of their friends found her to be the more socially outgoing – but he has the excuse that he is writing a novel, not an autobiography, and that he is not blind to his own self-centredness. A snatch of dialogue early in the novel shows something of the honesty with which he writes. Somers is speaking.

I want to do something with living people, somewhere, somehow, while I live on the earth. I write, but I write alone. And I live alone. Without any connexion whatever with the rest of men.

(p. 79)

This *cri de coeur* echoes what many an artist has felt about his social rôle. Harriet's reply, however, refuses to respond to the implicit rhetoric in what her husband has said: 'Don't swank to me about being alone, because it insults me, you see . . .' Her values are invested exclusively in their marriage, as legitimate in their way as Somers's. Lawrence draws no high-minded conclusions about the lonely genius and his uncomprehending wife, but he detects a kernel of irreconcilable differences between them. Indeed, this incompatibility may be, he suggests, at the core of any heterosexual relationship. Within the man lies a hard element of masculinity which cannot be shared by the woman: 'the pure male activity should be womanless, beyond woman. No man was beyond woman. But in his one quality of ultimate maker and breaker, he was womanless' (p. 108). The woman's knowledge of

her inevitable exclusion from one part of the man's life must lead
to pain and mistrust.

> Bitter the woman was, grieved beyond words, grieved till her face was
> swollen and puffy and almost mad or imbecile, because she had loved him
> so much, and now she must see him betray her love.
>
> (pp. 108–9)

Lawrence writes here with the pity, if not the savagery, of
Strindberg.

He dramatizes the conflict between the man and the woman
as the journey of a ship in a storm; but at the end of the day the
waters will be calm again, and the ship can continue if neither the
captain nor the crew (for there must be a captain) has broken
'that inner vital connexion which is the mystery of marriage'
(p. 182). In the chapter 'Harriet and Lovat at Sea in Marriage'
Lawrence wittily symbolizes his own marriage. The chapter
sustains the ship image with an ebullient skill and humour that
obviously please the writer as he tests how many variants he can
squeeze from the single conceit; but at its centre Lawrence confronts the crucial question: what kind of ship he is sailing, and
whether it is a houseboat or a pioneer vessel testing uncharted
waters in search of an unknown land. Clearly he imagines 'the
bark of their marriage' (p. 194) to be of the second kind, and so,
at the end of the novel, Harriet and Somers set sail for America.
In the closing words, however, Lawrence reminds himself of the
'cold, dark, inhospitable sea' over which they will travel. In
abandoning Australia he must necessarily opt for the continuing
struggle in marriage.

Lawrence entitles one chapter of *Kangaroo* 'Volcanic Evidence',
and the unpredictable energies of a volcano certainly seem to
well up and subside within the novel, justifying to some extent
Frank Kermode's opinion that it shows Lawrence 'as nearly as
possible careless of what he was doing in his narrative' (*Lawrence*,
p. 103). I tried earlier in this chapter to defend Lawrence against
this kind of charge, not so much by denying its validity as by
insisting that the disorder reflects the subject matter and the
author's state of mind at the time of composition. Lawrence's
uncertainty about his own life affects every page of the novel.
He confronts public responsibility more directly here than anywhere else, and consequently finds himself driven back into the
private reaches of his soul, from which even his wife is excluded.
He models his characters partly on his own contemporaries

(Kangaroo himself has elements of the translator S. S. Koteliansky and of the psychoanalyst Dr Eder), but sees each one as a mirror of himself. He remembers Italian fascism, though he had seen only its earliest manifestations, in his account of Australian politics. His 'dark god' is both phallic and Nietzschean, with gleanings of the Indian metaphysics he had learned about on his way to Australia. Binding these disparates together are the unifying images of the sea, the journey, flowers, ships and animals and, above all, the land of Australia itself.

Richard Somers's sense of marvel at the physical grandeur of Australia never diminishes. By the end of his stay there he has come to a reluctant respect for the breed of men who inhabit this land 'that as yet has made no great mistake, humanly' (p. 381). The phrases which predominate at the end – 'like the end of the world', 'absolutely broken hearted', 'the loveliest thing I've *ever* known' – suggest the victory of Australia's majesty and tenderness over the 'mad loathings' which both Richard and Harriet have sometimes known. The hurricane just before they leave sums up the hectic confusion of their feelings about Australia. The final departure, the whole of the last chapter, has a reconciliatory quality. The store of aggression in Somers–Lawrence is now reserved for America, and the reader is invited to wonder at the self-destructive streak which wants to throw away the hard-earned love for Australia. 'To be alone, mindless and memoryless, between the sea, under the sombre wall-front of Australia' (p. 365), ocean-surrounded, still in the fern age: this is Lawrence's vision at the end of the novel, yet he exchanges it, knowing that there are parts of the continent where it may be found, for another new land. The ribbons linking ship and land break as the ship leaves the quay; we feel that neither Somers nor Harriet, neither Lawrence nor Frieda, will be the same people again. They needed Australia to take stock of themselves. The farewell recalls the farewell to the English coastline months earlier; emotionally it is less of a wrench, but symbolically the umbilical contact with Britain and the imperial or European culture is only really severed now. Otherwise little is resolved at the end, though if we look at Lawrence's letter to Catherine Carswell, written on 22 June 1922, we know that part of his spirit would always remain in Australia. The writing of *Kangaroo* was Lawrence's way of admitting that to himself. When considering a novel so full of fracture and dissent it may be a restful note on which to finish.

I am doing a novel here – half done it – funny sort of novel where nothing happens and such a lot of things *should* happen: scene Australia. Frieda loves it here. But Australia would be a lovely country to lose the world in altogether. I'll go round it once more – the world – and if ever I get back here I'll stay.

# 9

## The Plumed Serpent

To us, God was in the beginning, Paradise and the Golden Age have been long lost, and all we can do is to win back.

To the Hopi, God is not yet, and the Golden Age lies far ahead. Out of the dragon's den of the cosmos, we have wrested only the beginnings of our being, the rudiments of our Godhead.

Between the two visions lies the gulf of mutual negations. But ours was the quickest way, so we are conquerors for the moment.

This passage comes from the penultimate essay in *Mornings in Mexico* (p. 89), a collection of travel pieces which Lawrence had written for miscellaneous journals and which he assembled for publication in 1927. It demonstrates his continuing concern, during his months in Central America, with the contrasts of 'western civilization' and 'primitive culture', with the evolution of man and his relationship to the wellsprings of life. It shows, too, in the phrase 'so we are conquerors for the moment' how Lawrence was still as interested as he had been when he wrote *Kangaroo* in the nature of colonized society, though he was now living in a land where, unlike Australia, the indigenous population had once possessed a deity as potent, a social system as hierarchical and an art as vigorous as that of the peoples, Spanish or American, who now dominated it. We come across all these issues in *The Plumed Serpent*, Lawrence's last 'foreign' novel and the only one, if we count the 'Nightmare' section of *Kangaroo* as part of the action, to be set entirely outside England.

Lawrence and Frieda arrived in Mexico for the first time on 24 March 1923. They had spent the last six and a half months in and around Taos, a small town in New Mexico north of Santa Fe. Though the name of Taos is associated with D. H. Lawrence as Haworth is with the Brontës, he spent only eighty weeks of his life in the region – all in the three years between September 1922 and September 1925. He and Frieda were together in Mexico, in various places, for five months, after which she returned to London to see her children. Lawrence remained behind until 22 November 1923, when he sailed for England, too. It was during this visit to Mexico that the first draft of *The Plumed Serpent* was composed. Four months later, on 22 March 1924, the two of them returned to Taos and then travelled back to Mexico the following October. There they stayed for several weeks, delayed at the end by a malarial attack so severe that it tended to over-shadow the diagnosis of Lawrence's tuberculosis, which was confirmed at the same time and which was eventually to kill him. During May and June 1925 Lawrence revised *The Plumed Serpent*, accepting with some reluctance this title suggested by the publisher, rather than *Quetzalcoatl*, which he had originally wanted.

All Lawrence's novels have their admirers and their detractors, but it is only in recent years that *The Plumed Serpent* has been treated with much critical sympathy. It had champions among its original readers, chief among them being Lawrence himself, who wrote to Curtis Brown on 23 June 1925, 'I consider this my most important novel, so far.' His friend Catherine Carswell thought it his best book, too. Others were less enthusiastic: 'a bad book and a regrettable performance' (F. R. Leavis), 'a monument to misused talent' (Anthony Beal), 'the only cynical and heartless book Lawrence ever wrote' (Julian Moynahan), 'inelastic and deficient' (Frank Kermode), 'the disaster of *The Plumed Serpent*' (Richard Swigg); and even the temperate Harry T. Moore wrote recently in *The Priest of Love* that 'The final effect is one of superb music with a foolish libretto' (p. 398). The balance has been redressed to some extent, not least by Dr Leavis in *Thought, Words and Creativity*, where he qualifies his judgement by insisting that 'it is a novel by a great novelist' (p. 57), but it certainly enjoys a reputa-tion as Lawrence's strangest work of fiction.

To help overcome the novel's alienating effect we can relate it to Lawrence's personal circumstances at the time he was writing it. He had abandoned England and neither saw nor heard of anything there in the 1920s which made him feel he had made the wrong decision. He had not found in Australia what he wanted. In Mexico he discovered a land where the oldest values of the community seemed on the brink of renewal. Here people talked seriously of going back to their 'primitive' origins. Lawrence does more than write enthusiastically of this spirit of regeneration which was rife in Mexico when he lived there. He imagines the consequence of such a revival, which has gone deeper than the imagined Australian politics of Kangaroo, and become religious in origin. What might come about in Mexico he believes might be an example for all cultures. Each must return to its own roots and nurture what it finds there. (In the industrial parts of Europe this will mean abandoning the forms of industrial society.) To bring this about each culture will have to revive its national religious cults, headed by a quasi-military hierarchy with a charismatic leadership. Since the actual Mexican attempt was anti-religious and eventually came to nothing, it has often been felt that Lawrence was dealing with wild fantasy, but this is not entirely so. Mahatma Gandhi, Mao Tse-tung, Jomo Kenyatta and Chè Guevara are all variants of Don Ramón in *The Plumed Serpent*, in the sense that they went to the bases of popular belief and brought about their revolutions by showing how the past might be used to revitalize the present. They all received a semi-religious devotion from their followers and eventually established a set of ethical and popular beliefs not so very far from a new religion. *The Plumed Serpent* was Lawrence's last and most intensely imagined attempt to deal with the possibilities of renewal through mass action under potent leadership. Even had he lived many years longer, it seems doubtful that he would have returned to a theme which had been so completely treated here. The subject was literally exhausted.

The last chapters of *The Lost Girl* and *Aaron's Rod* and virtually all of *Kangaroo* amply prove that Lawrence had one of the most attentive eyes among modern travel writers. His capacity to distil the essence of an atmosphere can also be seen in his specific articles on places he visited – in *Mornings in Mexico*, and in *Twilight in Italy* (1916), *Sea and Sardinia* (1921), *Etruscan Places* (1932) and various essays in *Phoenix*. He evokes Mexico with as much immediacy and graphic alertness as he does Italy or Australia, whether it be a market scene, the siesta hour, the strolling couples in the plaza, a dance rite or simply the bright variety of the landscape.

Before the long veranda of the old ranch-house the green pepper-trees dropped like green light, and small cardinal birds with scarlet bodies and blazing impertinent heads like poppy-buds flashed among the pinkish pepper-heads, closing their brown wings upon the audacity of their glowing redness. A train of geese passed in the glaring sun, automatic, towards the eternal tremble of pale, earth-coloured water beyond the stones.

It was a place with a strange atmosphere: stony, hard, broken, with round cruel hills and the many-fluted bunches of the organ-cactus behind the old house, and an ancient road trailing past, deep in ancient dust. A touch of mystery and cruelty, the stoniness of fear, a lingering, cruel sacredness.

(p. 104)

This combination of tropical plumage and ancient resonances has struck most essayists on the Mexican landscape, as it here strikes the heroine of *The Plumed Serpent*, Kate Leslie. Lawrence dwells on the implicit threat within the scene, a hostility partly of climate (for he shares E. M. Forster's view in *A Passage to India* that the personality of each race is determined by the temperature of its physical habitat) and partly of culture. He often describes Mexico in harsh images of male sexuality: phallic cacti and sperm-like water. The 'lingering, cruel sacredness' of this setting has been bestowed upon it by former peoples who have dwelt among these 'cruel hills'. Unlike Kate, who respects the scene with the curious half-fear, half-detachment of the western eye, the old inhabitants, like the 'automatic' geese, had a relentless knowledge of belonging here. There has been a partnership of man and nature in this landscape. Is there any chance that it may happen again?

*The Plumed Serpent* contains some philosophical obscurity, a certain amount of religious pastiche and, in episodes like Carlota's death, a measure of fanciful melodrama. Yet Lawrence has a strong story to unfold, with a lively sense of adventure (the attack on Jamiltepec, for example) and a forceful, if not altogether persuasive, triangle of human relationships. Many of the 'public' themes with which the novel deals – nationalism, guerrilla banditry, anti-American feeling, the desire for a new religion to compensate for the failures of the old and for charismatic leaders to inspire the working people – were true to the Mexico in which Lawrence stayed in 1923–5 but were unfamiliar to most of his readers then. Now that they are the clichés of our time, Lawrence's book has a strange topicality. Its absurdities – Aztec praise-poems arranged to the rhythms of chapel hymns, for instance – are the result of exerting the will on the imagination, but in many ways it is a novel which has only lately come into its own.

Richard Aldington, in his Introduction to the Penguin edition of *The Plumed Serpent*, asserts that 'this is one of the novels where Lawrence does not ostensibly appear as a character'. He adds, in common with most other critics, that 'Kate is obviously Frieda Lawrence'. Lawrence dramatized himself in many forms, however, some of them fairly evident (Paul Morel, Rupert Birkin, Rawdon Lilly, Richard Somers), others oblique. Lawrence even put something of himself into Gerald Crich, the character who most completely illustrates his indictment of modern western values. In *The Plumed Serpent* Kate Leslie's dilemma was very much his own in the mid-1920s: whether to end with Europe once and for all and align himself with a new faith, or to submit to the irrevocable blood-connection by returning home. All the talk of blood-forces in this novel, which so shocked Bertrand Russell and others, may have sprung from nothing more sinister than Lawrence wrestling with his uncertain feelings towards his homeland.

Kate, an Irishwoman and recent widow of one of those political activists (compare Paul Lensky in *The Rainbow*) whom Lawrence dismissed as part of the past, following dead causes – Kate has come to Mexico to sort herself out. She is forty, the same age as Lawrence when he finished the book. Like Frieda, she has left a family behind in England. Her instincts in the first chapters are all antipathetic to Mexico: the bullfight of the opening chapter expresses the barbarism she feels to be characteristic of the whole country. Yet the temptation to move on somewhere else is countered by Kate's instinct that 'Mexico lay in her destiny almost as a doom' (p. 29). Don Ramón and Don Cipriano embody that doom. Embittered by the subservience of Mexico to material, and predominantly American, influences, these two aristocratic soldier-mystics seek to revive the pre-Christian worship of the Plumed Serpent, Quetzalcoatl, god of the sun, the Morning Star and the wind. Cipriano falls in love with Kate, though it is the least personally explored of all Lawrence's central relationships. They eventually marry by civil regulations as well as 'in presence of the unfading star' (p. 344); the marriage is consummated; yet it remains essentially a union of the spirits, a kind of political–religious alliance, with Cipriano and Kate cast among the pantheon of the ancient gods as Huitzilopochtl and Malintzi. Kate both resents the 'bunk' of this religious revival and acknowledges its potency. At the end of the novel the religion of Quetzalcoatl has dethroned the religion of Christ and been adopted by the state. Kate still veers between staying in Mexico, feeling its power and beauty, and acknowledging the eventual futility of remaining in a land where, as Ramón predicts, she is likely to fall victim to the murderous treachery of the people. Race hostility will out. Ought she not return to her own people, even if, as a Celt, there is almost as close an affinity between her and the Mexican Indians as there is between her and Englishmen? Lawrence, always concerned as much with spiritual evolution as with social finalities, leaves the novel open-ended, as he does almost all his major work.

It has so frequently been assumed that the politico–religious elements in *The Plumed Serpent* are purely imaginative and unreal that it is worth noticing how attentive Lawrence was to the actual state of affairs in Mexico when he stayed there. The year after Lawrence left the country, open conflict, which had been threatened during the lives of several governments, broke out between church and state, and on 31 July 1926, for the first time since the landing of Cortés in 1519, no Catholic mass was said in Mexico. The clearance of Christian images from the churches and the revival of ancient rituals, which Lawrence used as the subject of some of the best writing in the novel, actually took place. It was not just a matter of atheistic iconoclasm, nor was it only among the European-descended and the politically 'western-izing' element; the instincts of the ordinary Mexican Indian, as Lawrence quickly perceived, were more pagan than Catholic. Under Quetzalcoatl these people had once been united and productive; since the god had gone into exile, promising his eventual return, they had been apathetic and submissive. This, at least, is the view which Lawrence presents in *The Plumed Serpent*, though the Quetzalcoatl myth has, like any other, many variants. Lawrence seems unable to make up his mind about it. Like Kate, he is fascinated by the mystery of this bird–serpent–god, yet bewildered by it.

All a confusion of contradictory gleams of meaning, Quetzalcoatl. But why not? Her Irish spirit was weary to death of definite meanings, and a God of one fixed purport. Gods should be iridescent, like a rainbow in the storm. Man creates a God in his own image, and the gods grow old along with the men that made them. But storms sway in heaven, and the god-stuff sways high and angry over our heads. Gods die with men who have conceived them. But the god-stuff roars eternally, like the sea, with too vast a sound to be heard. Like the sea in storm, that beats against the rocks of living, stiffened men, slowly to destroy them. Or like the sea of the glimmering, ethereal plasm of the world, that bathes the feet and the knees of men as earth-sap bathes the roots of trees. Ye must be born again. Even the gods must be born again. We must be born again.

(pp. 64–5)

The rhetoric here is looser and more hectoring than in *Women in Love*, but the sentiments are essentially Birkin's. Indeed, the rainbow image takes us back to the young Ursula Brangwen. Now, however, Lawrence seems to have accepted that the vision of the new world cannot be realized by the solitary individual. So he experiments in *The Plumed Serpent* with the possibility of a mass movement. He had studied mass political action in *Kangaroo* and *Aaron's Rod*; now it was the turn of religion. Both faith in a workers' revolution and the cult of revived religion eventually failed him.

Something remains of the vision which initiated *The Plumed Serpent*, however. When Ramón says he would like to see the Teutonic world 'once more think in terms of Thor and Wotan . . . a new Hermes should come back to the Mediterranean . . . Mithras again to Persia, and Brahma unbroken to India, and the oldest of dragons to China' (p. 261) we can easily imagine the bellicose dangers to which cultural nationalism of this sort can lead. Lawrence risks this in supporting the paradox implicit in Ramón's argument. If each set of peoples in the world, led by the inspiration of great leaders, revives what is true to their area, their climate, their history, then no one faith, whether it be socialist, communist, Christian or materialist, will be able to claim international dominance over the others: yet, as each local revival could be part of one global movement, a universal regeneration of the spirit might take place. As Ramón puts it, in his interview with the bewildered bishop, 'A Catholic Church is a church of all the religions, a home on earth for all the prophets and the Christs, a big tree under which every man who acknowledges the greater life of the soul can sit and be refreshed' (p. 277). Lawrence is not much interested in *The Plumed Serpent* in questions of goodness or redemption: saving the single unique soul. He desires man to rediscover his connections with the universal sources of existence in order to realize both his sensual and his spiritual being more fully. Justification before God hardly enters into it.

Lawrence seems to have tired of Quetzalcoatl and his religion almost before he finished the book. Ramón becomes more distasteful to him as, in his second marriage, he grows into a small sultan. Cipriano relies more than ever on the 'mindless communion of the blood' (p. 439). Yet if Kate should remain permanently in Mexico it will not be blood theories or the eye of the snake that will keep her there, but Cipriano's sudden capacity, shown in the last moment of the novel, to be loving in a human rather than a godlike way. That, and the soothing loveliness of the Mexican lakes and hills when the sun shines fierily upon them, will keep her there if anything does, not the ceremonies and intransigence of the revived religion. Lawrence believed too much in Ursula Brangwen's rejection of the past to believe ultimately that man's best prospect lay in its re-creation.

Lawrence was always hostile to the bland orthodoxies of modern liberalism, but even his most ardent champions are embarrassed by statements in the novel which can seem repugnant now. Often these result from the conversion of a true Lawrentian perception into an ugly generalization. This sentence, for example, is both compassionate and consistent with Lawrence's stance all his life:

Men and women should know that they cannot, absolutely, meet on earth. In the closest kiss, the dearest touch, there is the small gulf which is none the less complete because it is so narrow, so nearly non-existent.

(p. 265)

This sort of statement, sad but wise, becomes the basis for the racial thesis of the novel. Ramón's view that 'The races of the earth are like trees; in the end they neither mix nor mingle' (pp. 260–1) may seem hard to take in the more racially sensitive time in which we now read it, though in fact he is saying nothing about degrees of superiority between the races: merely reiterating the constant Lawrence theme that *all* individuals are separate and unique. As it happens, the races in the novel do both mix and mingle, for Kate probably opts to remain with the Indian Cipriano rather than to return to her family. Though Lawrence did not finally stay in Mexico he felt a real *rapport* with many of its ordinary people and assimilated both its recent and its ancestral history in astonishing detail. His espousal of the Aztec belief (not dissimilar from St Augustine's) that 'There is always and only Now' (p. 189) is comprehensible. However resistant a modern reader finds himself to the paradoxes of Quetzalcoatl's religion (blood-rites as creative arts, for example) there can be no doubt that Lawrence was elaborating on an actual philosophy, not fantasizing on a spurious creation of his own. That he believed for a while in the possible relevance to the modern world of its more grotesque notions justifies Leavis's view of the novel as 'regrettable'.

In the end Lawrence came to realize that the kind of religious excitement he investigates in *The Plumed Serpent* was unreal. Though he described something that was historically rooted in fact, he was also indulging in a strong measure of personal fantasy and wish-fulfilment. Just as Kate never whole-heartedly commits herself either to Mexico or to Cipriano, so Lawrence himself remained, in his inner being, greatly doubtful about the practicality of what he was saying in this novel. As a result, *The Plumed Serpent* is an unsettling text to read. If it appears too grandiose at times, it also contains brilliant incidental perception. The view of colonialism, for example, compares with V. S. Naipaul's in many astute observations: 'a conquered race, unless grafted with a new inspiration, slowly sucks the blood of the conquerors' (p. 86), 'Curious, the old gentle ceremonials of Europe, how trashy they seem in Mexico, just a cheap sort of charade' (p. 290). The powerful maleness of the book disturbs many readers, though much of it is as true to Mexican society as to Australian or Italian. It is a novel of sharp accuracies interspersed with idiosyncrasies, but it says nothing that is inconsistent with the Lawrence of the previous ten years. Perhaps because it deals so fully with the cult of leadership, with a religion that emphasizes Now rather than Hereafter, with the fulfilment of women in submission to men, and with the whole experience of confronting alien cultures and foreign countries, it had to be the final point in this phase of Lawrence's development. He was very ill for the rest of his life and was only to write one more novel, but it is significant that he abandoned in *Lady Chatterley's Lover*, not tentatively but whole-heartedly, the uglier philosophical and sexual premises upon which he wrote *The Plumed Serpent*.

# 10

## *Lady Chatterley's Lover*

After Mexico, the Lawrences lived entirely in Europe. Though their longest sojourn was at the Villa Mirenda, just outside Florence, these last four years of Lawrence's life were essentially peripatetic: astonishingly so for a man slowly dying. They visited Frieda's mother in Baden-Baden, returned briefly to England, stayed in Paris, in Majorca and finally in Vence, in the Alpes Maritimes, southern France, where, on 2 March 1930, D. H. Lawrence died. We should not be surprised that in this unsettled final period of his life Lawrence should look nostalgically yet critically at his own country, where he could no longer endure to live. *Lady Chatterley's Lover*, first published in 1928, is a sustained lament for that broken society. Yet Lawrence, even when mortally ill, refused to slide into total despair. A threnody upon dead England might have had the dignity of an obsequy or the bitterness of total disillusionment, but it could hardly have had the visionary determination which illuminates this last novel. For that is the character of Lawrence's vision now: a will to see some alternative to the impotent mechanization of modern living.

Lawrence had been seeking an alternative in several of his last stories (*St Mawr* and 'The Woman Who Rode Away' are both set in *Plumed Serpent* territory: deserts far from modern society) as well as in *Aaron's Rod*, *Kangaroo* and *The Plumed Serpent*; he had tested the possibilities of spiritual regeneration through the inspiration of potent leadership. Obviously a common feature of the relationships between Aaron Sisson and Rawdon Lilly, between Richard Somers and Willie Struthers, and between Don Cipriano and Don Ramón, is that they are of the same sex, though in the three novels Lawrence affirms his faith in the creative possibilities of heterosexual partnership with increasing enthusiasm, moving from the sterile Sisson marriage via the fraught but surviving Somerses to the guarded optimism of Kate and Cipriano. In *Lady Chatterley's Lover* he almost totally finishes with the 'mateship' theme which had been important to his work from *Women in Love* onwards. Though Oliver Mellors, the 'lover' of the novel's title, recalls the comradeship of army life with some wistfulness, his crucial relationships before the one with Lady Chatterley herself have all been with women. In a letter to Witter Bynner (an American caricatured as Owen Rhys in *The Plumed Serpent*), 13 March 1928, Lawrence confessed that

> the leader-cum-follower relationship is a bore. And the new relationship will be some sort of tenderness, sensitive, between men and men and men and women, and not the one up one down, lead on I follow, *ich dien* sort of business.

The key word here is 'tenderness': at one time this was to be the title of *Lady Chatterley's Lover*. Lawrence now put his faith in the intimate care of loving physical contact. The brutality inherent in the leadership novels is largely absent from *Lady Chatterley's Lover*; so, too, is the self-sacrifice implicit in the disciple-and-master relationship. Lawrence turns against power, embodied specifically in this novel by Clifford ('Power! He felt a new sense of power flowing through him; power over all these men' – p. 112), if not against all forms of guidance. Though Mellors leads Connie Chatterley to discover herself by putting her back in touch with the richness of life and by awakening her to the beauties of her natural surroundings, he cannot be thought of as a leader or educator or priest like Lilly or Struthers or Don Ramón. Leadership has ceased to be a thing of will or creed or might; it has become delicately tactile and soul-releasing.

In his last novel Lawrence created one of those archetypes of literature which pass into the daily currency of life even amongst those who do not read at all. Few people in English-speaking countries have not heard of Lady Chatterley and her gamekeeper. A 'Lady Chatterley type' is the quickest shorthand for a rich or well-connected lady who attaches herself to someone who, though of humbler means than herself, has the instinctive sexuality which Lawrence claims for the 'natural man' of the land. Lawrence creates his archetype by revising older ones: the legend of the Sleeping Beauty, awakened from her non-life by a stranger's kiss, and the Arcadian myth that the pastoral life has a purity and innocence which social man has lost. Lady Chatterley's story derives from both sources. Lawrence refashions this traditional material for a neurotic modern world. The nightmare or coma from which his heroine awakes is the world in which most of his readers are obliged to live; the Arcadia to which she escapes is the dream to which most of them aspire.

At the start of the novel Constance Chatterley is married to the author–industrialist Sir Clifford. Her background peculiarly mixes Scottish moral rectitude with artistic bohemianism: a blend more probable in novels than in life, one suspects. After the war, her husband has returned 'more or less in bits' (p. 5) to his estate at Wragby Hall, in the midlands of England: shattered physically, impotent sexually, firm only in the knowledge of his own superiority to the working men he employs in his coalmine and in his bodiless intellectuality as a writer. The Chatterleys evolve a relationship in which their cerebral rapport appears to compensate for the absence of any sexual connection. Clifford puts his whole being into his stories, which enjoy a popular success. Though a minor failing of the novel is that we have no chance to see exactly what kind of story he writes, they evidently exist as pert observations of life, utterly self-obsessed yet lacking the felt experience which Lawrence insisted was the life-blood of true literature. To his home Clifford brings the fashionable *literati*, a tedious crowd of 'highly mental gentlemen' (p. 37) like those we encounter in so much of *Aaron's Rod*. Connie has a sexual relationship with one of the visitors, a playwright called Michaelis. Though Clifford does not know of the affair, he would hardly care if he did, since he believes the sexual act to be one of the virtual irrelevances of existence, necessary only until a more efficient means of perpetuating the species is evolved. He has even given his wife permission to conceive a child by another man, since he cannot beget one himself, and he assumes unquestioningly that the instincts of her class will lead her to a man suitable to father the heir to Wragby Hall.

Connie's relationship with Michaelis makes her aware again of her sexual being, which she has kept subjugated since marriage: yet it makes her strangely detached and discontented, since Michaelis seems to want from it only the swift success of consummation with no obligation to the spirit. He has no regard for Connie herself, no tenderness. When he proposes marriage it is as though he were inviting her to an endless and particularly exclusive house party. Nevertheless, when his proposal ends the affair between them, Connie is plunged into a staleness of being which threatens her life. No Victorian heroine ever pined for lost love as debilitatingly as Lady Chatterley now drains away. She feels her sexual life drying up inside her. She wanders through the grounds of Wragby aching with forlornness. Her first encounters with the gamekeeper are merely neutral, but when she sees him washing himself, stripped to the loins, her system is shocked as though it had undergone a vision. Thereafter the love between keeper and mistress grows in passion and mutual fulfilment. Mellors has himself been bruised by a vicious marriage and has tried to pretend that sex can be put aside for ever. The two of them expose each other's vulnerability and reconstitute their faith in the possibilities of life. Their relationship, while life-enhancing, has to be conducted furtively and tensely. When Connie goes away on a long-arranged trip to Italy it is in the expectation that, whatever legal battles lie ahead (for both of them will need to be divorced), they will come together again. Connie returns from Italy, having had a momentary 'revulsion against the whole affair' (p. 276), and she reluctantly fulfils her promise to return to Clifford: but it is only to announce that she is pregnant, that Mellors is her lover and that she can never live again at Wragby. Clifford rages impotently, but Connie's escape is assured. Though legalities require them to live apart for a few months, she and Mellors will come together again. The novel ends on a note of tender promise and in the expectation of a new life being born. Between the two lovers the fulfilment of a right relationship seems probable – though by no means certain: and it may contain in its tenderness some germ of a better life.

Lawrence took great trouble over this novel. The 'rushed' methods of the leadership novels and the hasty revisions of *The Lost Girl* were replaced by careful planning and meticulous rewriting. The editorial history of *Lady Chatterley's Lover* only became clear to the general reader in 1972 when the second draft of the story, *John Thomas and Lady Jane*, was published. This is the longest of three versions, the first of which, *The First Lady Chatterley*, came out in 1944. The version familiar to most people is the third draft, *Lady Chatterley's Lover*, which Lawrence certainly intended to be the 'official' text. Comparisons between the three versions are fascinating, showing much more than Lawrence's tendency to change names (Mellors is Parkin, for example, in the first two drafts) or to tinker with his plot. Critics have their preferences among the three: Frieda Lawrence preferred the first version, Harry T. Moore most admires the second. I opt for the third because Lawrence sculpts his material free of much extraneous matter. In some ways it is the most dogmatic of the three versions. Clifford is allowed none of the compensating humanity of the first draft. In *John Thomas and Lady Jane*, Parkin–Mellors is mellower in his attitude to Clifford and the established class he has to serve. Some writers have objected to the hardening of contrasts which the third version displays. I suspect, however, that Lawrence saw no point in beating about the bush: the failure of contemporary values had to be pointed as strongly as possible by a viable alternative. *Lady Chatterley's Lover* is much less concerned than its two predecessors with giving a fair analysis of modern society or with proper roundness of character: it works more diagrammatically, offering clearly differentiated types. The bones of allegory which always lie embedded in a Lawrence novel are clearly evident beneath the surface of the third *Lady Chatterley* draft. Death versus life, the mechanical in opposition to the phallic: Lawrence saw no point in dressing up the central battle in modern life with distracting complexities of character, so his third draft whittles away all the impedimenta of Forsterian 'roundness' to leave a purer, more elemental work than any of the other novels. The existence of the two earlier drafts demonstrates that it was not a failure of technical ability nor any kind of creative tiredness which led Lawrence to write in the more functional, spare, black-and-white manner of *Lady Chatterley's Lover*. He arrived at the clarity and explicitness of his last novel only by the most careful craftsmanship. In doing so he does not just look to the Arcadian and Rousseauist back-to-nature models of earlier periods but forward to the linear simplicity and deliberate spareness of many later novelists.

The third version is much the most widely known. Indeed, there was a time in the 1960s when, in Britain at least, it rivalled the Bible as the best-selling book in the English language. Lawrence was dogged all his life by legal proceedings, but no prosecution in his lifetime rivalled the astonishing 'Lady Chatterley Trial' of autumn 1960. Penguin Books, following an American publisher's lead, decided to publish the unexpurgated *Lady Chatterley's Lover*, which, in Lawrence's own time, could only be printed privately in Florence. The consequent court proceedings resulted in the vindication of the novel as 'serious literature': of course, it had been an impertinence to Lawrence's reputation to suggest it was otherwise. Penguin could scarcely keep up with the demand for the book, and sales of brown paper are said to have gone up as respectable citizens chose to read it 'under plain cover'. The irony, implicit in all prosecutions of serious art, was that the very thing the book was meant to counter was now encouraged, a prurient ferreting for sexual titbits. It is hard now to see why anyone thought of prosecuting *Lady Chatterley's Lover*, for it possesses an innocence which seems almost unworldly in contrast to so much which has been published since; but that we find it inoffensive partly results from the more liberal aesthetic mood ushered in by its successful defence before the law.

Lawrence knew from the start that his book would cause a stir. He enjoyed its effect among his English friends, which he described as 'like a bomb . . . they're still suffering from shell-shock'. His only surprise was that the book was the subject of some of the most industrious pirating in publishing history. He introduced few social or private themes into *Lady Chatterley's Lover* with which his regular readers would not already be familiar. He set out, however, to release the English language from some of its inhibitions by using all the old words traditionally thought of as 'dirty' because they were the popular or unliterary words in which sexuality was expressed. In the process he hoped to rescue them from the two usages into which the English sexual vocabulary had fallen: as meaningless swear-words or as 'dirty' in the sense that by their associations they soiled the experiences. The attempt was almost certain to fail, for language has its own natural ways of developing, and no individual can by his own act of will arrest the evolution. Though the Lady Chatterley Trial undoubtedly publicized the so-called 'four-letter words' and helped to make them acceptable in print instead of forms like 'f---' or '****' there is no evidence that their ordinary usage has been redirected. They continue to flourish both as expletives and in mild pornography. Lawrence himself does not know how to use them in print without automatically appearing over-studied.

'Th'art good cunt, though, aren't ter? Best bit o' cunt left on earth. When ter likes! When tha'rt willin'!'

'What is cunt?' she said.

'An doesn't ter know? Cunt! It's thee down theer; an' what I get when I'm i'side thee, and what tha gets when I'm i'side thee; it's a' as it is, all on't.'

'All on't,' she teased. 'Cunt! It's like fuck then.'

'Nay nay! Fuck's only what you do. Animals fuck. But cunt's a lot more than that. It's thee, dost see: an' th'art a lot beside an animal, aren't ter? – even ter fuck? Cunt! Eh, that's the beauty o' thee, lass!'

(p. 185)

The tone of affectionate banter between Mellors and Connie cannot overcome the sense of self-conscious daring in the choice of words. The facility with which the keeper switches from standard English, where such words would be out of place, to a regional speech where they are supposed to sound natural is itself a suspect device, for it reminds us that he is not simply the natural man but a moderately educated, travelled, experienced person whose decision to work on the land is partly forced upon him by the economic necessity to do something and partly a deliberate opting out of the industrial alternative. We sentimentalize Mellors if we fail to see that in being a gamekeeper he does not enjoy total release from the bonds of society; on the other hand, we ought to recognize that there is an element of luxury in his opportunity to be a keeper rather than a miner, for in the Lawrentian scale he can enjoy some personal freedom as a feudal servant but would have precious little if he were the servant of capitalism. And being a keeper means being alone; to be a miner entails comradeship and a sense of community. Lawrence saw that all lives which are circumscribed to any degree by economic considerations must be only part-existences. The full self remains unrealized. Part victim and part free agent, therefore, whenever Mellors slides into dialect he sounds *less* natural than when he talks conventionally. The four-letter words, being part of his dialect, cannot avoid sounding over-deliberate, plopped into his speech as Lawrence plopped them into the novel, in order to create a few ripples.

In the end Lawrence proves more successful at finding prose rhythms to articulate virtually inexpressible sensations than he is at a single-handed rescue of the English language from its natural evolution. This applies to the best sexual descriptions.

And it seemed she was like the sea, nothing but dark waves rising and heaving, heaving with a great swell, so that slowly her whole darkness was in motion, and she was ocean rolling its dark, dumb mass. Oh, and far down inside her the deeps parted and rolled asunder, in long, far-travelling billows, and ever, at the quick of her, the depths parted and rolled asunder, from the centre of soft plunging, as the plunger went deeper and deeper, touching lower, and she was deeper and deeper and deeper disclosed, the heavier the billows of her rolled away to some shore, uncovering her, and closer and closer plunged the palpable unknown, and further and further rolled the waves of herself away from herself, leaving her, till suddenly, in a soft, shuddering convulsion, the quick of all her plasm was touched, she knew herself touched, the consummation was upon her, and she was gone. She was gone, she was not, and she was born: a woman.

(p. 181)

Lawrence seeks for a language in which to express the sensual depths, mystery, yielding and abandonment of an orgasm. No prose can *describe* this. The essence of the experience, like pain, lies outside language. The writer can only find an equivalent expressing the sense of the sensation. The rolling waves of the phrases (especially the sustained accumulation of the second sentence) imply, but do not describe, the rhythm of the inter-course. The tidal image suggests the utterly female cyclical exper-ience, but it does not state anything. The directing words are really 'disclosed', 'uncovering', 'touched' and 'born', for these we can relate to character. They express Connie's discovery of her own inner being. The rest of the prose can only hope, through its orchestrated rhythm and its urgency, to give a vibration of the feeling we assume Connie to have. Lawrence himself is often 'the plunger' going 'deeper and deeper, touching lower' into the mysteries of sensation, but he implicitly admits here, as he does at the end of *Women in Love*, that no literature can substitute for life or penetrate the private tenderness of total consummation. 'She was gone, she was not, and she was born': transportation, extinction, birth, climax: states without language. The limitation of his art is a necessary condition for the vindication of his faith.

Much of the language of *Lady Chatterley's Lover* continues the motifs of earlier novels. We find the rind–husk–kernel pattern of images, for example, in the crustacean view of Clifford as a 'hard, efficient shell of an exterior and a pulpy interior, one of the amazing crabs and lobsters of the modern, industrial and financial world' (p. 114). The descriptions of the woods and seasons have Lawrence's characteristically fresh eye for detail.

The wood was silent, still and secret in the evening drizzle of rain, full of the mystery of eggs and half-open buds, half-unsheathed flowers. In the dimness of it all trees glistened naked and dark as if they had unclothed themselves, and the green things on earth seemed to hum with greenness.

(p. 127)

However disenchanted Lawrence became with the social reality of England he never ceased to savour the best of its landscape. Of course, a passage like this carries its symbolic resonance – 'the green things on earth seemed to hum with greenness' because Connie is on her way to Mellors's hut. The woods themselves are a relic of an ancient forest, a small surviving part of the displaced world.

Lawrence knows of the other England, too, 'the vast bulk' (p. 159) with its blackened cottages and serried modern dwellings, its factories and railways and its abandoned castle and its dimin-ished church, the landscape through which Lady Chatterley drives in chapter 11. This England is literally falling apart.

This is history. One England blots out another. The mines have made the halls wealthy. Now they were blotting them out, as they had already blotted out the cottages. The industrial England blots out the agricultural England. One meaning blots out another. The new England blots out the old England. And the continuity is not organic, but mechanical.

(p. 163)

Though he was to claim in one of the last letters he wrote that 'When I began *Lady Chatterley*, of course I did not know what I was doing – I did not deliberately work symbolically' (letter to D. V. Lederhandler, 12 September 1929), Lawrence always worked through symbolism. His fastidiousness as a symbolist sometimes wavered, but in all the novels we have been examining, the prose takes its muscle from the patterning of symbol. Lawrence had an intensely concrete perception of the world which, when it fused with his evolutionary view of creation, produced images like that of the geological strata. In the beginning was vegetable matter which became the coal within the land. Man dug the land and discovered the coal, gnawing away at it to make himself rich but exhausting the land as he did so. From their wealth the rich men built great houses and founded a servile class to work for them. The land was blotted out by the evidence of their wealth, by mines and cottages. Then this excretion of wealth itself overcame the great houses and suffocated the rich men. Layers of blots: that, for Lawrence, was man's social history. The tragedy was that he had chosen to evolve like this; he had made his history 'mechanical' where it should have been 'organic'. His salvation might lie in recognizing that the process was not yet completed. The flowers bloom in quiet corners, the sun shines through lace curtains, the birds fly and the eggs hatch. The natural world needs rescuing, but it has not died. Thus, when Connie and Mellors thread forget-me-nots in their sex-parts they celebrate not only the tenderness of their private relationship but the survival of nature and an unforgotten England in which they deeply believe.

Much of what Mellors says recalls Birkin. He too anticipates a world without the corruption of people in it – 'To contemplate the extermination of the human species and the long pause that follows before some other species crops up, it calms you more than anything else' (p. 227) – but he likewise cannot resolve the problem of how a humanless world can be contemplated at all. What conscious force does the contemplating? Mellors tends to recognize this inconsistency more readily than Birkin. 'I'd wipe the machines

off the face of the earth again and end the industrial epoch absolutely, like a black mistake. But since I can't an' nobody can, I'd
better hold my peace, an' try an' live my own life' (p. 230).
Lawrence affirms, in other words, that whatever social ideal or
moral revolution he may posit in theory, the way out of the modern
nightmare remains an individual responsibility.

  *Lady Chatterley's Lover*, like *The Rainbow* and *Women in Love*,
concerns the attainment of wholeness of being. Mellors and
Connie find their wholeness through the harmony of sharing.
Both of them seek to escape their past. Mellors has been damaged
by life and marriage; Connie has been thwarted and sidetracked.
Through their vital sexual relationship they look for a way out.
They do so in a world, like Clifford, shot all to bits. 'Ours is
essentially a tragic age' are the famous opening words of the novel;
'. . . we are among the ruins'. Images of disintegration proliferate
in the book: the big houses are pulled down, their estates are
eroded, the trees are chopped, the pits are running out, there is
talk of babies being bred in bottles and the impact of broadcasting
destroys the natural harmony of communities. The atmosphere is
full of smut 'like black manna from the skies of doom' (p. 14).
Clifford talks of holding Wragby together, but in the process of
defending the heart of old England he fails to see that the heart
itself is diseased. 'Things fall apart; the centre cannot hold':
Yeats's words in 'The Second Coming' constantly come to mind
as we read Lawrence's last novel.

  Yet *Lady Chatterley's Lover* should not be read as a document of
despair. The love between the two central characters is a force
sufficiently potent to be weighed against the national fragmentation. Lawrence makes any sensitive reader understand the importance of tenderness and fidelity in human relationships. He
approaches them cautiously, but the hope exists that they can
defeat all the modern evils. Life matters, but we must learn why it
matters if we are to preserve it. Lawrence surely wants *Lady
Chatterley's Lover* to be morally instructive, not in a condemnatory
way but as an exhortation to value rather than to abuse life. For
this reason, the notion that the novel encourages promiscuity or
that no clean-minded person should read it has always seemed
not just silly but offensive to anyone who understands it. Lawrence
himself thought it 'tender and delicate', and the earliest serious
reviewers agreed. Catherine Carswell's judgement, 'very truly
moral', should be ours, too. Morality and sex have often been
separated in the public mind, however. British culture has been

particularly laden, for many reasons, with the doctrine that sex is innately moral and ought not to be discussed in a decent society. Lawrence wrote all his novels to criticize the sterility of this attitude, nowhere more obviously than in *Lady Chatterley's Lover*. The novel is indubitably about sex but it is also indubitably moral.

Lawrence distinguishes between various moments of sexual intercourse. He distinguishes each occasion when Connie and Mellors make love together. The key word the first time is 'instinctive' (p. 120). They are drawn together by inevitable attraction: their sharing is natural. Yet 'the activity, the orgasm was his, all his' (p. 121). On the next occasion, Connie wills herself into a hard separateness; then comes the triumph of mutual orgasm; later, fierce passion, though the novel vehemently criticizes the bacchante attitude to sex in which the woman uses the man only to humiliate him and to celebrate the victory of the female will. Each occasion has its own character. We do wrong to read the sexual passages as though they were all written in the same way. Lawrence carefully distinguishes them, emphasizing the uniqueness of each individual moment in human partnership. Nor does he restrict his study to Connie and Mellors alone. Mrs Bolton, the housekeeper on whom Clifford comes to rely more and more, contains within the shell of a rather prim morality her tender memories of her dead husband. We remember the passage quoted earlier on page 49 of this study:

That's it, my Lady, the touch of him! I've never got over it to this day, and never shall. And if there's a heaven above, he'll be there, and will lie up against me so I can sleep.

(p. 170)

Lawrence hardly wrote in all his work more poignant support for physical love.

*Lady Chatterley's Lover*, being Lawrence's last major fiction, must be read as the work of a man tired of England, tired of modernity, tired of all things superficial, brutal or mechanical, but far from tired of life or tired of the novelist's art. He exercises his craft here more sharply than in any novel since *Women in Love*. The famous episode in which Clifford's wheelchair crushes the bluebells as he tries to jerk its impotent machinery into life wonderfully illustrates the man's assumption of class superiority to Mellors, whom he instructs to push him, his contempt for nature, his reliance on mechanism, his vanity, arrogance and futility. Less obviously 'set' episodes nonetheless show a concern for the craft of good novel-writing. When, for example, Connie returns to the house after her first lovemaking with Mellors she finds the door bolted against her and has to ring for admission: a vignette of her new relationship with Wragby.

In certain obvious ways *Lady Chatterley's Lover* brings Lawrence back full circle to *The White Peacock*. They share elements of pastoralism, with a similar triangle of central relationships, and correspondences between Mellors and Annable. *Lady Chatterley's Lover*, however, is long past the vestiges of *fin-de-siècle* prettiness we find in *The White Peacock*. It could only be the product of the post-war period. Lawrence wrote it in sad rebellion against the drift of modern life, but he testified to the possible endurance of the best human values. If not a greatly hopeful novel, it is not without hope either, exhorting us, if we are powerless to change the tide of human history, to settle for an integrity in personal relationships: shut the curtains on the world and get on with a real emotional life. For this reason his novel remains widely read now after the notoriety following its prosecution has died down. Lawrence wrote in his last novel about things in which he really believed. It is hard to feel that he was ever utterly convinced by the theses of the leadership novels; but *Lady Chatterley's Lover*, like all his best work, is a true declaration of faith. In the last lines of one of his last poems, 'Shadows' (1929), Lawrence expresses the hope which directs all his best work and which bears witness to his humility:

> then I must know that still
> I am in the hands of the unknown God,
> he is breaking me down to his own oblivion
> to send me forth on a new morning, a new man.

The tone is calm here; he said something similar, but with more urgency, in the essay 'A Propos of *Lady Chatterley's Lover*' (1930): 'We *must* get back into relation, vivid and nourishing relation, to the cosmos and the universe.'

# Select Reading List

D. H. Lawrence's novels, short stories, essays and most of his other major writings are published in paperback by Penguin Books Ltd, Harmondsworth, from which editions all quotations in this book have been taken.

Letter quotations are from *The Letters of D. H. Lawrence* (edited and with an introduction by Aldous Huxley), London, Heinemann, 1932.

Critical works mentioned in the text:

Richard Aldington. Introductions to the Penguin editions of D. H. Lawrence's novels.

Anthony Beal. *D. H. Lawrence*. Edinburgh, Oliver & Boyd, 1961.

Emile Delavenay. *D. H. Lawrence: The Man and His Work*. London, Heinemann, 1972.

Graham Hough. *The Dark Sun*. London, Duckworth, 1956.

Frank Kermode. *Lawrence*. London, Fontana Modern Masters/Collins, 1973.

F. R. Leavis. *D. H. Lawrence: Novelist*. Harmondsworth, Peregrine Books in association with Chatto & Windus, 1964. First published 1955.

— —. *Thought, Words and Creativity: Art and Thought in D. H. Lawrence*. London, Chatto & Windus, 1976.

Harry T. Moore. *The Priest of Love: A Life of D. H. Lawrence*, rev. edn. London, Heinemann, 1974.

Julian Moynahan. *The Deed of Life: The Novels and Tales of D. H. Lawrence*. Princeton, N.J., Princeton University Press, 1963.

Bertrand Russell. *Autobiography*, vol. II, *1914–44*. London, George Allen & Unwin, 1968.

Richard Swigg. *Lawrence, Hardy, and American Literature*. Oxford, University Press, 1972.

Kenneth Young. *D. H. Lawrence*. British Council series, Writers and Their Work, no. 31, rev. edn. Harlow, Longman, 1969. First published 1952.

See also:

Keith Alldritt. *The Visual Imagination of D. H. Lawrence*. London, Edward Arnold, 1971.

Michael Black. *The Literature of Fidelity*. London, Chatto & Windus, 1975.

L. D. Clarke. *Dark Night of the Body: A Study of 'The Plumed Serpent'*. Austin, University of Texas Press, 1964.

Harry T. Moore. *The Life and Works of D. H. Lawrence*. New York, Twayne, 1951.

Alastair Niven. 'D. H. Lawrence's The Plumed Serpent', *British Council Notes on Literature*, no. 164 (1976).

Keith Sagar. *The Art of D. H. Lawrence*. Cambridge, University Press, 1966.